Psychology for Professional Groups

Psychology for Managers

Psychology for Professional Groups

Series Editors: Antony J. Chapman and Anthony Gale

Psychology for Professional Groups is a new series of major textbooks published with The British Psychological Society. Each is edited by a teacher with expertise in the application of psychology to professional practice and covers the key topics in the training syllabus. The editors have drawn upon a series of specially commissioned topic chapters prepared by leading psychologists and have set them within the context of their various professions. A tutor manual is available for each text and includes practical exercises and projects, further reading and general guidance for the tutor. Each textbook shows in a fresh, original and authoritative way how psychology may be applied in a variety of professional settings, and how practitioners may improve their skills and gain a deeper understanding of themselves. 'Psychology and People; A tutorial text' incorporates the complete set of specialist topics and their associated teaching materials.

Other titles

Psychology for Social Workers. Martin Herbert
Psychology for Teachers. David Fontana
Psychology for Physiotherapists. E. N. Dunkin
Psychology for Speech Therapists. Harry Purser
Psychology for Occupational Therapists. Fay Fransella
Psychology for Careers Counselling. Ruth Holdsworth
Psychology and Medicine. David Griffiths
Psychology for Nurses and Health Visitors. John Hall
Psychology and People: A tutorial text. Antony J. Chapman
    and Anthony Gale

Psychology for Professional Groups

Psychology for Managers

Cary L. Cooper and
Peter Makin

First published 1981 as **Psychology and Management**

Second revised edition 1984

Published by THE BRITISH PSYCHOLOGICAL SOCIETY and MACMILLAN PUBLISHERS LIMITED.

Distributed by Higher and Further Education Division MACMILLAN PUBLISHERS LTD., London and Basingstoke. Associated companies and representatives throughout the world.

ISBN 0 333 36522 4 (hard cover)
ISBN 0 333 36523 2 (paper cover)

Printed in Great Britain by Wheatons of Exeter

Note: throughout these texts, the masculine pronouns have been used for succinctness and are intended to refer to both females and males.

The conclusions drawn and opinions expressed are those of the authors. They should not be taken to represent the views of the publishers.

Contents

Foreword

This book is a revised edition of Psychology and Management: A Text for Managers and Trade Unionists (1981). It is one of a series, the principal aims of which are to illustrate how psychology can be applied in particular professional contexts, how it can improve the skills of practitioners, and how it can increase the practitioners' and students' understanding of themselves.

Psychology is taught to many groups of students and is now integrated within prescribed syllabuses for an increasing number of professions. The existing texts which teachers have been obliged to recommend are typically designed for broad and disparate purposes, and consequently they fail to reflect the special needs of students in professional training. The starting point for the series was the systematic distillation of views expressed in professional journals by those psychologists whose teaching specialisms relate to the applications of psychology. It soon became apparent that many fundamental topics were common to a number of syllabuses and courses; yet in general introductory textbooks these topics tend to be embedded among much superfluous material. Therefore, from within The British Psychological Society, we invited experienced teachers and authorities in their field to write review chapters on key topics. Forty-seven chapters covering 23 topics were then available for selection by the series' Volume Editors. The Volume Editors are also psychologists and they have had many years of involvement with their respective professions. In preparing their books, they have consulted formally with colleagues in those professions. Each of their books has its own combination of the specially-prepared chapters, set in the context of the specific professional practice.

Because psychology is only one component of the various training curricula, and because students generally have limited access to learned journals and specialist texts, our contributors to the series have restricted their use of references, whilst at the same time providing short lists of annotated readings. In addition, they have provided review questions to help students organize their learning and prepare for examinations. Further teaching materials, in the form of additional references, projects, exercises and class notes, are available in Tutor Manuals prepared for each book. A comprehensive tutorial text ('Psychology and People'), prepared by the Series Editors, combines in a single volume all the key topics, together with their associated teaching materials.

In devising and developing the series we have had the good fortune to benefit from the advice and support of Dr Halla Beloff, Professor Philip Levy, Mr Allan Sakne and Mr John Winckler.

Antony J. Chapman
University of Leeds

Anthony Gale
University of Southampton

September 1983

Acknowledgement

The Editors would like to thank Dr Jean Hartley, Chairperson of the Section of Occupational Psychology for her detailed comments on an earlier draft of the book.

Part one

The organization

Chapter 1
Introduction to Part 1
Cary L. Cooper and Peter Makin

This book is intended for managers in organizations that are both large and small, public and private, who wish to know something about psychology and its applications to our lives at work.

Most people's knowledge of what psychologists do is very limited. The best known areas of applied psychology are those of educational and clinical psychology. The former concerns itself with children and their emotional and intellectual development, while the latter deals with the emotionally disturbed and mentally ill, and it is parts of these areas that most people would describe if asked to say what psychology entailed. There are, however, other areas of psychology that describe the lives of normal, adult individuals, and one of these is concerned with people at work. (The most widely used titles for this area of psychology are occupational, organizational or industrial psychology. Each means something slightly different but it need not concern us here.)

In this book we concentrate on those aspects of psychology which are of most relevance to the manager and assume no previous knowledge of psychology. First, however, what is work? Bertrand Russell (In Praise of Idleness, 1962 p. 11) divided work into two kinds:

> first, altering the position of matter at or near to the earth's surface relatively to other such matter; second, telling other people to do so. The first is unpleasant and ill paid; the second is pleasant and highly paid. The second kind is capable of indefinite extension; there are not only those who give orders but those who give advice as to what orders should be given.

Few managers would, we suspect, accept Russell's analysis concerning pleasure and pay, but many will have suffered from the extension of advice. It is interesting to note, however, that the piece was originally written in 1932 at a time when the emphasis in industry was still on 'power'; for example, using steam or electricity to power large machines. Since the Second World War, however, the emphasis has shifted from 'power' to 'control': what has become known as the 'cybernetic revolution' and 'information technology'.

It is interesting that the same period has seen the rise of 'the manager' and a recognition of the manager's role as a control mechanism. Within this role are, of course, aspects that require particular specialist knowledge but of equal, and some might argue, greater importance is a manager's skill at managing people. It is with such skills that the present book is concerned.

We would have no trouble finding definitions of the role of managers or management from among the best-sellers of Drucker or other management gurus, but the approach that appeals to us is to try and categorize the different types of managers by acknowledging the reality that individual managers behave in quite different ways. This allows us to get a feel for the generic role of management; all the activities that should be performed if 'superman-ager' existed.

Handy (1976) recently remarked that 'the last quarter century has seen the emergence of "the manager" as a recognized occupational role in society'. He then goes on to suggest that managers seem to be increasingly playing two primary sets of roles: the manager as a person or the manager as a GP. The manager as a person alludes to the increasing professionalization of managers, so that managers are acquiring a set of skills which are, and arguably should be, independent of any organization for whom he does, or could, work. Since organizations seem to care less for the home/work interface concerns of their managers than previously (Cooper, 1979), it is in their interest to make sure they continue to make themselves marketable by further education and career-management. The manager as a GP concept, on the other hand, is based on the premise that the manager is the 'first recipient of problems' which require solutions or decisions. It is the role of a manager in this context to carry out four basic activities at work: (i) identify the symptoms in the situation; (ii) diagnose the cause of trouble; (iii) decide how to deal with it; and (iv) start the treatment or make the decision or create the action plans. Handy argues that all too often the symptoms are treated like diseases in the 'industrial wards' of the country, and that managers who do not follow the medical model above in dealing with issues and problems, but stop at stage one, find that the illness or sources of grievance return in the same form or in disguise. Frequently we find managers who can diagnose the symptoms, such as poor morale or bad communications, but then provide solutions without knowing the cause: for example, poor communications - start in-house journal; late arrivals to work - introduce time-clocks, etc. In order to identify adequately and accurately problems or situations, it is absolutely essential to understand the needs of individual workers, be they other managers or unskilled labourers. Diagnosis not only involves understanding individual behaviour but also the dynamics of groups within the organizations and the consequences of actions/plans that may affect groups outside.

Handy also suggests that the manager as a GP, when considering strategies for improving the health of the organization, should consider and be aware of three sets of variables; the people, the work and the structure, systems and procedure of the organization. In terms of 'people concerns', he should be aware of individual needs, training and education potential, career development, motivation, need for counselling or support, etc., whereas in terms of the organizational structure and systems he should be aware of the nature of roles, inter-group conflict, small group behaviour, decision making, negotiating processes, reward systems, etc. The general practitioner manager is not only expected to be aware of these factors and processes but also to understand their interaction: that is, how change in one may produce change in another.

And finally, a crucial characteristic of any skilled manager is to be aware of change and how to implement it. This requires an understanding of learning theory, the various strategies for change (counselling, behaviour modification, etc.), the dilemmas people experience at different times in their lives, identifying an initiating person or group, creating an awareness of change, and so on. This is part and parcel of any GP role whether in the medical field or in organizations.

To obtain a further and more amusing yet informative view of the role of the manager we turn to Mant's (1977) historical styles of management, which has its contemporary meaning in today's managers (by sleight of author's licence). First, there is the RESPECTABLE BUCCANEER or the British proto-manager. This is the swashbuckling Sir Francis Drake type who uses 'who he knows' and 'who he is' to achieve results. The success of this style depends to a large extent on a highly developed sense of social skills and timing, but little else. He is the entrepreneur in its most extreme form.

The next managerial prototype is the AGENT. He acts on behalf of others, takes no decisions himself and has historical roots in the commercial world of nineteenth-century England. His contemporary counterpart is the 'middle manager' of today, who feels, not by choice, that his power and ability to influence decisions is declining (due to the power of the trade union movement, greater participative decision making, etc.).

The SCIENTIFIC MANAGER is another breed of executive who is seen in organizational jungles from time to time. He tends to make decisions based on what appear to be rational and appropriate data, but frequently ignores the 'people problems' that result from his decisions or are created by them. Sheldon writing in 1923 (quoted in Mant, 1977) summed it up from a historical perspective: 'management is no longer the wielding of the whip; it is rather the delving into experience and building upon facts'. In contrast to the factual manager is the MANAGERIAL QUISLING, or as Mant puts it, 'the manager in the role of the pal'. This stems from the human relations school of management of the 1940s and 1950s. This prototypic manager is one who is supposed to be concerned with the quality of worklife and the well-being of workers. It is our view that this species of manager comes in different varieties. First, there is the GENUINE QUISLING, who really is concerned about the worker's health and well-being. Incidentally, this type of manager is usually so naive about the politics of his organization that he fails to achieve his objectives, or achieves them at the expense of other people. Second, there is the ENTREPRENEURIAL QUISLING, who 'appears to care' but is really using the 'flavour of the month' managerial style to achieve recognition, or enhance his own image, or accomplish some political manoeuvre. He is the classic Milo Minderbinder in Heller's Catch-22; 'it's all in the syndicate and everybody has a share'.

Another managerial prototype is the MANAGER AS A TECHNOCRAT. He is a breed that grew up as the technology around them developed, particularly during the 1940s when we were increasingly looking to engineers for our salvation. This type of manager handles all issues as if they were technical problems capable of stress analysis, critical path analysis, etc. His concern for the 'people component' is once again a mere 'given' in the decision-making process.

And finally, there is the MANAGER AS A CONSTITUTIONALIST. This form of managerial style seemed to emerge from the Glacier Metal Company study undertaken by Brown (1965). This style of management is not unlike the Tavistock approach to applied problems in industry, in that it relies heavily on contractual arrangements. That is to say, it believes fundamentally that psychological contracts between individuals or representatives of groups are essential for harmonious relationships at work. Managers are effective, according to this strategy, if they work with their subordinates and colleagues in designing contractual arrangements on most issues of importance. This reduces ambiguity and heightens the boundaries on tasks, roles and organizational units.

What Mant (1977) has done in trying to identify managerial types is to suggest implicitly that each of the caricatures of prototypic executives is ineffective, but in different ways. And although some managers utilize (consistently) one or more of these styles than others, the well-rounded and Twenty-First-Century manager will require a behavioural repertoire that encompasses nearly the whole range, but used flexibly and appropriately. We need to educate and train managers to understand the needs of people so that they take a scientific or diagnostic approach to problems and decision, but with a socio-technical, humanistic, and risk-taking orientation as well. To do this, one might follow the advice of many managers that 'behavioural scientists are incapable of telling us anything we don't already know'. This was epitomized in a piece that appeared in 'The Financial Times' a few years ago:

> Good evening gentlemen, welcome to the X management education establishment. You will have noted, perhaps with relief, the absence of faculty or curriculum. This is a regular feature of this programme and a closely-guarded secret of its alumni, present and past. If you should require any inducement to keep this secret you may be influenced by the £500 in crisp ten-pound notes which is to be found in a brown envelope in your bedroom. This represents half the fee paid by your employers and approximated expenditure that would other wise have been incurred with respect to teaching staff salaries and related costs. In the meantime, meals and other services will be provided and the bar will remain open at normal opening times. You will have discovered that your colleagues are drawn from similar organizations to your own and contain amongst them a wealth of practical experience in all manner of managerial roles. There is also a first-rate library at your disposal. How you decide to pass these six weeks is your own managerial decision; we trust you will enjoy it and find it beneficial. Thank you.

On the other hand, we could begin to provide managers with information that behavioural scientists have accumulated over the last 30 years of empirical and theoretical development. It is this latter approach that we have decided to take in this volume, to make available psychological knowledge that may be of some use in dealing with individual, interpersonal, group and organization behaviour, and in creating change among individuals and organizations.

Structure of the book

The chapter by Payne is intended to act as an introduction to the whole field of behaviour in organizations and some of the later chapters will build upon the ideas that Payne presents. As with all the chapters in this book, you will find that the authors provide a useful list of books for those who wish to follow up particular topics as well as a list of thought-provoking questions.

There follow three further parts, the first concerned with individual behaviour, the second on dealing with others, and finally we take a look at some specific problem areas. Each of these sections is preceded by an introduction which sets the scene for the chapters which follow.

Finally, we include three appendices. Obviously we are limited by space in such a book and we realize that there are some interesting topics that we have had to omit. In the first appendix, therefore, we have given a short list of books in some of these areas that will provide a useful starting point. We also give a brief list of some of the most important academic journals in the field for those who want to see what research and theories are currently receiving (or not receiving) attention. The second appendix is meant to supplement the chapter on personality and describes the requirements of a good psychological test. The final appendix is unusual in a book of this nature and we are grateful to Allan Sakne of The British Psychological Society for suggesting it. He pointed out that some indication of where managers could seek expert advice would be useful and so we have included a number of contact addresses, including that of the Occupational Division of The British Psychological Society.

References

Brown, W. and Jacques, E. (1965)
Glacier Project Papers. London: Heinemann.
Cooper, C.L. (1979)
The Executive Gypsy. London: Macmillan.
Handy, C. (1976)
Understanding Organizations. Harmondsworth: Penguin.
Mant, A. (1977)
The Rise and Fall of the British Manager. London: Pan.
Russell, B. (1962)
In Praise of Idleness. London: Unwin.

Chapter 2

Organizational behaviour

R. Payne

Organizational behaviour is concerned with refining our knowledge about the behaviour of individuals and groups in organizations and their role in the growth, development and decline of organizations. These various outcomes are also determined by the financial, political and technical environment in which the organization functions, so researchers also study these organization-environment relations and their consequent impact on the behaviour of individuals and groups. It is a multi-disciplinary enterprise involving economics, politics, engineering, management science, systems theory, industrial relations, sociology and psychology. Given this complexity the student will not be surprised to discover that our ability to predict accurately what will happen to individuals, groups and organizations is very limited. In searching to achieve this 'scientist's stone', however, a variety of frameworks, conceptual schemes and even a few facts have emerged which can facilitate our ability to perceive, interpret and organize this social complexity. This chapter concentrates on presenting some of these frameworks.

What are organizations like?

As with men an organization is:

> Like all other organizations
> Like some other organizations
> Like no other organizations.

In your professional work roles you encounter a unique organization, like no other organization. In this chapter we deal with the ways in which organizations are the same as each other and the ways in which groups of organizations are similar to each other, but different from other types of organizations. Apart from its intrinsic interest such information should enable you to appreciate the ways in which your own organization is unique, and also help you understand something about why it is the way it is.

We are concerned with work organizations so part of our definition must be that an organization exists in order to get work done. They differ in the way they achieve this and two of the major reasons for the differences are (i) the way

the organization divides its work into different tasks and
(ii) how it co-ordinates those tasks. Most organizations
contain several or many people but according to the present
definition an organization could consist of only one person.
Two different silversmiths may divide the different parts of
their work in different ways and co-ordinate the tasks differently. One might choose to design and make one complete
article at a time. Another might make bowls one week,
handles the next week, assemble them the next week and then
polish and finish them.

They represent two different organization structures.
Similarly, seven people may work together and agree that
each is capable of doing all the tasks that are required to
get the work done and the co-ordination of these tasks will
be left to the whim of the individuals on a day-to-day
basis. Another seven people might have six people each doing
different tasks with one person left to co-ordinate the work
they do. One thing that is well proven is that once the work
of the organization requires more than just a handful of
people there is a strong preference for dividing work into
different tasks and giving some people (managers)
responsibility for supervising and co-ordinating them.

Henry Mintzberg (1979) describes five main ways in which
organizations achieve co-ordination amongst people doing
different tasks. They are:

*   mutual adjustment which relies on informal, day-to-day
    communication and agreements;
*   direct supervision where one person takes the
    responsibility for ensuring that other people
    satisfactorily complete the tasks they have been
    allocated;
*   standardization of work processes: this refers to the
    situation where work has been carefully designed from
    the outset so that the system or technology determines
    what work gets done. As they say in the car industry,
    'the track is the boss'. That is, the operator's work is
    so organized that he can only screw nuts on wheels, or
    only place the front seat in the car, or only spray the
    right side, etc.;
*   standardization of work outputs achieves co-ordination
    by specifying the nature and quality of the completed
    task. The salesman must take X orders, the craftsman
    make so many articles. How they do it is not specified,
    but what they must achieve is;
*   standardization of skills is what has produced
    professions. Doctors, lawyers, teachers and engineers
    are replaceable parts. In theory anyone with the correct
    training can be substituted for any other without
    creating major difficulties of co-ordination. This
    substitutability is captured in the colloquialism, 'He's
    a real pro!'

Mintzberg proposes that organizations divide activities into five broad categories. At the top of the organization there are people whose main role is to determine the goals and policies of the company. These occupy the 'strategic apex'. Below them are the managers and supervisors who have the responsibility of ensuring that policies and procedures are followed: 'the middle line'. They manage the people who work most directly on the outputs or services of the organization and these Mintzberg describes as the 'operating core'. To the right and left of the middle line, and subordinate to the strategic apex, there are people supporting the main workflow of the organization. There are those in the 'technostructure' whose job is to assist the middle line and the operating core by analysing problems and providing solutions and systems for monitoring and implementing them. They include professional workers such as work study analysts, planning and systems analysts, accountants and personnel analysts. The latter assists this analysing and control process by standardizing skills and rewards. The support staff are not directly connected to the main workflow of the organization but they provide services enabling the rest of the organization to function. They include payroll staff, mailroom, cafeteria, reception, legal advice and research and development. In large organizations any one of these departments may be large enough to have the same five-fold structure so that one gets organizations within organizations.

This very general model is most easily recognized in production organizations but it can also describe the structure of schools, universities or hospitals. In a hospital, however, professionals are the operating core: the doctors, nurses, physiotherapists, occupational therapists and radiologists who provide the treatment and care. Other professionals such as planners and trainers are in the technostructure and basic research scientists or laboratory staff are in the support staff. Thus professionals serve different functions within the same organization. Figure 1 presents a conventional tree diagram of a secondary school structure with Mintzberg's concepts overlaid. Note the small technostructure which is provided mainly by the local authority and the inspectorate. They are, strictly speaking, outside the school and this is indicated by a dotted line.

Building on these two sets of concepts and reviewing a large body of literature, Mintzberg concludes there are five basic types of organizations. They are theoretical abstractions but some of them approximate to the pure types and many larger organizations are hybrids of the types or contain examples of more than one pure type within them. Mintzberg continues his fascination with the number five by offering a pentagon model of the pure types. A simplified version appears in figure 2.

The different forms of co-ordination pull the organization towards different structures. The strategic apex pulls the organization structure upwards to centralized decision making and direct supervision. The name for this

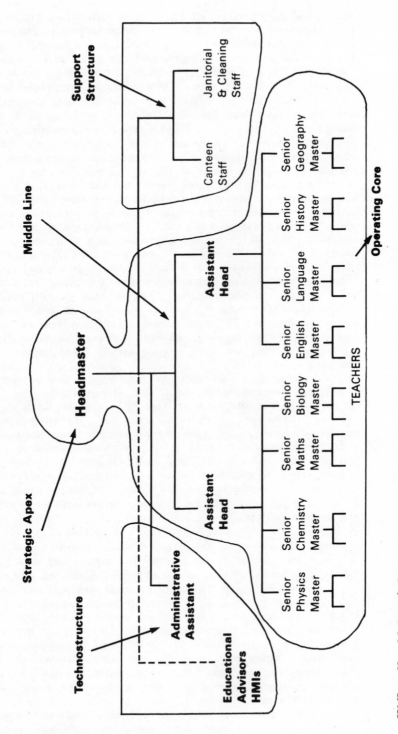

HMIs = Her Majesty's Inspectorates

Figure 1

A tree diagram of a school with Mintzberg's elements of structure superimposed

type is 'simple structure' and some of the organizations that frequently take this form are newer, smaller, autocratic organizations. The technostructure's function is to standardize and control the work processes so it pulls in that direction. Mintzberg mixes two metaphors to describe the resulting structure as a 'machine bureaucracy'. The bureaucratic element in the metaphor conveys the written procedures and documents designed to prescribe and control the system, and the machine element conveys the rationality, predictability and reliability of the design that has gone into it. A car or television assembly line plant are good examples.

The third pull is that exercised by professionals. They wish to exercise the skills their training has provided and argue the case for the quality of what they do within the discretion of their professionalism. This striving for autonomy is reflected in the small technostructure that these 'professional bureaucracies' have (see figure 1 for the school example). Note they are still bureaucratic. Despite their professionalism, organizational size leads to greater complexity which requires records to be kept, minutes taken, standard procedures followed, and professional standards maintained. Hospitals, universities and craft organizations tend towards this form because the services they supply need people with complex skills and professional training. Since they employ so many professionals it is not surprising that their needs and values influence the way the organization functions.

The fourth group to bid for influence in the design of the organization is the middle management. They too wish to be regarded as professionals and have the responsibility for their production or workflow units. They achieve this only by agreeing to conform to set standards in the production of the output or service: that is, standardization of outputs. The strategic apex co-ordinates the different units and supplies financial and technical resources but each unit acquires reasonable autonomy to create the 'divisional structure'. This is common in conglomerates such as Imperial Chemical Industries which has separate divisions dealing with organic chemicals, agriculture, fibres and plastics. Within each autonomous division, of course, one may find a different structure: the machine bureaucracy is prevalent, but if a separate research division exists it may be a professional bureaucracy or adhocracy.

The support staff represent the final force. Their preference is to co-ordinate by mutual adjustment and they are frequently supported in this by the 'operating core'. This would be the case in the Research Division just mentioned since the operating core would be scientists who are imbued with values of freedom and innovation. This produces a structure Mintzberg calls 'adhocracy'. The title attempts to convey the fact that there are limited formal structures and that action and responsibility are defined by the current problem rather than past precedents or personal

Figure 2

Mintzberg's pentagon
From H. Mintzberg (1979), 'The Structuring of Organizations: A synthesis of the research'.
Reprinted by permission of Prentice-Hall Inc., Englewood Cliffs, New Jersey.

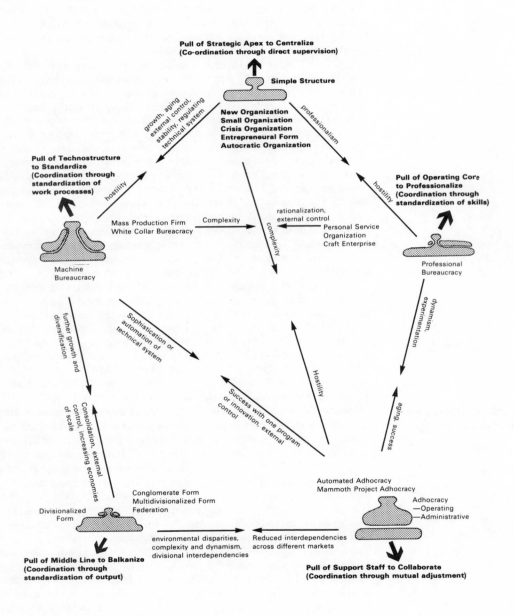

prestige. Large research and development projects sometimes take this form, as do smaller groups of professionals such as advertising organizations. It can also serve the needs of the automated factory. Since automation itself controls and monitors the workflow process, the executives and their technical staff can concentrate on designing new products and the processes to market, produce and distribute them.

Mintzberg's thesis is that all organizations experience these five forces and that in a search for harmony one of the forces becomes dominant at any particular point in the organization's history. The dominant force pulls towards one of the five configurations. As circumstances change, however, the dominant forces change.

The arrows in figure 2 indicate the main forces acting on each type trying to move it towards another type. The results of these forces are the myriad of organizational forms we actually find in the world.

In summary, the very essence of organization is the co-ordination of activities. There appears to be a limited number of ways in which co-ordination is achievable. They are co-ordination by mutual adjustment, direct supervision, standardization of work procedures, standardization of work outputs and standardization of inputs or skills. If any of these forms of co-ordination dominates in an organization they tend to lead to a structure of a particular type. Thus co-ordination by mutual adjustment tends to produce an 'adhocracy'. Direct supervision leads to 'simple structure', whilst standardization of work processes tends to produce the pure 'machine bureaucracy'. The 'divisionalized struc-ture' arises from the desire to co-ordinate by standardizing the quantity and quality of work outputs, whilst standar-dizing inputs (skills) results in a 'professional bureau-cracy'. These are 'pure' types and most organizations contain elements of more than one. We now consider some of the factors that produce these hybrids.

Why are organizations the way they are?

Because people choose, with more or less awareness, to make them that way. It is only too easy to start talking as if organizations make choices, but it is the men and women in them who determine their nature. This is not to say they are totally unconstrained. The fundamental purpose of the organization sets constraints, though organizations doing the same things may organize very differently to do them. A basic distinction is whether the organization manufactures things or provides a service. The latter could include providing treatment, providing education, selling goods or doing research. One reason that this is such a basic choice is that the decision to manufacture almost certainly involves the use of energy, tools and technology to a much greater degree than is likely in providing a service. This area of organizational theory has become known as the 'technological imperative', implying that certain forms of technology force certain kinds of organizational structures.

Quite a lot of empirical research has been done on this subject. Joan Woodward's work (1965) has had a lasting impact. She developed a way of classifying different kinds of production or workflow technology. Note this concept applies to the way products are manufactured, not the nature of the product itself. Woodward constructed a scale of production technology which can be described as ranging along a dimension from simple to complex or, more accurately, as smoothness of production. The least smooth form she called 'unit production'. This is where things are produced one at a time. A craftsman producing hand-made furniture would come into this category, but so would an organization producing ships, railway engines or large, complex computers. Each item is assembled as an individual product. Further along this production technology dimension one moves into mass production, which can be sub-divided into small-batch production such as might characterize a toy manufacturer, and large-batch production which occurs in the motor industry. The most complex and integral form of production technology is in continuous-flow or 'process production', where the product never, or rarely, ceases to be produced. Oil refineries and certain parts of the chemicals industry are good examples.

Table 1 contains an example of the relationship between production technology and an aspect of organizational structure. The table contains information about three different size bands of companies and the average number of people per supervisor in each size band for each of the three product technologies.

Table 1

Number of operators per supervisor classified according to production technology and organizational size
From Woodward (1965); reprinted with permission of Oxford University Press.

Production technology	Size of organization		
	400–500	850–1000	1000–4000
Unit	1:22	1:35	1:26
Mass	1:14	1:14	1:18
Process	1:8	1:8	1:8

In organizations employing unit production technology, the medium-sized organizations (850–1,000 employees) tend to have more employees per supervisor. Regardless of size, unit production employs fewer supervisors than the other two forms of production technology. This is largely because the operating core consists of skilled workers whose training and skill controls the quality of the output: the building of ships or railway engines is a relevant example. Mass production technologies are designed to use relatively unskilled labour and therefore they have to be more closely supervised. Process production employs the most supervisors because the technology is complex and mistakes can be very costly, so the whole process is very closely monitored. Toxic chemicals and float glass manufacturing illustrate such processes. In mass production and process production technologies size appears not to affect the number of supervisors employed. This latter conclusion from Woodward's data is perhaps the most tenuous (see Hickson et al, 1969).

There is some controversy in the literature as to whether organizational size or production technology is the more important determinant of organizational structure. A large body of work carried out by researchers from the University of Aston in Birmingham (Pugh and Hickson, 1976; Pugh and Hinings, 1976) showed organizational size to be a much stronger predictor of degree of bureaucratization. By bureaucratization they meant that the organization had divided its work into specialist roles (high division of labour) and that co-ordination was achieved by a hierarchical system supported by standardization of procedures which were formalized into written documents and records. In Mintzberg's terms it was a machine bureaucracy. Organizational size was correlated with bureaucratization 0.69, whilst production technology correlated only about 0.30. The Aston workers did qualify their findings by showing that technology had a greater impact on the structure at the bottom of the organization (the operating core). In medium-sized mass production organizations the operating core would have more precisely defined jobs and duties than would operators in a medium sized unit production technology. However, the roles and role definitions relating to managers in the two organizations would be very similar.

Summarizing briefly, both the decision to employ a particular mode of production and the decision to grow bigger begins to put important constraints on how the organization should structure and/or organize itself if it is to succeed. One of Woodward's findings was that organizations which had deviant structures for the technology they used tended to be the least successful. Other factors influence the design of the organization, however. Some are external to the system and some are internal.

External influences on structure

The external ones include the market/clients the organization is trying to serve; the knowledge/technical change that is occurring in the world; the economic situation resulting from changes in the availability of resources such as raw materials and finance; and the political changes resulting

from government legislation. Space prevents a separate
discussion of these, but together they may be construed as
factors which create environmental uncertainty or turbulence
(Metcalfe and McQuillan, 1977). To cope successfully with
such turbulence requires different structures from those
required to survive and develop in a stable and benign
environment. One strategy large corporations adopt is to buy
the suppliers or competitors who may be causing uncertainty.
This diversification also increases the complexity of the
organization so that the divisionalized structure tends to
emerge. One of the general principles for dealing with
environmental complexity is the 'Law of Requisite Variety'
(Ashby, 1956). This states that the variety/complexity
inside a system must be sufficient to match the variety/
complexity of the environment outside the system. Thus the
diversification strategy not only reduces uncertainty but
increases intra-organizational variety which also aids in
coping with turbulence. Less rich organizations cope by
relying much more on their own flexibility and ability to
respond to the uncertainty with new strategies and behaviour. One way they achieve this flexibility and responsiveness is by employing a variety of professional, technical and scientific people, each of whom participates
intimately in the decisions taken within the company. Such
organizations have few rules and regulations. This internal
diversity, however, creates problems of communication and
integration. To achieve co-ordination and integration
special groups are sometimes formed to ensure that the
necessary communication takes place. These 'liaison roles'
(Lawrence and Lorsch, 1967; Chandler and Sayles, 1971) come
to demand special skills and qualities of their own.
    A structure specially designed to facilitate co-
ordination in such situations is the 'matrix structure'.
This structure was developed and extensively used by NASA
to complete the US lunar programme. Problems of this scale
do not come neatly packaged by function or department, so
'project groups' were formed which combined specialists from
different functions (e.g. engineering, human factors,
physics, finance). The structure is described as a matrix
because the groups were formed by project and held responsible to the project leader (see table 2) but each member
was also responsible to the head of a functional department.
It is this dual membership which provides the expert back-up
of the function combined with the good communication and
involvement of belonging to a project team. These two responses, the liaison group and the matrix structure, are
variations of the Mintzberg adhocracy. The existence of
these two structures implies that co-ordination by mutual
adjustment sometimes needs some structural support if it is
to succeed in complex environments.

Internal influences on structure
If we turn to Mintzberg's pentagon in figure 2 we can see
some of the forces within the organization which may
influence its structure. Th se consist of the tensions

Table 2

The matrix structure

		Functional departments			
		Engineering Head + 7 subs*	Physics Head + 5 subs	Finance Head + 2 subs	Maths Head + 4 subs
Project groups	A. leader + 4 members	2		1	1
	B. leader + 8 members	2	3	1	2
	C. leader + 8 members	1	3	1	3
	D. leader + 6 members	4	1	1	

* A member of a functional department may be a member of more than one project group.

between the major groups in the organization: the top managers/owners, the professionals in the technostructure and the support structure, and the middle and lower parts of the workflow, the middle line and the operating core. Those in the strategic apex want to maintain as much control as they can, but the technocrats, the middle manager and the professionals in the support structure, fight to increase their autonomy and influence. The technocrats wish to consolidate and automate the successes of the creative research staff, but the latter prefer to continue creating new products and processes. The operating core strive to professionalize their skills and provide better products and/or services to their clients, but the technocrats wish to rationalize and improve what already exists. As Mintzberg says, at any one time there may be harmony amongst these forces, but if the external environment changes the internal environment must respond to it or the organization as a whole will fail. The internal tensions arise again and a new stability emerges through death, amputation, amalgamation or reconciliation.

The professional can now see how he may be caught in any of these cross-fires. The accountant can find himself attached to the apex, the technostructure, the operating core or the middle line. In a hospital the nurse could be in the technostructure, the middle line, the operating core or the support staff. Doctors are trained to diagnose and treat illnesses, teachers to instruct and educate and each pro- gresses in his profession on the basis of his ability in these specific skills. Eventually, however, they become managers, administrators and policy makers with little formal training in these skills. No wonder hierarchical organizations have been accused of promoting people to the point where they reach their level of incompetence (Peter, 1969). This only goes to emphasize the flexibility required of professionals in complex organizations, for the roles they create extend far beyond those for which the professional was originally trained. Indeed, roles provide the link between the broad abstractions so far discussed and the actual behaviour of people at work.

Roles in organizations

The term 'structure' refers to the pattern of offices or positions existing in an organization, and to the nature of the behaviour required of the people filling each of the offices. It is this dramaturgical aspect of structure, the definition of the parts to be played, that leads to the use of 'role' as the central concept. In their work on organizational structure, the Aston group (Pugh and Hickson, 1976) relied heavily on the concept in constructing their major measures, 'role specialization' and 'role formalization', and it is important in other concepts such as 'standardization of procedures' (for roles) and 'configuration' (distribution of roles). A major research project which utilized the concept contains some useful definitions and distinctions (Kahn et al, 1964).

ROLE: the activities and patterns of behaviour that should be performed by the occupant of an office: for example, the nurse must administer drugs and follow the correct procedures in so doing.

ROLE-SET: all other office holders who interact with another office holder, the latter being designated the focal role. Figure 4 illustrates the role-set of a senior occupational therapist in a psychiatric day hospital.

ROLE EXPECTATIONS: the attitudes and beliefs that members of a social system have about what the occupant of any office ought to do; for example, as well as doing their job, teachers are expected to be honest, moral and dedicated to children.

SENT ROLE: the expectations sent to an office holder by other members of his role-set; for example, the head of a department presses a scientist for more research, whilst his colleagues expect him to be a creative theoretician.

RECEIVED ROLE: the role as understood by the occupant based on the expectations sent to him by his role-set; for example, the above-mentioned scientist interprets the message to mean, 'publish as much as you can'.

There may well be a difference between the sent role and the received role. This may be partly due to inadequate information/communication, but can also occur because the receiver, consciously or unconsciously, wishes to see the world in a way which is comfortable or acceptable to him. Cognitive dissonance and perceptual defence are terms used elsewhere in this volume to describe these distorting processes). The disparity may also occur because the role is not clearly specified: small, expanding organizations have often not stopped to clarify who does what and have never written role specifications. Larger organizations are called bureaucracies because they do write rules and they are kept in the 'bureau'. The written word is being used here to delineate the role. We can see from the role-set in figure 3, however, that the senior occupational therapist is at the focus of a disparate set of expectations. Even if all expectations are transmitted accurately (low role ambiguity) they are likely to be in conflict. The psychiatrist may want more group work but the nurses and trainees more individual treatment. Kahn et al defined a number of types of role conflict.

INTER-SENDER CONFLICT: the expectations of two or more role senders are incompatible.

INTER-ROLE CONFLICT: two or more of the roles we occupy are in conflict; for example, manager and trade union representative, worker and father.

INTRA-SENDER CONFLICT: the same role sender has conflicting expectations, for example, increase output and improve quality.

ROLE OVERLOAD: this simply means being unable to meet the legitimate expectations of role-senders.

The fact is, of course, that role-senders also develop illegitimate expectations. This is partly because individuals in organizations are not only concerned with meeting the organization's needs: many are more concerned at meeting their own needs. The ambitious manager may develop all sorts of illegitimate ways round the rules to improve the performance of his department so that he gets promotion and leaves the clearing up to somebody else! On the other hand, we, as the general public, know from bitter personal experience that 'working to rule', the organization's carefully thought out, written down, legalized prescriptions, means inefficiency and frustrations for all. That is, some bending of the rules is actually highly functional for the organization. The universality of this slip between what is and what is supposed to be has been recognized by the concept of 'the informal organization'. The concept of role enables us to see how and why the slippage occurs. More generally the concepts relating to role enable the occupant of an office to analyse why his role is the way it is, and why it is not the way he expected it to be!

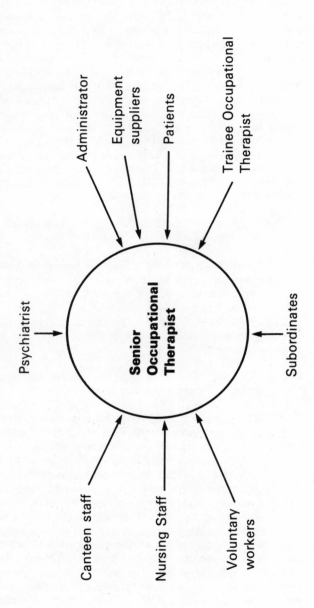

Figure 3

The role-set of a senior occupational therapist in a psychiatric day hospital

The informal organization

In work organizations role-sets do not occur randomly. They arise from the tasks to be done. In figure 3 we depict one based on the senior occupational therapist. If we were to search for others in the hospital setting we would find them centred on the surgeon's 'firm', on the portering staff, on the accident department, on the administrative office, on the junior doctors, and so on. Within each of these role-sets there would be frequent face-to-face interaction and high levels of communication. Relationships between them, however, would be much less clear-cut. In the current jargon they would be 'loosely-coupled' systems (Weick, 1976) whereas within a role-set it would be a 'tightly-coupled' system. It is also obvious that members of one role-set are often members of another. The surgeon's 'firm' will contain some of the junior doctors. The surgeon will be on committees guiding policy-making which will also contain members of the administration. These formally required interactions open up informal communication channels. It is much quicker, and perhaps more revealing, to make a direct, informal approach to another department than to work through the formal channels where the information has to go up, along, back, along and then down. It is faster, and perhaps more satisfying to take the organizational hypotenuse than the organizational right angle. The fact that many people in organizations do prefer them is confirmed by studies of how managers spend their time. About 45 per cent of their time in communication is spent communicating outside the formal chain of authority.

These informal 'grapevines' appear everywhere and are very vigorous. Caplow (1966) studied rumours in war-time conditions and found they travelled surprisingly quickly and were often surprisingly accurate. Davis (1953) studied an organization of 600 people and traced the pattern of various decisions. For one letter from a customer he found that 68 per cent of the executives received the information but only three out of the 14 communications passed through the formal chain of command. Getting things done at all, and certainly getting them done quickly, depends heavily on knowing and understanding the nature of the informal organization. It seems impossible to regulate the behaviour of human beings by fiat and authority alone. Professional, ideological and social interests cross the formally defined boundaries and these reciprocal relationships very quickly begin to twine themselves around the organization's neatly designed trunk and branches. As with vines they provide extra support and bear rich fruits but they sometimes need pruning, or replanting. And if they are accidentally uprooted they can leave the ground exposed, as it may be if a consultant recommends and installs a different, perhaps more clearly prescribed structure, but one which breaks up established relationships. An organization risks relying too heavily on the informal system which is why formalization and bureaucratization are utilized in the first place, but there is danger in trying to eliminate it all together. Farris (1979) contrasts the formal with the informal as in table 3 and it

shows clearly how the informal relies heavily on expectations rather than rules. He quotes several examples of how
the formal organization, or at least the managers representing it, can make use of the informal organization better to
achieve its purposes; for example, by placing newcomers with
people at crucial cross-over points in the informal network
in order to teach them quickly how the system really works.
Effective organizations then allow the formal and informal
to work symbiotically: to sustain and support each other.
Less effective ones fight a battle for the dominance of one
over the other. We can see from Farris' table that the
informal is, in fact, very similar to the co-ordination
principle of mutual adjustment. As Mintzberg's model indicated, all organizations face the problem of resolving the
tensions between the five co-ordinating mechanisms. From the
universality of the informal organization it seems that
adhocracy is never completely defeated. This incipient
victory of adhocracy has an influence on managerial
behaviour as we see in the next section.

The nature of managerial work

The difference between what is specified in a job (role)
description and what actually happens can also be illustrated by the study of how managers actually spend their
time. The classical description of management is that it
involves planning, organizing, co-ordinating and finally
controlling systems and people in order to achieve the
goals outlined in the plans. A relatively small number of
researchers have actually studied what managers do and one
of the most influential of these pieces of research has
again been done by Henry Mintzberg (1973). In 1975 Mintzberg
compared folk-lore to fact. The first element of folk-lore
he discussed was that the manager is a reflective, systematic planner.

His own intensive study of five chief executives showed
that only one out of 368 verbal contacts was unrelated to a
specific issue and could be called general planning. A diary
study of 160 British top and middle managers found they
worked for a half hour or more without interruption only
once every two days (Stewart, 1967). Mintzberg concludes
that not only is a manager's work characterized by brevity,
variety and discontinuity but that they actually prefer
action to reflection. Plans, if they exist, are formulated
and re-formulated in the executive's head: they are not
written down and rationally elaborated.

On the other hand, our folk-lore of the modern super-
hero is that the effective executive has no regular duties
to perform. He sits on the Olympian heights waiting the
calls of us lesser mortals. The facts show that he is down
in the valley dealing with the unexpected directly,
encouraging the peasants, negotiating with neighbours, and
even mending the fences.

Executives spend much time meeting important customers,
carrying out regular tours round their organizations, and
officiating at rituals and ceremonies. Much of their time is

Table 3

Some contrasts between formal and informal organizations
From Farris (1979): reprinted with permission.

	Organization	
Element	Formal	Informal
Salient goals	Organization's	Individual's
Structural units	Offices/positions	Individual roles
Basis for communication	Offices formally related	Proximity: physical, professional, task, social, formal
Basis for power	Legitimate authority	Capacity to satisfy individuals' needs (often through expert or referent power)
Control mechanisms	Rules	Norms (expectations)
Type of hierarchy	Vertical	Lateral

spent scanning the environment for information which can then be passed to their subordinates. This is not 'hard', easily-available information but 'soft', given in confidence or as a favour, but which becomes available only as a result of maintaining regular contacts: informal contacts!

A third piece of conventional wisdom is that senior managers need aggregated information which a formal management information system best provides. Computers have fostered this view as they seemed to be able to make such information up-to-date and easily available. The evidence suggests that managers do not use the information even if it is there. They strongly prefer to rely on meetings and telephone calls. Burns (1954) found managers spent 80 per cent of their time in verbal communication, and Mintzberg 78 per cent. The latter's five managers produced only 25 pieces of mail during the 25 days he investigated them. Only 13 per cent of the mail they received was of specific and immediate use. Managers appear to operate this way because they are future-orientated and their active scanning for hints and gossip is felt to be more useful than detailed understanding of the past. Such behaviour puts a heavy premium on their personal ability to store and sort information. It also makes it difficult for them to transfer their personal images and maps to others in the company.

A related piece of folk-lore is that management is a
science and a profession. It is true that the technostructure in large organizations uses mathematical modelling and
sophisticated planning and control techniques, but these
have little influence on senior managers or even on the
managers of the specialists running such facilities. All are
still reliant on their intuition and judgement. This is
because they manage (i) people and (ii) very complex situations: imagine the problems facing the head of a department
of management services in a regional hospital authority who
manages 70 professional staff ranging from computer specialists, through work study to behavioural science change
agents. That it is correct to give people problems priority
over situational problems is reflected in Mintzberg's
conclusions about the different roles a manager must perform. These appear diagrammatically in figure 4.

The titles of the ten roles are useful enough not to
require further elaboration. The arrows indicate that the
organization gives the manager the authority and status to
perform the 'interpersonal roles', that this requirement
leads him to perform the 'informational roles', and that
this forces his involvement in the 'decisional roles'.

Figure 4

The ten roles of the manager
Reprinted by permission of the Harvard Business Review.
Exhibit from H. Mintzberg, 'The Manager's Job: Folklore and
fact' (July-August, 1975). Copyright c 1975 by the
President and Fellows of Harvard College; all rights
reserved.

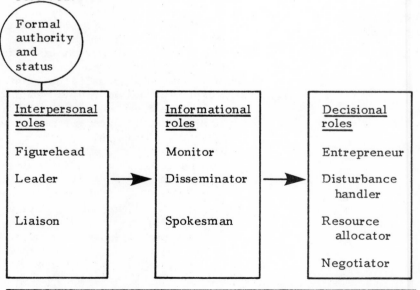

The effective manager is the one who carries out all ten
roles but who does so by finding ways to:

* gain control over his time: he tends to be bombarded by others so he must find ways of using these obligations to others to suit his own ends. His only other hope is that people do things for him because of their personal commitment to him. In hierarchical and competitive situations this highly desirable state is often lacking. He may have to be political and devious to achieve his goals;
* some of the time thus gained must be used to determine which issues are really important in the overall picture. This ability has been called the 'helicopter capacity';
* to use the rest of his saved time to ensure that he regularly and systematically shares with colleagues and subordinates his privileged information and how it fits into the images and plans that are guiding his actions.

With this amount of preparation the manager has a good chance of sneaking through the interpersonal barrage that makes up his weekly war. This applies to managers and supervisors at all points in the organization: low, middle or high, in the technostructure or the support structure. For these different positions the task changes in quantity rather than quality, and in the severity of the consequences which result from failure.

Earlier, we reviewed the major forms of organizational structure, the forces which helped to produce them, and the sorts of work they produce for managers and other professional workers. We now wish to examine some of the psychological concepts relevant to understanding the behaviour of people in organizations.

Motivation in organizations

Steers and Porter (1975) distinguish three aspects of motivation:

* what energizes or initiates behaviour?
* what directs or channels the behaviour towards a particular goal or in a particular direction?
* what maintains or sustains the behaviour once it is activated?

The various theories of motivation can be classified under each of these three headings (Hamner and Organ, 1978).

Energizer theories
The most widely known of these is Maslow's (1954) theory of human needs. Simply, men and women are motivated to act in order to satisfy their needs. According to Maslow these needs are arranged in hierarchy of pre-potency. The hierarchical order implies that needs higher up the hierarchy (lower pre-potency) do not motivate behaviour unless there is some degree of satisfaction of the lower-order needs.

Maslow's hierarchy of human needs in order of pre-potency is shown below:

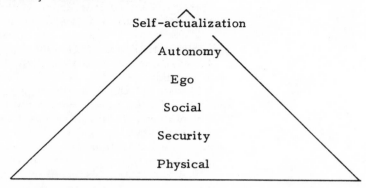

Self-actualization

Autonomy

Ego

Social

Security

Physical

It is helpful to think of them as following the course of development from infancy to full human maturity. Physical needs refer to food, water, shelter and reproductive needs. Safety needs motivate or direct behaviour when the physiological needs are more or less satisfied or satiated. They force us to seek protection against threat, danger and deprivation. Once we feel this measure of security we are emboldened to seek contact with others in search of friendship, affection and a sense of belonging to an identifiable group. That is to satisfy our social needs. The next set of forces to energize us arises from our need to be valued, liked or esteemed by the groups around us. These are the esteem needs, sometimes called ego needs. Once we have discovered that we compare well with other people we may begin to find that we are not totally happy, either with the standards they set, or with what they actually esteem. We begin to develop our own standards and values which signals the motivating force of our autonomy needs. Provided we achieve sufficient autonomy, and Maslow's view is that many organizations prevent us from achieving it (1965), we may begin to find ourselves driven strongly to develop our talents and potential even to the detriment of the satisfaction of our lower-order needs. The drive to fulfil oneself in this way arises from our self-actualization needs, sometimes called growth needs (Alderfer, 1969). It must be understood that the amount it takes to satisfy any particular need varies enormously across individuals. Gluttons need more food than hermits, risk-takers less security than bankers, extraverts more friends than introverts, the Smiths more cars than the Jones, adventurers more freedom than nuns, artists more fulfilment than executives.

A second energizing theory is proposed by Scott (1966) and is called activation theory. It is a very general theory about how people are energized. High activation occurs as a result of (i) physiological/biochemical differences between people and (ii) the liveliness or demandingness of the environment. The theory states that moderate levels of arousal are the most preferred. Too little and we experience boredom, too much and we experience anxiety or fear. The right amount is pleasant and motivating. We are likely to seek out these conditions again. This takes us to the question of how behaviour is channelled.

Channeller/director theories

As suggested in the previous paragraph we strive to achieve situations that have satisfied our needs. Two theories are relevant. The first is goal-setting theory. Locke (1976) is its chief proponent. His major point is that individuals strive to attain that which satisfies them. But the goal, and not the pleasure from achieving it, is what actually directs their efforts. Logically and temporarily it comes prior to the satisfaction. What we value and desire determines the goals we strive for but what directs us are the goals (intentions) themselves. Locke has done several experiments showing that setting specific, even difficult goals leads to more effective performance than setting general goals such as 'I'll try my best'.

A major management tool incorporating goal-setting is 'management by objectives' (Humble, 1970) or MBO. This is a systematic technique whereby boss and subordinate agree on the objectives for the job, agree what would indicate the successful achievement of the objectives and meet periodically to review if the objectives have been achieved.

A more complex and popular theory with researchers has been expectancy-instrumentality theory (Vroom, 1964). Efforts to demonstrate its empirical value have not been impressive (Campbell and Pritchard, 1976), but it has intellectual appeal. The theory assumes objects and states of affairs have differing value, attractiveness or valence. Valence can be positive (we want it), neutral (we do not care), negative (we want to avoid it). Our acts lead to outcomes and in expectancy-instrumentality theory outcomes are either first-order or second-order. A first-order outcome enables us to achieve a second-order outcome. For example, a manager may wish to be promoted (second-order outcome) and in order to achieve this he works hard, increases his team's output and is given a merit increase (first-order outcome). One can see straight away that this person's strategy depends upon the assumption that increased performance will lead to promotion. Instrumentality refers to the strength of this belief: how confident the manager is that increased performance will lead to promotion. Instrumentality is measured by asking people how certain they are of this relationship. They can be certain it will, uncertain, or certain it will not. The final concept is expectancy. This refers to the person's subjective beliefs about the probability of his behaviour leading to the first level outcome. The person can be 100 per cent certain to totally unsure. The strength of the person's motivation to proceed in a particular direction will be a function of these various factors. We are strongly motivated to do something if we are confident (high expectancy) that the act will lead to a given outcome (first order) and that this outcome is highly likely (instrumental) to lead to our attaining something we value (second-order valence). Students are likely to work hard for exams if they are confident they can achieve a good result, and are reasonably certain that a good result will lead to the kind of career they have long wanted. Managers will not be motivated if they see no hope of achieving a goal, no matter how certain they are that it will lead to something they dearly want.

Put like this it sounds like a tautology or truism, but it has proved difficult to demonstrate empirically because (i) our success is determined by other factors such as our skill or ability, or the intrusion of unexpected factors; (ii) because it is very difficult for people actually to know what the probabilities connecting instrumentality and expectancy are; and (iii) because real-life behaviour entails several sets of both first- and second-level outcomes making it easy for errors in estimating the probabilities to become compounded.

Nevertheless, the theory highlights some practical aspects of motivation: (i) the organization must provide rewards its employees value: money, fringe benefits, interesting work, security, etc.; (ii) there must be a relation between variations in performance and variations in reward: in many professional/salaried jobs promotion is the only variation in reward; (iii) the organization must make clear what the relationships between effort, performance and rewards are; (iv) the organization must be free to vary the size of rewards sufficiently to encourage people to work harder: some companies employ merit reward systems where extra payment is given solely for higher performance. But sometimes the maximum reward as a percentage of salary may be only three or four per cent which can be so low as to seem demotivating to the dedicated worker.

Maintenance theories of motivation

The most influential maintenance theory has been Herzberg's (1966) two-factor theory. Herzberg set out to understand what it was that gave people satisfaction at work, with the assumption that this would reveal what motivated them to work harder. He proceeded by asking accountants and engineers to describe times when they were dissatisfied and times when they were highly satisfied. Analysis of these interviews showed that these two emotional states were caused by two different sets of conditions.

The things that caused dissatisfaction if they were absent or inadequate were:

* salary or pay;
* relationship with peers;
* job security;
* status;
* company policy;
* working conditions;
* relationship with boss.

Herzberg called these hygiene factors. Following the analogy of public health measures, he argued that if they were adequate they would prevent one from becoming dissatisfied, but they would not make one satisfied, just as good sanitation alone will not make one healthy. He argued further that no matter how good the hygiene factors were people would always want more. Most people could always use more money, have better relationships with others, have better working conditions, etc.

The things which people said made themselves satisfied with their work Herzberg called motivators. These were psychological factors such as the interesting nature of the work, feelings of significant achievement, feelings of personal growth and being responsible for worth-while activities. The promotion and recognition that went with these were also motivators. These same findings have been replicated with shop-floor groups, though there is some controversy about whether things are quite as neat as Herzberg's early work showed (cf. House and Wigdor, 1967).

This work has been influential, however, since it played an important part in encouraging organizations to enrich jobs, to make them more complex, more demanding in skill and to increase the degree of control the worker has over his work activities. For example, instead of having each person assemble one part of an electric fire, one could design the job so that each person assembled a complete fire. The principles can extend to allowing workers to set targets and quality standards.

The relevance of the two-factor theory in the present context is that it is interesting work and achievement that sustains high commitment and performance. Pay may get us to work but excitement turns us on once we are there. There is evidence that people low on self-actualization needs do not conform to this pattern. There is also evidence that some people are strongly motivated by money and a good deal of agreement that it has importance for most of us.

Another theory about what maintains our behaviour is social comparison theory. The theory proposes that we compare ourselves with others doing similar work in similar conditions, with similar qualifications and experience, and if the comparison is equitable we continue to sustain our efforts. If the comparison is unfavourable we reduce our input to maintain equity. The skilled coal miner who, when asked why he only attended work four days a week, replied 'because I can't earn enough money in three', may well have been comparing himself with better paid, unskilled car workers. This is quite a good example of why the hygiene factors remain insatiable and why parity arguments are such a powerful force in trade union bargaining. The challenge to the organization is to maintain equity at minimum costs. This means remaining alert to pay rates and working conditions and being flexible in adjusting to changes in them. It also means treating people fairly and equitably.

When we talk about motivating individuals we are usually talking about a change in their behaviour: we want people to work harder, or give a better service, or follow the organization's rules. Learning is defined as a change in behaviour and not surprisingly learning theory has some relevance to understanding behaviour in organizations.

Learning theory and work behaviour

If learning is defined as 'a change in behaviour' we have to ask, 'What causes the behaviour to change?' A common-sense answer might be, 'I decided to do things differently'. 'Why?' would be our next question. The person might reply, 'Because I felt it would be more rewarding to me', or 'Because I would be punished if I didn't'. If we analyse this we can see that learning involves dealing with situations and that depending upon how we behave or respond we may get rewarded or punished: that is, there is an outcome.

Situation ——▶ Behaviour ——▶ Outcome (reward/punishment)

Given we wish people to deal with particular situations and the behaviour is what we want to change, the only things we can manipulate are the outcomes associated with the behaviour. Much research on learning has concentrated on what happens when the outcomes are manipulated in different ways. Two major factors are, first, the nature of the outcome and, second, the frequency with which the behaviour is rewarded/ punished: this is known as the study of schedules of reinforcement.

The nature of outcomes

Four types of outcome are distinguished. Two encourage the behaviour to be repeated and two discourage repetition of the behaviour. Either way behaviour is changed.

1. REINFORCING OR ENCOURAGING OUTCOMES: (i) positive reinforcement: this occurs when the behaviour is followed by a reward which the person likes and wants. The reward encourages the person to repeat the behaviour in the same circumstances or even to generalize the learning by repeating the behaviour in similar circumstances: for example, a worker solves a problem and his superior congratulates him. The solution will be tried again. (ii) Escape learning: by behaving correctly a person escapes being hurt or punished. This is rewarding too and the person is likely to repeat the behaviour: for instance, a worker escapes injury because he was wearing proper safety equipment. This may generalize to his always wearing a seat belt in his car.

2. DISCOURAGING OUTCOMES: (i) expected rewards do not materialize: this is known technically as extinction. A person has got used to being rewarded for a particular behaviour and the rewards cease to be given. Under these conditions the behaviour will eventually cease; for example, under one boss a subordinate is encouraged to read the

technical journals. A new boss never comments on the behaviour so he stops reading. (ii) Punishment occurs when
behaviour is followed either by something painful or disliked, such as being publicly told off by one's boss or
something one wants is withheld: for example, an expected
promotion is not given.

How well the behaviour is learned depends on two things:
first, how valued the reward is, or how severe the punishment might be: most people do not deliberately touch a hot
iron twice; and second, how frequently the behaviour has
been rewarded/punished in the past; that is to say, there
are different schedules of reinforcement.

3. SCHEDULES OF REINFORCEMENT: there are two basic
schedules: continuous reinforcement and partial reinforcement. Continuous reinforcement refers to the situation where
the behaviour is followed by the same outcome every time the
behaviour occurs. In real life this situation very rarely
applies. When the conditions are approximated, however, it
results in very rapid learning but also in rapid extinction
once the reward is withdrawn. This is true unless the behaviour has been rewarded enough for it to become automatic
or habitual.

For example, a supervisor can rapidly stop a person
making an error if he stands over him, but the error will
quickly return unless the behaviour has been overlearned and
become a habit. Nurses are carefully watched when preparing
drug doses and always punished for mistakes until it does
become a habit; and like riding a bike it is probably never
extinguished.

Partial reinforcement schedules mean the behaviour is
only followed by the outcome some of the time. There are
four types, based on whether the rate of reinforcement is
fixed or variable, and whether the rate is based on intervals of time or the ratio of reinforced to unreinforced
behaviours. Thus fixed interval schedules mean that
reinforcement occurs at a fixed time interval: weekly or
monthly as does a pay cheque. Fixed-ratio schedules mean
that reinforcement is given after every nth response: for
example, after every fifth sale is made a saleswoman
receives a bonus. The variable schedules mean that the time
period or the ratio of responses varies around an average.
Research on animals has shown that behaviour which is
learned under the variable schedules is more resistant to
extinction. One continues the behaviour because one is less
sure whether the outcome has really stopped occurring.
Gambling behaviour is an obvious example. The reinforcement
occurs randomly. The size of the reward varies randomly and
the reward immediately follows the behaviour.

An ideal payment schedule based on these ideas might
look something like this:

*   a reasonable fixed amount to attract you to the
    workplace;

* bonus payments based on higher output and paid daily/weekly;
* extra 'lucky draw' tickets, with extra ones being given for exceptional performance, and the lottery being drawn irregularly but including small chances of winning really valuable prizes.

Examples of such systems do exist and these principles for 'shaping' behaviour have been applied to problems such as lateness, absence, under-utilization of public transport, reducing scrap rates, training, and improving the quality of supervisory behaviour. Examples can be found in 'Organizational Behavior Modification' (Luthans and Kreitner, 1975). See also chapters 5 and 6.

Research in this area has been heavily dominated by B. F. Skinner and a statement of his work and the philosophy of behaviourism which has guided it can be found in 'About Behaviorism' (Skinner, 1976). Much of Skinner's research has shown the superiority of positive reinforcement over punishment as a means of controlling and shaping behaviour. The natural world, however, seems to have been uninfluenced by Skinner. It still punishes us viciously, but we learn from the punishments. Many men and women have not heeded Skinner either, the cynics say because giving punishments is rewarding to the punisher. There is doubtless some truth in this. More practically, if we only rely on positively rewarding desired behaviour we have to wait until the behaviour occurs to be able to reward it: it may never do so. So punishment is here to stay, but research indicates that if it has to be used, it is more effective if it is administered immediately following the undesired behaviour, that the person is given an explanation as to why the behaviour is undesirable, that it is administered because of the behaviour and not the person themselves, that it is administered in private to avoid public shaming, that the punishment fits the crime, and that we do not immediately do something nice to the person to make up for the punishment! Such 'model' behaviour leads us to consider a third form of learning: imitation.

Imitation learning
We often change our behaviour by copying someone else. No doubt we learn to model by copying our parents who reward us through the processes of positive and negative reinforcement, but imitative behaviour seems to develop a life of its own. Often we copy behaviour that is not apparently reinforced by outside contingencies. It may be that we just like it, but regardless of its origins it is certainly a major way in which we learn. We can exploit this capacity for ourselves by looking for good models to copy or we can use the process to encourage learning in others. It is a technique frequently used in training (see Goldstein and Sorcher, 1974). Factors which affect the degree of learning through modelling are:

* CHARACTERISTICS OF THE MODEL: they are good at what they do; they are of high status; they control resources desired by the learner; they are similar in age, race and same sex; they are helpful and friendly; the model is rewarded for helping the learner.
* THE PROCESS OF MODELLING: the behaviour is vivid, but detailed; is organized from least to most difficult; is repeated enough for overlearning to occur; avoids irrelevant behaviours; uses several similar models rather than a single model.
* CHARACTERISTICS OF THE LEARNER: is instructed or wants to model; has similar attitudes and background to the model; likes and admires the model; is positively reinforced for modelling.

Our treatment of learning so far has been of a rather mechanical nature: know which carrot to wave when, or how and when to apply a suitable stick and behaviour becomes controllable. Implicit in this sort of learning is the assumption of a standard of desirable behaviour. Otherwise the learner, and the teacher/influencer, would not know when to stop their respective activities. We used the analogy of a machine because machines are designed to behave to specified standards. Recent thinking about human learning and changing human behaviour has raised the important question, how do we learn to change the standards? Argyris and Schon (1974, 1978) call this Model II learning.

Model II learning
One thing that distinguishes man from the animal or physical world is that he can represent, interpret and value it for himself, so that he constructs reality. Man decides whether democracy is good, whether better performances should be better rewarded and whether red is a colour or a communist. In the psychosocial world there are not just facts, but facts and appreciations (Vickers, 1968) of them. Much of the time we are not aware of the nature of our appreciations or value systems and even less aware of how they are influencing our perceptions and the actions we base on them. An everyday example is our injunction to children, 'Don't do as I do; do as I say'. Clearly the message received by the child is not the one we wish to convey; but which message reflects what we really value? Argyris and Schon (1974) refer to the 'do as I say' part of the above statement as the espoused theory. The 'don't do as I do' element they call the theory-in-use; that is, the theory, standards, values which are actually guiding our behaviour.

Based on their research and consultancy Argyris and Schon have concluded that people find it very difficult to understand and to change the principles which are guiding much of their social behaviour. Furthermore, the very principles guiding that behaviour are the ones which prevent the learning of new values or standards. Table 4 contrasts some of the properties of the two models.

Table 4

A comparison of Model I and Model II learning
From Argyris and Schon (1978); 'Organizational Learning: A theory of action perspective'. Addison-Wesley, chapter 6, p. 137, figure 6.1: 'Model II Theory-in-Use'. Reprinted with permission.

Model I		Model II	
Governing variables	Behavioural consequences	Governing variables	Behavioural consequences
1. Define goals achieve them	Actor is: defensive, about self, controlling	1. Striving for information	Minimal defensivesness, collaborator, facilitator, choice creator
2. To win, not lose	Define, and control what's done	2. Free and informed choice	Trust, risk-taking with support, shared responsibility
3. Minimize generating or expressing negative feeling	Defensive norms (mistrust, conformity, emphasis on diplomacy, power-centred competition)	3. Freely chosen commitment to choices and monitoring of implementation	Norms orientated to learning (open confrontation) on difficult issues)
4. Be rational	Low freedom of choice, calculated commitment and calculated risks		

OUTCOME - THINGS STAY AS THEY ARE EVEN IF THEY APPEAR TO HAVE CHANGED

OUTCOME - NEW, PERHAPS ORIGINAL PATTERNS EMERGE

One can see that if we start with the goals of being rational and avoiding hurt, of remaining in control and of avoiding defeat, that it becomes painful, irrational and an admission of self-defeat to ask if these guiding principles are wrong! Since we have strived to avoid hurt we have, of course, avoided being punished for using the principles. In other words, our world has reinforced us positively for following them, frequently and over many years. They are habits of thought.

Argyris and Schon (1978) have found them deeply ingrained ones, but ones which many individuals and organizations need to discard if they are to break out of the closed loop such principles create. Sometimes this breaking out occurs naturally as a result of disaster such as bankruptcy, divorce or severe illness. These events force us to recognize the real nature of our theories-in-use and the costs of following them. Since creating crises is hardly a marketable commodity, the main strategy used to develop Model II learning is for the consultant to model the behaviour and force public testing of the effectiveness of current theories in use, and the design and public testing of alternative theories in use. This requires the establishment of open and trusting interpersonal relationships, great skill and integrity on the part of the consultant, and an initial willingness to experiment on the part of the learners. Argyris' (1974) descriptions of his efforts in a major newspaper corporation illustrate the difficulties even when these factors are present. But the evidence that we are victims of our values is incontrovertible: and poignantly emphasized by Vickers (1968). 'The sanest, like the maddest of us, cling like spiders to a self-spun web, obscurely moored in vacancy and fiercely shaken by the winds of change' (Vickers, 1968).

Leadership in organizations

Whilst there is a large and distinctive body of research on leadership, it overlaps with the study of managerial behaviour and decision making. Its importance lies in its evaluation of the effectiveness of particular styles of managing and in determining which styles are most appropriate in different situations.

The word manager is derived from the French word 'la main' which conveys handling and manipulating. In contrast, 'lead' means heading in a direction with the assumption that others will follow. The essence of leadership then is influencing people to follow your lead. French and Raven (1959) propose people can be influenced in several ways: they call them the bases of social power. They are described below.

* Coercion or the power to punish.
* Reward or ability to allocate resources.
* Authority or legitimate power.
* Referent power: one is liked or admired.
* Expert power: the authority of knowledge.

In the numerous studies of leadership behaviour there has been a striking consensus about the major and most frequently used styles. The two most frequently discovered are (i) a concern for people and (ii) a concern for ensuring the task is done and done properly. Some of the labels used to describe these two basic styles are listed below:

People		**Tasks**
Employee-centred	versus	Production-centred
Consideration		
structure	versus	Initiation structure
Democratic	versus	Autocratic
Concern for people	versus	Concern for production
Consults, joins	versus	Tells, sells

A less frequently identified aspect of behaviour is one which Cooper (1966) called 'leader's task relevance' and which Bass (1967) called 'task-orientation'. It refers to the leader's personal commitment to and competence in the skills and knowledge inherent in the task. If the leader was a surgeon the commitment would be to surgery, if an academic to scholarship, if a manager to management, if a trade unionist to labour history and union organization. We prefer to call it the technical-professional style because task-centred has been used to describe the production-centred autocratic style too. The parallels between these empirically discovered styles of leadership and the bases of social influence is, we hope, apparent.

All three styles have been shown, and have not been shown, to be related to the effectiveness of the group. It is differences in the situation which cause these variations. Fiedler (1967) was the first to collect a body of empirical research from which he developed his 'contingency model of leadership effectiveness'.

Fiedler measured three aspects of the situation:

* leader-member relations: were they good or poor?
* task structure: highly structured tasks have (i) clearly stated goals, (ii) low variety of tasks, (iii) low requirements for members to co-operate with each other, and (iv) involve decisions where it is easy to verify the success of failure of the decision. Assembly lines are highly structured; governing boards are low.
* leader's position power: the degree of power the leader has by virtue of his formal authority and his informal influence.

These three measures were combined to produce an eight-fold classification of situations. Underlying this classification, however, is the important theoretical proposition that the relationship between leadership style and group effectiveness is moderated by the degree to which the situation allows the leader to influence his team members. Figure 5 shows these eight situations ordered from most to least favourable in allowing the leader to influence sub-ordinate behaviour. If leader-member relations are good, the task is highly structured and the leader has strong position power (situation 1) so he can more easily influence his group. Beneath each of the eight situations we have indicated by the letters P, N and T the most effective leadership style. This summarizes many studies on many different kinds of groups. Fiedler only measured person (P) and task-centred (T) styles of leadership. 'N' refers to situations where there is no relationship between these leadership styles and group performance. Task-centred styles are more effective if the situation is either very favourable or very unfavourable, and obviously for very different reasons. People-centred styles are most effective in situations where it is only moderately easy for the leader to influence team members. Three practical suggestions arise from this work:

*   change the leader's style to match the situational demands;
*   change the situation to match the leader's style;
*   select people to match situations.

There is some debate as to whether leaders can change their behaviour so easily. One study of UK managers showed that subordinates were most dissatisfied with managers who had no consistent style. Fiedler believes behaviour is difficult to change and favours changing situations, but others have shown that leaders treat sub-groups of their teams differently anyway. The inner 'cadre' of a team are given freedom and respect and the rest, the 'hired-hands', are treated more formally and autocratically. Freedom to change both situations and behaviours are also frequently constrained by organizational rules, practices and the physical plant. Once again the findings are best used as general guidelines for understanding particular situations. A short, up-to-date summary of leadership can be found in Evans (1979).

The difficulties encountered by lone individuals (leaders) attempting to create change in large organizations are universal and are partly responsible for the growth of a new breed of behavioural science consultants who practise organization development (OD).

Organizational development

OD has two major strands to its short history. One is the evidence that management development alone does not improve an organization. A second is the increasing recognition that emotional and interpersonal factors play a major role in determining behaviour. Even well-educated men are not totally rational, or even reasonable beings. It was also recognized that understanding feelings, emotions and attitudes requires different learning and teaching methods from passing on cognitively-based knowledge. In the late

Leader: member relations	Good				Poor			
Task structure	Structured		Unstructured		Structured		Unstructured	
Leader position	high	low	high	low	high	low	high	low
	1	2	3	4	5	6	7	8
Type of leader most effective in the situation	T	T	N	P	P	N	T	T

Favourable for leader ←———————→ Unfavourable for leader

KEY
P = Person-centered leadership style
T = Task-centered leadership style
N = No relationship

Figure 5

Leadership effectiveness in situations
Adapted from F. E. Fiedler, 'A Theory of Leadership
Effectiveness', New York: McGraw-Hill.

1940s psychologists, psychiatrists and their students began to work together in groups to understand what was happening within the group itself. The distinction between teacher and student was suspended, people were encouraged to say how they felt about things and why they felt the way they did. Group members were pressed to be honest about what other people's looks, actions or mannerisms did to them. Openness, honesty, sharing and trust were encouraged in order for people to understand themselves and the processes going on within groups. This grew into a world-wide movement with a vast array of techniques for helping people understand themselves and others. They range from groups where everybody is nude and which last continuously for 48 hours to conventional counselling. I do not know of any organizations which have used the nude marathon but many have used less risky techniques to develop their social skills and actually to work with each other to solve personal and interpersonal problems. The OD consultant's job is to help them to do this without them damaging each other.

For many years this 'sensitivity-training' or 'process consultation' was the OD consultant's main role. Experience taught them, however, that it is not enough merely to get people talking and listening to each other effectively. The communication needed to be used to get the organization's work done more efficiently and effectively. This required an understanding of the technology and tasks of the organization and the role structures associated with them. Organization development requires creating harmony amongst people, tasks, technology and structures. It is about helping the organization to develop its capacities to learn for itself, to do its own Model II learning. The consultant's job is to facilitate the processes that lead to this. The truly successful consultants make themselves redundant forever.

Table 5 outlines an OD programme to illustrate how all levels and parts of the organization are involved in the change programme. If it is a success people feel a greater sense of integration with each other, with the goals of the company, and have a greater willingness to risk new ventures. It becomes a genuine learning system as opposed to a set of individual learners.

This is an idealized view. In practice few organizations have experienced such total OD programmes. It is more typical to find consultants working with parts of the organization or using OD techniques and principles to assist the implementation of a technological or structural change, such as job enrichment or decentralization. The author and three colleagues (Warr et al, 1978) carried out an intervention in a steel works where we did work with groups from the top to the bottom of the organization. But the focus was on problems facing each particular group and ways the group might go about solving them for themselves. This actually raised problems which could only be resolved by the Steel Corporation more generally and there was little success with these issues, but many local problems were successfully tackled.

Table 5

A six phase OD programme
From: Blake and Mouton (1978): reprinted with permission of
Gulf Publishing Company.

0. The top management give the go-ahead.

1. Learning the language and principles: small groups of
managers from different parts and levels of the company meet
for one week to learn about the programme, its language and
their own leadership styles. An open climate is encouraged.

2. Team development: actual work teams meet for a week
to work on how they work. Starts with the top group and
works down. Openness, trust encouraged.

3. Inter-group development: groups and departments that
have important working relationships spend several days
exchanging views of each other and working out plans to
improve relationships. Plans implemented.

4. Top management team's relationships should now be good
enough to develop an ideal model for the organization. They
spend a week developing the basic ideas and months refining
them.

5. The ideal strategic model is implemented. Special teams
are set up to achieve this. The consultant may still be
involved.

6. The strategic model is systematically evaluated and
adjustments planned, made, and evaluated ...

In his fascinating book 'Behind the Front Page', Argyris
(1974) describes how he acted as a consultant to the top
management team of a major American newspaper. He concentrated on developing good interpersonal relationships
amongst the team and worked with them over many months.

Concepts in organizational behaviour: some common threads
This chapter is replete with concepts and labels. Figure 6
attempts to show that there are some common threads amongst
most of those used. There is a progression from left to
right implying that organizations develop certain dominant
forms and patterns of behaviour if the individuals who lead
them make particular assumptions about what motivates men
and women at work. The philosophies of man are taken from
Schein (1965) and follow Maslow's need hierarchy up until
complex man where Schein proposes that men learn and adapt,
circumstances force them to change and that motivation is a
complex, ever-altering force. Historically, however, and in
different organizations now, these different philosophies
have been more or less popular. It is proposed in figure 6

that these motivational assumptions lead to different learning/shaping processes, that they depend on different bases of social power which lead to different leadership styles and decision-making procedures. These processes are most easily supported by structures of particular types. Once again, they are pure types, but figure 6 is intended to convey the nature of their purity, the possible combinations of impure types and to act as a summary of essential facts.

Before finishing, however, let us deal briefly with the role of professionals in organizations.

Professional roles in organizations

We saw at the beginning of this chapter that professionals can be located in all parts of the organization's structure and that this would demand different responses from them. A general model for examining the nature of these tensions has been proposed by Gowler and Legge (1980). They use it to derive a table showing the methods that different professional groups use to deal with the varying demands made upon them. This table is shown with the addition of trade union official (table 6). Apart from revealing the variety of professional relationships it shows how professionals need to change roles within their organization. The scientist who manages research becomes a professional manager. The trade union official also becomes a manager of his staff. The values and methods of these different professions are rarely in sympathy.

The stresses in professional roles are further elaborated by Gowler and Legge with the model in figure 7. This

Table 6

The variety of professional roles
From Gowler and Legge (1980): reprinted by permission of J. Wiley & Sons.

Provider	Values/Beliefs	Core Method	Outcomes	User
Scientist	Cognitive/ technical	Experimental	Prediction	Other scientists
Doctor	Therapeutic	Diagnostic	Prescription	Patient
Lawyer	Judicial	Negotiated adjudication	Proscription	Client
Administrator Manager	Bureaucratic Entrepreneurial	Organization Pragmatic	Regulation Transaction	Employees Customers
Trade union official	Welfare and protection	Negotiation	Agreements	Membership

Figure 6

Concepts in organizational behaviour – some common threads

Dominant philosophy of man	Dominant learning process	Dominant basis of social power	Dominant style of leadership	Dominant organizational form
Economic man →	Punishment and extinction →	Coercion/ authority →	Initiation structure (tells/sells) →	Simple structure/ machine bureaucracy
Social man →	Reward and avoidance learning →	Reward →	Consideration structure (consults) →	Professional bureaucracy
Self actualizing man →	Imitation/ learning →	Referent/ expert (about facts) →	Task orientated (joins) →	Adhocracy
Complex man →	Model II Learning/ appreciative behaviour →	Referent/ expert (about process) →	Facilitator (unites) →	? (Flexitocracy)

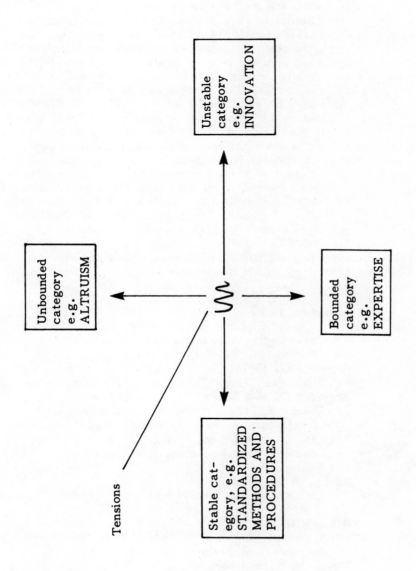

Figure 7

The cruciform effect in professional roles

model describes 'the cruciform effect' to emphasize the competing tensions inherent in professional roles. The tensions can only be resolved by the choices of the professional himself. As figure 7 shows, the professional is expected to provide a service to his clients based on the expertise derived from his training. Professionals as 'worthy' people, however, are expected to demonstrate goodness, kindness and other altruistic behaviour. But this is not clearly defined and takes them outside their expertise. Similarly they are pulled in opposing directions by demands to provide a reliable and comprehensive service requiring the application of standard methods and procedures, and yet as good professionals to be either using or actually creating the latest innovation. In these authors' words, 'The professional is trapped between morality and expediency as he attempts to match the absolutism which vindicates professional authority with the relativism which vindicates professional practice'. How these tensions will appear in specific roles in specific organizations it is not possible to predict. You will have to fill out the boxes for yourself, but the models will help to identify the general nature of the issues you are likely to face. The cruciform effect has a visual similarity to a role-set, of course, and that model would be helpful too in putting bones on this ubiquitous skeleton.

Indeed, the whole chapter is a series of skeletons, but they do constitute an introduction to the anatomy and physiology of organizations.

References

Alderfer, C.P. (1969)
An empirical test of a theory of human needs. Organizational Behavior and Human Performance, 4, 142-175.

Argyris, C. (1974)
Behind the Front Page. San Francisco: Jossey-Bass.

Argyris, C. and Schon, D.A. (1974)
Theory in Practice: Increasing professional effectiveness. San Francisco: Jossey-Bass.

Argyris, C. and Schon, D.A. (1978)
Organizational Learning. Reading, Mass.: Addison-Wesley.

Ashby, W.R. (1956)
An Introduction to Cybernetics. London: Chapman & Hall.

Bass, B.M. (1967)
Social behavior and the orientation inventory. Psychological Bulletin, 68, 260-292.

Blake, R.R. and Mouton, J.S. (1978)
The New Managerial Grid. Houston: Gulf Publishing Co.

Burns, T. (1954)
The directions of activity and communication in a departmental and executive group. Human Relations, 7, 73-97.

Campbell, J.P. and Pritchard, R.D. (1976)
Motivation theory in industrial and organizational
psychology. In M.D. Dunnette (ed.), Handbook of
Industrial and Organizational Psychology. Chicago: Rand
McNally.

Caplow, T. (1966)
Rumours in War. In A.H. Rubenstein and C.H. Haber-
stroth (eds), Some Theories of Organization. Homewood,
Ill.: Irwin-Dorsey.

Chandler, M.K. and Sayles, L.R. (1971)
Managing Large Systems. New York: Harper & Row.

Cooper, R.C. (1966)
Leader's task relevance and subordinate behaviour in
industrial work groups. Human Relations, 19, 57-84.

Davis, K. (1953)
Management communication and the grapevine. Harvard
Business Review, Sept.-Oct., 43-49.

Evans, M.G. (1979)
Leadership. In S. Kerr (ed.), Organizational Behavior.
Columbus, Ohio: Grid Publishing.

Farris, G.F. (1979)
The informal organization in strategic decision-
making. International Studies of Management and
Organization, 9, 131-152.

Fiedler, F.E. (1967)
A Theory of Leadership Effectiveness. New York:
McGraw-Hill.

French, J.R.P. Jr and Raven, B. (1959)
The bases of social power. In D. Cartwright
(ed.), Studies in Social Power. Ann Arbor, Mich.:
Institute for Social Research.

Goldstein, A.P. and Sorcher, M. (1974)
Changing Supervisor Behavior. New York: Pergamon
Press.

Gowler, D. and Legge, K. (1980)
Evaluative practices as stressors in occupational
settings. In C.L. Cooper and R. Payne (eds), Current
Concerns in Occupational Stress. Chichester: Wiley.

Hamner, W.C. and Organ, D.W. (1978)
Organizational Behavior: An applied psychological
approach. Dallas: Business Publications Inc.

Herzberg, F. (1966)
Work and the Nature of Man. Cleveland: World
Publishing.

Hickson, D.J., Pugh, D.S. and Pheysey, D.C. (1969)
Operations technology and organizational structure:
an empirical reappraisal. Administrative Science
Quarterly, 378-397.

House, R.J. and Wigdor, L.A. (1967)
Herzberg's dual-factor theory of job satisfaction
and motivation: a review of the evidence and a
criticism. Personnel Psychology, 10, 368-389.

Humble, J. (1970)
Management by Objectives in Action. London: McGraw-
Hill.

Kahn, R.L., Wolfe, D.M., Quinn, R.P., Snoek, J.D. and Rosenthal, R.A. (1964)
Organizational Stress. New York: Wiley.

Lawrence, P.R. and Lorsch, J.W. (1967)
Organization and Environment. Boston: Harvard Business School.

Locke, E.A. (1976)
The nature and causes of job satisfaction. In M.D. Dunnette (ed.), Handbook of Industrial and Organizational Psychology. Chicago: Rand McNally.

Luthans, F. and Kreitner, R. (1975)
Organizational Behavior Modification. Glenview, Ill.: Scott, Foresman & Co.

Maslow, A.H. (1954)
Motivation and Personality. New York: Harper & Row.

Maslow, A.H. (1965)
Eupsychian Management. Homewood, Ill.: Irwin-Dorsey.

Metcalfe, L. and McQuillan, W. (1977)
Managing turbulence. In P.C. Nystrom and W.H. Starbuck (eds), Prescriptive Models of Organization. Amsterdam: North-Holland Publishing Co.

Mintzberg, H. (1973)
The Nature of Managerial Work. New York: Harper & Row.

Mintzberg, H. (1975)
The manager's job: folklore and fact. Harvard Business Review, July-August, 49-61.

Mintzberg, H. (1979)
The Structuring of Organizations. Englewood Cliffs, NJ: Prentice-Hall.

Peter, L.F. (1969)
The Peter Principle. New York: William Morrow.

Pugh, D.S. and Hickson, D.J. (eds) (1976)
Organizational Structure in its Context. Farnborough: Saxon House/Teakfield Press.

Pugh, D.S. and Hinings, C.R. (1976)
Organization: Structure Extensions and Replications. Farnborough: Saxon House.

Schein, E.H. (1965)
Organizational Psychology. Englewood Cliffs, NJ: Prentice-Hall.

Scott, W.E. Jr (1966)
Activation theory and task design. Organizational Behavior and Human Performance, 1, 3-30.

Skinner, B.F. (1976)
About Behaviorism. New York: Vintage Books.

Steers, R. and Porter, L.W. (1975)
Motivation and Work Behavior. New York: McGraw-Hill.

Stewart, R. (1967)
Managers and their Jobs. London: Macmillan.

Vickers, G. (1968)
Value Systems and Social Process. London: Tavistock.

Vroom, V.H. (1964)
Work and Motivation. New York: Wiley.

Warr, P.B., Finemen, S., Nicholson, N. and Payne, R.L. (1978)
Developing Employee Relations. Farnborough: Saxon House/Teakfield.

Weick, K.E. (1976)
Educational organizations as loosely coupled systems. Administrative Science Quarterly, 1-19.

Woodward, J. (1965)
Industrial Organization: Theory and practice. Oxford: Oxford University Press.

Questions

1. Describe the different ways by which organizations attempt to achieve co-ordination. Give examples of each.
2. What is a matrix organization? When is it likely to be used? What are its strengths and weaknesses?
3. What type of organizational structure(s) would you expect to find in (i) a medium-sized general hospital; (ii) a department store?
4. Illustrate your understanding of the concepts related to role-set by analysing the role of student (or any suitable variation of that).
5. Compare and contrast the formal versus the informal organization. Provide examples from an organization of which you are a member.
6. Why do informal organizations develop?
7. What is the cruciform effect? How might it apply to the job of social worker (or any suitable variant)?
8. Why is it not possible for organizational psychology to make the kind of predictions that the physical sciences can make?
9. Imagine you are a newly appointed manager and find your workers are not putting in much effort. What would the motivational theories of how to energize behaviour suggest about changing this situation?
10. What theories of motivation deal with the channelling of behaviour? Use one of them to explain/illustrate the behaviour of you and your fellow students.
11. Illustrate your understanding of Herzberg's two-factor theory by comparing the following jobs: coal miner, general medical practitioner and a travelling salesman paid partly by commission.
12. What factors enable one person to influence another? Which ones would be dominant in (i) a military organization; (ii) a college or university?
13. Describe the different ways in which people learn. Do some seem to be superior to others? If so, why?
14. What advice would you give to a young manager who asked you about how to discipline people?
15. What would be an optimally reinforcing payment system according to reinforcement theory? What sorts of jobs would it be applicable to? What sorts of jobs would it not be applicable to?

16. Why is there no one best leadership style?
17. Describe Fiedler's contingency model of leadership effectiveness.
18. A leader is in octant 8 of Fiedler's contingency model. He is doing badly. What kind of situation is he in and what kind of leadership style is he likely to have? What should be done to make things better?
19. What is organization development and why did it develop as an activity?
20. Compare and contrast stereotypes about managerial roles with what managers actually do.
21. Why might the training of a professional worker fail to prepare him properly for a career in a large organization?
22. Which of the main types of organizational structure most appeals to you personally? Why?
23. What is model II learning? Why is it difficult to get people to do this sort of learning?
24. Can motivational theory help explain why it is difficult to get people to do model II learning?
25. What factors influence the structural characteristics of organizations? Give examples.

Annotated reading

Mintzberg's ideas are only available in Mintzberg, H. (1979) The Structuring of Organizations. Englewood Cliffs, NJ: Prentice-Hall.
> This is a detailed review and synthesis of a mass of literature on organizations. The first chapter describes the five co-ordinating mechanisms and the last describes the five types of structures and the pentagon model.

Child, J. (1977) Organization: A guide to problems and practice (paperback). New York: Harper & Row.
> A readable and informed account of the meaning of organizational structure. It discusses the choices managers have when faced with designing an organization around the issues of shaping the jobs/roles people do, having tall or flat chains of command, grouping activities by function, product or some mixture, mechanisms for integrating the divisions so created, and how to control the humans working in the system. Child also discusses how to change organizations and the future forms they may need/choose to adopt.

Handy, C. (1976) Understanding Organizations. Harmondsworth: Penguin.
> This is an extremely well-written and lively book, rich with pertinent examples. The first part introduces basic concepts for understanding organizations: motivation, roles, leadership, power and influence, group processes, structure and politics. The second part applies the concepts to problems such as how to design organizations, how to develop and change them and the working

of the various aspects of organizations as systems (budgets, communications, computers, bargaining). The last chapter describes what it is like to be a manager and the dilemmas they face. The book has a very useful third section which is a guide to further study for each of the 12 chapters.

Warr, P.B. (ed.) (1978) Psychology at Work (2nd edn). Harmondsworth: Penguin.

This book contains 16 chapters, each written by different authors. It is moderately technical in places, but much of it is quite understandable to the non-psychologist. The chapters cover the following topics: hours of work and the 24-hour cycle, workload and skilled performance, training, the design of machines and systems that optimize human performance, accidents, computers and decision making, selection, interviewing, negotiation and collective bargaining, leadership, attitudes and motives, job redesign and employee participation, work stress, counselling in work settings, how to change organizations and organizational systems as psychological environments.

Some journals which cover these subjects but which aim their content at practitioners and which are widely available in UK are: Harvard Business Review, Personnel Review, Personnel Management, Management Today.

Part two

Individual behaviour

Chapter 3

Introduction to Part 2
Cary L. Cooper and Peter Makin

If we were to say that no two people are exactly the same, in other words, people differ from one another, we might be thought to be laying ourselves open to the charge of 'stating the obvious'. On reflection, however, the statement does not appear to be as trivial as might be thought. In many ways, people are very similar and can be described in similar terms. Although people's bodily structures vary, in height, weight, bone structure, proportion of fat to muscle, etc., nevertheless the medical professions have increasingly precise explanations of how our bodies function and how we can attempt to correct things that can go wrong. For example, specific drugs can be used to treat the same complaint in everybody. On the other hand, no two patients react in exactly the same way to the same drug; indeed sometimes particular patients may develop a severe reaction to such treatment. In many cases the initial stage of treatment consists of trying to identify which of a range of similar drugs is best suited to the patient concerned.

In psychology we are concerned with understanding and explaining not biochemical phenomena, but people's behaviour. In so doing, however, we will concentrate on the two aspects of our medical analogy; in certain respects we are seeking general rules which apply to everyone, but we have also to bear in mind that there will be individual deviations from these rules.

The first chapter in this section is about personality and as we will see, there are many different ways of describing the patterns of behaviour, attitudes and abilities which characterize individuals. It is obviously important from the point of view of organizational effectiveness to know something about a person's personality and ability. Jobs differ in their requirements for different skills (mental, physical and social) and, if we are to ensure that people are placed in the positions for which they will perform effectively, we need to know their strengths and weaknesses. Indeed, as we will see, such knowledge can also be of considerable use to the individual in guiding career decisions. In order to make use of such information, however, we have to classify personality and ability in such a way that we can produce methods of assessing them. We will also be looking at ways of assessing the components of jobs in order that the 'matching' of jobs and person can be undertaken, and also at ways in which we can assess the performance of someone doing that job.

However, as every manager knows, having the necessary attributes to be able to do a job, does not mean that the person will do the job effectively. We have all come across people who, while perfectly capable of doing a particular job, do not appear to have the inclination to do so. In other words, they lack the necessary 'motivation', and it is to this that we devote the second chapter of this section. Beginning with the work of Fredrick Taylor (1911) at the start of the century, we examine how successive theories have sought to discover what motivates employees. Once again, however, you will see the influence of theories which attempt to give answers that apply to everyone and those which emphasize the differences between what motivates different people. There are some useful guidelines to be learnt from both types of theories.

In addition to ability and motivation, there is another requisite for successful job performance: the specific skills and knowledge required by the job encumbent. Therefore, the most mundane job involves some form of training, even if this consists of 'take that and put it there'. The jobs of professionals often involve a training period that lasts over a number of years. Indeed, some would say that we never stop learning. In order to ensure that our training techniques are effective, we need an understanding of the factors that influence learning. The basic principles of successful learning are equally applicable to any form of training, whether it be in the workplace or in school. In fact, most forms of industrial and commercial training involve a period of classroom instruction, whether it takes place in the training school, the local technical college or even university.

Finally, and especially in the chapters on personality and motivation, we have been describing people as if they did not change with time; but this is not the case. As Van Maanen and Katz (1976) have shown, people's satisfactions with various aspects of work vary over time. This change is in fact often larger within a career than between people in different careers. Bartolome and Lee Evans (1979) have also charted the changing values of managers. In the early part of their careers (up to early 30s), the emphasis is upon their career, often to the detriment of their families. In mid-career, however, the family comes into its own but sometimes too late to save the marriage. This is also often a time of regret for the lost experience of their children's early years. From there on Bartolome and Lee Evans chart a number of possible routes through the later stages of the career. As well as such gradual changes, however, there are the far more acute changes brought on by traumatic events and it is with such events that we are concerned in the final chapter of this section. An understanding of the changing patterns of reaction to traumatic events can be of considerable benefit to managers when dealing with them, whether they occur to the managers themselves, colleagues or subordinates.

References

Bartolomé, F. and Lee Evans, P.A. (1979)
Professional lives versus private lives - shifting patterns of managerial commitment. Organizational Dynamics, 7, 3-29.

Taylor, F.W. (1911)
Scientific Management. New York: Harper.

Van Maanen, J. and Katz, R. (1976)
Individuals and their careers: some temporal considerations for work satisfaction. Personnel Psychology, 29, 601-606.

Chapter 4

Personality and individual differences
Cary L. Cooper and Peter Makin

Cary L. Cooper and Peter Makin

What is personality?

Everyday language is full of words to describe personality: shy, aggressive, dominant, ingratiating - the list is huge. Each word applies to a pattern of behaviour, usually across a range of occasions and situations. This pattern, which remains relatively stable, can be used to predict the individual's future behaviour in similar or nearly similar situations. We would expect for example that someone who has been described as shy would be rather reticent when introduced to strangers or sent to complain about service in a shop.

In using these descriptions, we are attempting to generalize in a few words a person's usual or preferred way of behaving. Personality therefore, can be seen as the relatively enduring and stable patterns of behaving, thinking and feeling which characterize an individual. As we will see later there is disagreement as to whether it is meaningful to talk about 'stable' personality, given the differences we observe in our own and other people's behaviour in different situations. Initially, however, we shall accept the commonly held view that people have stable personalities.

There are many differing psychological theories of personality but they all have one thing in common. They attempt to simplify the more important ways of describing individual patterns of behaviour into a more manageable (and measurable) number of dimensions (typically between 2 and 16). In following these theories we inevitably make over-generalizations and lose individuality and the subtlety of everyday language, but we gain in being able to make fairly accurate descriptions and predictions about large groups of people - whether for example they would be likely to make good salespersons or teachers, or managers.

First let us consider how personality is formed. We have stated that personality is relatively stable over time and is, except in the case of severe physical or psychological trauma, likely to change only slowly. An interest in how personality is formed is not merely academic, it has implications for management.

How is personality formed?
As with the controversy about the development of intelligence (see page 79), theories about the formation of

personality can be divided into the nature or the nurture schools. The naturalists would have us believe that personality is due to our genetic and physiological make-up, whilst others believe that it is the environment, and the individual's experience of it, which are of crucial importance. However, this is a crude split; indeed you will find few who believe totally in one or the other. Indeed, not only are both genetics and the environment involved, but the way in which they interact is of crucial importance.

Let us start with those theories which maintain that personality is largely genetically controlled and hence less likely to be susceptible to a great deal of change.

Instincts

It is clear that some behaviour is automatic and common to the whole of a particular species. Such instinctive behaviour does not have to be learnt: it is in some way wired-in to the animal's nervous system, in much the same way as the human knee jerk reflex. Young babies, for example, will look at patterns that resemble a human face more readily than at other patterns. The influence of instincts is even more recognizable in animals. Konrad Lorenz has shown how greylag geese, when hatched, will 'imprint' on the first large moving object they see, following it as they would their mother. This mechanism guarantees that the infant goose has immediate protection. In his provocative but controversial book 'On Aggression', Lorenz shows how animals have built-in systems of preventing fights to the death between members of the same species. When one of the fighting pair is beaten, it admits defeat by a certain pattern of behaviour, often by exposing a crucial weak spot to its opponent, and this has the effect of 'switching off' the victor's aggression. Thus, for example, the vanquished wolf will turn its head to expose its neck but, rather than take advantage of this and going for the kill, the victor's aggression subsides. In the more controversial later sections of his book Lorenz argues that, because the weapons of human conflict are manmade, nature has not wired in the instinct in man that would prevent the use of such tools for killing. When people speak of human nature they are often expressing a view of human behaviour that is based on instincts. Most psychologists however, would not accept that much, if any, of the behaviour patterns of humans are controlled by instincts. If our instinct is 'wired-in', the same stimulus should elicit the same behaviour in every member of the human race without it having to be learnt. Such a pattern is virtually impossible to find, for every pattern of behaviour that might be considered human nature, for example maternal love or keeping oneself alive at all cost, there is an individual or society somewhere in the world that does it differently. So in answer to questions like 'Are people by nature lazy or dishonest etc.?', we can answer almost certainly not: they can be influenced to be otherwise.

Physique

There are certain stereotypes that we have about people's character based upon their physical build. For example, we think of large round individuals as being jolly and extraverted, while thin people are introverted and moody. Sheldon (1954) classified people into three types according to their bodily build. The endomorph is well rounded, often with a paunch, who loves to eat, seeks bodily comforts and is sociable. The ectomorph on the other hand, has a delicate build and is sensitive, given to worry and is nervous in groups. In between is the muscular mesomorph who is energetic and direct in action. Sheldon claimed that genetic factors determined both an individual's build and his/her personality. Scientific study has not produced much support for Sheldon's theory however, and the message should be: avoid stereotypes - because a person is built like you they may not have your temperament. Indeed the editors of this volume are both tall, thin extraverts!

This stereotyping may however act in some cases as a 'self-fulfilling prophecy', the endomorph is expected and even encouraged to be the 'life and soul of the party'. It has been suggested that there may be a causal link between fatness and sociability. Stereotypes plus expectations make the connection.

Basic drives influenced by experience

Genetic and body-build theories place the responsibility for our personality firmly on our genetic structure - if you want a particular personality choose your parents carefully! Most psychologists however would want to stress the importance of experience, especially in early life. A mixture of such early experience, plus the operation of basic instinctive drive for pleasure is the basis of the theory of personality of the most famous person in psychology, Sigmund Freud.

Freud

We include a brief description of Freud's theory for interest rather than because of its direct application to management. Nevertheless there are a few books which do take a Freudian (or psychoanalytic) view, notably De Board (1978), and acceptance of the theory has implications for managerial styles. Freud (1973) believed that we are all born with a basic drive for pleasure (the libido). The source of this energy is the ID and its whole method of operating is to satisfy the drive for pleasure. Obviously if we merely pursued pleasure without any concern for the reality of the physical world, we would soon be killed, so the EGO (or I) develops to deal with reality and either modify or keep under control the demands of the ID. As well as the physical world, however, there is the social world to be considered and hence the SUPEREGO or conscience develops which operates according to the social rules of the particular culture. A particular means devised by the ego to satisfy the id, might not be culturally acceptable. In the developing child, the main area for satisfaction of the id changes with time. First it is the mouth (oral stage), then the rectum (anal) and finally the sexual organs (phallic). The development of a particular personality depends upon whether the pleasure at each stage has been adequately satisfied or not. Thus, for example, severe potty training during the anal phase in which the child is required to retain his/her faeces may lead to a tidy parsimonious personality. This fixation at a particular stage then shows up in later life. Not enough satisfaction at the sucking stage, it is argued, may lead to a desire for oral gratification. For example, smoking would be seen to reflect the ego's failure to satisfy the needs of the id during the oral stage.

Few psychologists in the organizational behaviour field consider Freud to be of any great relevance but, to be fair, his more recent followers (e.g. the neo-Freudians) place less emphasis upon the id and its animal drives, and more upon the ego and the way in which people consciously develop themselves. Indeed, Loevinger and Knoll (1983), have charted the resurgence in psychology of the self. As they point out 'rereading Freud is a growth industry' (p. 197). Acceptance of a Freudian view of personality has two major implications. First, like instinct theories, personality is seen as unchangeable (except possibly by deep, long and expensive treatment by a psychoanalyst), at least once childhood is passed. Second, the method of dealing with people who have a weak superego (conscience) or ego is to repress their basic drives by the use of authoritarian methods.

Anxiety and frustration

Although he recognized that there would be genuine rational anxiety brought about by uncertainty or fear, Freud's major concern was with what he termed 'neurotic' anxiety. This anxiety is caused not by real or actual occurrences in a person's environment but by the conflicting demands of the id, ego and superego. Such anxiety is an unpleasant experience, which can have effects upon our physical and psychological wellbeing if it is allowed to continue for any length of time. Individuals therefore adopt 'defence mechanisms' to protect themselves from neurotic anxiety. The function of the defence mechanism is to release the anxiety by displacing it onto more acceptable views of reality. Several defence mechanisms are described below. While Freud concentrated upon these defence mechanisms in the context of neuroses they can also be considered as methods of adaptation to the anxieties and frustrations of everyday life. Although Freud and other psychoanalysts first drew attention to them, their existence and purpose are now accepted by many psychologists who do not support other aspects of Freudian theory.

Adapting to frustration

Frustration is a fact of life. All of us experience it in our working lives and have varying reactions to it. These reactions can be both immediate and long term and each individual's reactions will be a complex mix of the behaviours we will now describe. It should be borne in mind that we all use such methods of adaptation and that they have a positive value in reducing anxiety and maintaining our self-esteem. Although, as we will see, they all involve self-deception of one form or another, it is only when they are carried to extremes that they become abnormal.

Short term frustration

We are often faced with obstacles that block our path and, while some are tolerated many, especially those that appear suddenly, give rise to a feeling of frustration. It could in fact be argued that it is the unexpected interruption of our plans that gives rise to such emotions. Different people will react to different frustrations in different ways but there are some common reactions which it will be useful to describe.

AGGRESSION. This is most probably the most common reaction and, although often inappropriate, some writers (e.g. Kahn, 1972) have suggested that its suppression merely directs that aggression inwards, with adverse stressful physical effects for the individual. Aggression can be experienced in a number of ways, either physically, or verbally and may be directed towards objects or people. For example, who has not kicked or sworn at their car when it refused to start? Such direct aggression, however, is usually not advisable when other individuals, especially superiors, are involved and we then may resort to indirect aggression. Such indirect aggression can be directed at someone in a weaker position than ourselves (and often quite innocent). For this reason we tend to keep out of the way of the boss if he's having a rough time. The effects of aggression are usually, however, counter-productive, giving rise to feelings of resentment or anger on the part of those attacked. The problem is to redirect such aggression into more appropriate channels. Perhaps like the Japanese we should make available straw models of the managers together with some baseball bats.

APATHY. Some individuals, perhaps because of past experience, react to frustration by doing nothing and become apathetic. More usually, however, apathy is the end result of repeated attempts to cope, none of which has been successful. If nothing you can do can alter the situation, why bother doing anything? Consider for example a situation where a large factory is threatened with closure because the firm is uncompetitive. Despite this the workers do not seem interested in attempts to improve productivity. Why? From the point of view of the individual worker the situation may appear to be hopeless. It is unlikely that the particular

individual can save their job by working harder, even if
everyone in that particular section did so. Indeed the
workers may well be aware that in the past even highly
productive parts of the same company have been closed
because of lack of demand or political decisions at a
national level.

Continuing frustration and conflict

While the short-term mechanisms we have described are
adjustments to particular situations, psychological defence
mechanisms come into play when the anxiety results from a
frustration caused by conflicting values within the individual. By either denying or disguising the conflicting
motives, anxiety is reduced and self-esteem maintained.
There are many methods of defence but we will cover the most
common.

RATIONALIZATION. We all want to see ourselves, and have
others see us, as behaving rationally and according to
acceptable motives. In order to do so we often construct
elaborate 'rational' reasons to explain behaviour that may
have other, less socially approved reasons. It is not
considered quite right for example, to buy goods for their
status value (a fact which is not lost on the people who
advertise such goods, in that they offer the status symbol
and the 'rational' reason for having it in the same advert).
If you care to ask your chief executive why he has an
American Express Gold Card or has just changed his two-year-
old Jaguar for a new one, it is unlikely that status reasons
will be given. The reasons are more likely to be along the
lines of 'I have to entertain a lot' or 'I have to have a
car I can rely on'. This is not to deny that these are not
perfectly rational reasons, but when the reasons given
invoke the cry from others 'who does he think he's kidding?'
then it can be assumed that rationalization is taking place.

PROJECTION. There are certain aspects of everyone's own
character of which they are not particularly proud but, in
the majority of cases we come to terms with them. Sometimes
however it is easier to cope with if, rather tl an disliking
ourselves, we can 'project' our own faults onto someone else
and then dislike them instead. By thus projecting our faults
we have created a scapegoat who is responsible for all our
ills. To an outsider however it is often apparent that,
although the scapegoat may bear some element of blame, the
reaction of other people to him is out of proportion to his
culpability. In organizations, scapegoating often enables
people to avoid facing up to more fundamental sources of
difficulty.

In some respects, projection can also be seen as a form
of rationalization. By projecting certain motives onto other
people 'in general' we can justify some of our own less
desirable behaviours. For example consider so-called 'white-
collar' crime, the practice of 'adjusting' expenses or

using the firm's time, stationery or telephone for private purposes (we suspect that most calls to the cricket test match score service are from firms' telephones). By convincing ourselves that 'everyone else does it', we can remove some of the anxiety caused by our dishonest behaviour. If white-collar crime is as widespread as believed, reading this paragraph will have caused anxiety to many of us. What are you doing at the moment to reduce it? We suspect that many of you will have started one of those little mannerisms that people use to relieve anxiety, like lighting a cigarette, tapping a pencil, fiddling with their watch or even shutting the book!

DISSOCIATION. The behaviours we have just described above are probably the most common forms of dissociation. Like indirect aggression the arousal produced by the anxiety is directed into other, and often inappropriate activities. For example, think about that job you have been putting off for weeks! The effect is most probably to make you feel anxious and one way of reducing this anxiety (short of actually doing the job) is to do something else instead. You will of course then rationalize as to why the alternative job needed doing - but is that really the case?

We have described a few of the more common forms of defence mechanism but with all of them you should bear the following in mind. As presented above they appear to be maladaptive ways of behaving, but each has its positive aspect. So, for example, the positive aspect of rationalization is logical thought, while that of projection is the ability to understand and empathize with the feelings of others. It is only in their extreme form that they become dysfunctional. An understanding of defence mechanisms can, however, be of value to managers. For when defence mechanisms are operating, they must be in reaction to anxiety and conflict. Sometimes the underlying causes may be incapable of resolution but some may be susceptible to change. The problems of the group that has a scapegoat, for example, may lie not in the scapegoat but within the group itself.

Type and trait theories

There are thousands of words that are used to describe people. Indeed, in 1936, Allport and Odbert set themselves the task of listing all the English words that were used to distinguish between the behaviour of one person and another. In all they found 17,953 and the list has most probably grown since then. Each of these words or phrases can be considered a 'trait'. There are of course physical traits: tall, blonde, etc., but it is with traits which describe personality that we will concern ourselves here.

The type and trait theories which we will now consider are attempts to reduce the plethora of traits in common language to a small number of more important and more general ones. As we will see, the main difference between

type and trait theories is their level of generality.
Because of the close relationship between types and traits
you may well find some of the type names also appearing as
trait names.

Type theories

Type theories of personality have been with us for a long
time - indeed some of the types take their names from
ancient Greece. In addition they are most probably the most
widely known to the general public. The term extraversion
coined by C.G. Jung (one of Freud's early disciples) has
become part of everyday language. You may have noted that
some of the theories about the development of personality
already discussed can be classified as type theories.
Sheldon's theory about personality and physique is a type
theory as is that of Freud.

Of particular interest are the type A and type B
behaviour patterns identified by Friedman and Rosenman
(1974). They have described A behaviour as 'hurry sickness',
characterized by a striving for achievement, extreme haste,
impatience etc. This pattern of behaviour, which appears
stable enough to be described as personality, has been shown
to be related to a number of physical illnesses, including
coronary heart disease. Because of its interest and
importance this typology is dealt with in more detail in
chapter 14.

The major criticism of type theories of personality is
that they tend to over-simplify individual differences. Very
few people fit 'purely' in one type or another. Despite this
apparent oversimplification, type theories can still be
useful so long as the variation between people of different
types (or groups) is larger than the variation between
people of the same type, i.e. within the same group.

Trait theories

Rather than classifying people into a relatively few classes
or 'types', trait theories consider that a person can best
be described by their score on a number of scales, each of
which measures a different trait. The assumption is that
everyone may obtain a score to a higher or lesser degree,
for every trait. Extraverted and introverted people are at
two extremes of a continuous category of behaviour. Thus you
could draw a profile of an individual indicating the degree
to which they possess (or lack) such traits.

We concentrate upon the trait theories of H. J. Eysenck
and R.B. Cattell, not only because of the amount of research
and data that they have generated, but also because the
tests they have developed to measure personality, the EPQ
(the Eysenck Personality Questionnaire) and the Cattell 16PF
are the most widely used.

H.J. Eysenck

The British psychologist Hans Eysenck considers that there

are two major dimensions of personality, introversion/extraversion and neuroticism/stability.

Although Eysenck (1983) has attacked the idea of personality 'types', the fact that he uses a small number of dimensions means that they can be easily combined to produce 'type-like' categories. For this reason some writers on personality consider Eysenck's theory to be 'type-trait' (e.g. Pervin, 1980).

Bearing this reservation in mind however we might look at the four combinations produced by the two dimensions, stable extravert, stable introvert, neurotic extravert and neurotic introvert.

Extraverts are sociable and have many friends. They also crave excitement, acting on the spur of the moment and take chances. They are optimistic and happy-go-lucky but are also aggressive and tend to lose their temper quickly. They are not always reliable.

The introvert, as might be expected, is a mirror image of the extravert being a quieter individual, often fonder of books than people. Except with intimate friends introverts are reserved and distant. They tend to plan ahead and take life seriously. They keep their feelings under control and are reliable, placing a high value upon ethical standards. They can also be somewhat pessimistic.

The neurotic is an anxious, moody individual who worries a lot and frequently becomes depressed. Another name Eysenck uses for this scale is emotionality: the neurotic is highly emotional, sometimes behaving in irrational ways.

The stable individual is again a mirror image, responding only slowly to emotions and quickly returning to placidity after upsets.

Since every individual has a rating on both scales, thumb-nail sketches of four different types therefore might be obtained by combining extreme scores:

stable-extravert : responsive, easy-going, a leader

stable-introvert : thoughtful, controlled, reliable

neurotic-extravert : aggressive, changeable, impulsive

neurotic-introvert: anxious, rigid, moody

Since his original theory Eysenck has introduced a third dimension, psychoticism or toughmindedness, but space precludes us from discussion here; for a full account see Eysenck and Eysenck (1975).

R.B. Cattell
Cattell started with Allport's list of 17,953 words and, by a complicated statistical process called factor analysis, eliminated words whose meanings overlapped, to produce 171 variables which described the whole range of personality and temperament. Each of these he measured by means of a 10-

point scale, usually with a normal position in the middle
and with opposite extremes at either end (e.g. cheerful to
gloomy). He then went even further to try and reduce the
dimensions to a manageable number by seeing how people's
scores on the traits clustered together, and produced a list
of what he called 'surface traits'. More important than
these surface traits however were the underlying and more
general 'source traits'. These were determined by factor
analysing the scores of a large number of people in order to
discover the underlying 'pure' traits. Factor analysis is a
complex mathematical technique for determining which scores
cluster together or alternatively, are wholly unrelated to
each other. In this way he managed to reduce the dimensions
to 16 source traits - hence the name of the test - 16 Personality Factor (16 PF). These traits, supposedly representing the main underlying dimensions of personality, are
labelled in rather technical phraseology; for example,
affectothymia/sizothymia are the opposite ends of one
dimension, but Cattell also gives everyday alternatives. For
the dimension just mentioned, these are good-natured and
trusting as opposed to critical and suspicious. It is worth
noting that Cattell derives more general 'second order
factors' from the original 16 and two of these he calls
extraversion and anxiety.

D. McClelland

Although not strictly a trait theory, the theory of David
McClelland is worth mentioning at this point as it has
particular relevance to management. McClelland (1961)
argues that people differ in the relative importance of
their needs according to their need for achievement (nAch),
their need for affiliation, and need for power. Of these,
McClelland considers nAch to be the most important; indeed
he believes that differences in achievement motivation can
explain not only the levels of success of individuals, but
also whole societies. Thus, for example, the 'Protestant
work ethic' of many Western countries with its emphasis upon
work and achievement leads to their higher economic performance. These cultural differences are according to
McClelland, transmitted to the child in early life. For
example those individuals with high nAch will, as children,
have been rewarded (usually with signs of love such as
hugging) very specifically for success in competitive
situations. This need for achievement has to be balanced
against a competing motive: fear of failure. For individuals
whose nAch overcomes the fear of failure, those tasks will
be attractive which are perceived as moderately difficult
and hence offering a reasonable chance of success. For those
high in fear of failure the most attractive tasks will be
the very simple or the almost impossible. In the former case
success is guaranteed while failure in the latter can be
blamed on the situation. Within a culture, values about
achievement and acceptable ways of striving are embodied in

folklore and even in the content of children's stories and readers.

The theory and the supporting research is not without its critics. Indeed McClelland himself has come to the conclusion (McClelland and Winter, 1969) that nAch levels are not totally determined by upbringing and that they can be increased by appropriate training. Steers and Spencer (1977) have concluded that, whilst individual nAch may have some effect on performance, the amount is small when compared with other variables such as pay levels.

Personality determined by experience

Trait theories, in particular that of Eysenck, stress the importance of inherited genetic factors as determinants of an individual's personality: we are born with a tendency to behave in certain ways because of our genetic inheritance. Other theorists stress the importance of the external environment in determining how a person behaves. Indeed, the operant conditioning theory of Skinner (1974) sees personality as merely a shorthand way of describing, rather than explaining, patterns of behaviour. The emphases of such theories are upon behaviour and the way that the environment rewards or punishes it. Behaviour therefore is learnt and, because it is learnt, it can also be unlearnt and/or other patterns of behaviour learnt anew. The pattern of behaviour that we refer to as 'personality' is nothing more than a set of habits acquired on the basis of previous rewards. Personality is only stable, therefore, because it is a set of habits that has been deeply ingrained over a long period.

As far as the behaviourists are concerned, although an individual can behave in many different ways, the way in which the environment rewards or punishes such behaviour will determine which behaviour patterns will be encouraged and hence increase in frequency. For example, if a hungry rat is placed in a box which contains a lever, the pressing of which delivers a pellet of food, the rat will not immediately press the lever. Instead it will move about the cage in a largely random fashion until eventually it will accidentally press the lever and a food pellet will arrive. The rat will not learn immediately that the pressing of the lever caused the food to be delivered but, over a period of time and as long as the rat is hungry, the rate of lever pressing will increase because this behaviour has been rewarded. In technical terms it has been positively reinforced. Behaviour can also be negatively reinforced by removing an unpleasant stimulus. The distinction between this and positive reinforcement can perhaps be illustrated as follows. Performing well in a job leads to more money (positive reinforcement) or leads to withdrawal of redundancy notice (negative reinforcement). Behaviour can also be punished, which leads to its temporary suppression, but a better method of eliminating undesirable behaviour is non-reinforcement which causes it to be extinguished. We return to these processes in chapter 5 when we discuss motivation.

Personality, therefore, is merely the pattern of behaviour that has been reinforced for an individual. The extravert has been reinforced for outgoing behaviour, while the introvert is the opposite. The reinforcement may have been, for example parental or peer-group approval. Neuroses, especially phobias, rather than reflecting deep inner conflicts, are examples of learning that has been inappropriate, and they can therefore be treated by systematic unlearning. For example, someone who is afraid of spiders experiences unpleasant feelings when in their presence, so the method of behavioural treatment is first to produce a relaxed state (which reduces tensions) and then teach the person to maintain the relaxed state whilst in the presence of the spider. Initially the person relaxes with the spider at a distance. Then the spider is progressively brought closer, always ensuring that feelings of relaxation are stronger than feelings of anxiety. In this way, an old inappropriate pattern of behaviour (anxiety) is unlearnt by substituting a more normal one (being relaxed).

This approach suggests, therefore, that behaviour and the pattern of behaviour we call 'personality' can be changed, so long as the environment can be arranged to reinforce some aspects and extinguish others. Reinforcement does not always have to be experienced by the individual directly for it to influence that individual's behaviour. We can also experience vicarious, or social learning, by seeing others being reinforced or being punished for behaving in certain ways.

Genetic vs environmental factors

In our consideration of how personality is determined we have looked at theories which range from those that stress purely genetic factors to those that stress the importance of the environment. What evidence is there for each?

Anyone who has had a close acquaintance with more than one young child will be aware that there are distinct and characteristic differences between them, almost from birth. They vary, for example, in their general level of activity, rate of sucking and smiling, and many other behaviours. This would suggest that there are differences which are, in the main, due to genetic factors. It has to be borne in mind however, that not all differences at birth are due to heredity. The womb is also an environment and the child may be affected by, for example, the mother smoking during pregnancy. There is, however, considerable evidence to suggest that some differences in personality, especially extraversion, are strongly influenced by genetic factors.

Adherents of the alternative view, that personality is determined by environmental factors, point to studies which show that even identical twins, when reared in different environments, exhibit different personality patterns (see Pervin, 1980).

Given this conflicting evidence, the only conclusion that can be safely drawn is that not only do both genetic and environmental factors have an influence, but that the nature of their interaction is important. Genetic factors determine what has been called a 'reaction range', in other words, the limits within which personality characteristics may develop. Which characteristic pattern develops and becomes apparent in adulthood, however, will depend upon environmental factors. As Pervin (1978) points out, 'Just as you can get the number ten through different numerical combinations, you can get extraversion or introversion through different gene-environment relationships' (p.50).

Internal vs external determinants of behaviour

In our definition of personality and in our discussions so far, we have assumed that personality is 'internal'. Whilst the way in which it develops is due to both internal (genetic) and external (environmental) factors, once adulthood stability is attained, the individual's behaviour is seen as being caused by internal traits.

This view of personality, which was particularly important in the 1950s and early 1960s and which is still the underlying theoretical basis for many personality tests, came under attack from those who suggested that behaviour, rather than being caused by internal traits, was determined by the external situation.

The most influential statement of this 'situationalist' theory was made by Mischel (1968). His two main points may be summarized as follows:

(i)   with the possible exception of intelligence, there is little or no consistency in an individual's behaviour.

(ii)   Personality 'traits', rather than describing consistencies in the individual being observed, instead describe the observer's concepts of personality.

The first of these points is most probably the easiest to understand. It is apparent to us all that an individual's behaviour does vary, both from one situation to another and also from one point in time to another. For example, most of us would describe ourselves as 'honest', but there will inevitably be situations in which we would behave dishonestly. Similarly, there are situations in which someone we would normally describe as quiet and shy becomes loud and aggressive. Given these obvious inconsistencies, is there any meaning that can be attached to a 'trait'?

If we accept that there is little or no consistency other than that created by similar situations, where does it leave our common sense view that different people have different personalities? Indeed, more immediately, how can we view ourselves as distinct individuals if our behaviour is determined by the situation rather than our own personality? This extreme view, that behaviour is totally externally determined, is not held by many psychologists and, indeed, as Rorer and Widiger (1983) point out, they have never met anyone who is not, in some respect, a trait theorist. If behaviour were totally controlled by the situation, interviewing someone for a job would be point-less, all that is needed is to structure the situation properly: 'picking a mate would simply be a matter of finding someone whose physical characteristics appeal to you' (p. 445).

On the other hand, no trait theorist would claim that a particular trait will predict specific behaviour in a specific situation. We all accept that there are 'rules' that govern behaviour and decide what is appropriate in a given situation. For example, behaviour that would be acceptable as a spectator at a football match would be unacceptable in church. In this respect, behaviour is obviously determined by the situation, but your traits will most probably determine which of the two events you would rather attend (see Argyle's chapter for a further dis-cussion). In short, traits do not predict behaviour, they are probablistic: they give a range of likely behaviours. In addition, it is likely that some traits exhibit greater stability than others for particular individuals. For example, someone may be consistently truthful but un-predictably aggressive, for someone else the relationship may be the reverse (there is considerable disagreement as to whether there is a trait of consistency).

The second point is more difficult as it is likely that there is no experiment that could be devised to prove Mischel's contention one way or the other (Rorer and Widiger, 1983). Do our words reflect the real structure of the world or merely the way our brains and/or minds construe it? Put in this way, the question is philosophical rather than psychological. This being said, however, there is some support for what is called Implicit Personality Theory: that certain traits 'go together' and that some are more important than others. Indeed, many studies have shown that observers, even when they are asked to rate a number of traits, tend to use only four or five traits, and that there are a number of particular traits that are used most frequently (see Argyle's chapter).

The discussion as to whether behaviour is internally or externally explained does not, however, end here. It has become apparent to psychologists that whether we attribute behaviour to the person or the situation itself depends upon both the person involved and the particular situation.

Attribution theory

Attribution theory assumes that individuals are motivated to see their social environment as predictable. We all like to think that, to some extent, we can control our social environment, and this control is only possible if we can predict the behaviour of others.

What we seek when we observe the behaviour of others therefore, is some degree of cause and effect. The effect is their behaviour but what has caused this behaviour? There are two major factors that we use to explain both the behaviour of others and of ourselves, one is internal: a disposition or trait; the other external: the situation. The way in which we 'attribute' the cause of behaviour has, as we will see, important implications for our perceptions of personality.

SITUATION OR PERSONALITY: there are several studies (e.g. Jones and Nisbett, 1971), which suggest that in general, people attribute other people's behaviour to personality dispositions while we consider our own to be influenced more by the specific situation. In role-playing interviews for example the interviewer often describes his behaviour in terms of a reaction to the behaviour of the interviewee: 'He wouldn't talk, so I did most of the talking.' Observers, on the other hand, often use trait items such as 'domineering' to describe the same behaviour. Interestingly enough when the interviewer is changed into an observer by seeing a video recording of the interview then he also gives a description in terms of dispositions (Storms, 1973). This general tendency can, however, be influenced by other factors. Consider for example that you are given a task to do which will require the co-operation of two other people, one of whom is a few levels above you in the company hierarchy (but not your direct superior), and the other who is a few levels below you (but not your direct subordinate). You ask each of them for help and both give you their assistance: their behaviour is the same. What reasons do you give as to the cause of their behaviour and what are the consequences? Thibaut and Riecken (1955) carried out such a study and came to the following conclusions. People tended to attribute the high status individual's behaviour to internal causes: 'he did it because he wanted to'. The same behaviour by the low status individual was more commonly attributed to external causes: 'he did it because he had to'. In addition, the high status individual was rated more favourably: he did it because he wanted to, therefore he must be a good guy!

SUCCESS, FAILURE AND BLAME: we have seen how there appears to be a desire for consistency in explanation of behaviour. This consistency is often extended to such an extent that whole groups of traits cluster together and the presence of just one or two key pieces of evidence is taken as proof of the presence of the others. This is commonly known as 'stereotyping'. For example, tell a shop steward that someone he is about to meet is a merchant banker or vice versa, and it is likely that each will have a general view of the other's life style, personality and motivation. None of their descriptions are likely to be flattering and many may be inaccurate. These expectations of behaviour also influence our attribution of praise or blame for success or failure. In general, success is attributed to the individual but failure to the situation, but this also is influenced by expectations based upon previous experience. Thus, for example when someone who has previously been very successful fails, the reason is often given in terms of the situation rather than the individual's abilities. Also the converse occurs, if a failure suddenly succeeds then the cause is often seen as 'luck'. Perhaps a successful leader is not one who performs well but one who can ensure that he gets recognition for the good results of his group, and can place the blame for the bad results on the situation (which includes others not in his group). If someone we like succeeds it is due to his personal qualities, if he fails, it is the situation. The opposite is the case for someone we dislike.

This attribution, based upon expectations, has been suggested by Deaux (1976) as a possible explanation for the relatively low number of women in management. Women are not expected to do well in management: therefore, when they do well, it is attributed not to their personal qualities but to a favourable situation. Women therefore have an uphill task in areas where they are not expected to perform well, in showing that their performance is due to their efforts and abilities and not the situation.

LOCUS OF CONTROL: although we have considered the attribution of causes as a general characteristic of people, there do appear to be differences in the extent to which individuals believe they can control their environment. Individuals who are 'internal' believe that they have control of their environment whilst 'externals' believe that the major influences on their environment are either 'luck' or 'powerful other people', and that they themselves can have little influence on what happens to them. Such beliefs obviously influence behaviour and internals are much more 'active' in seeking to control their own destiny. Andrisani and Nestel (1976) found, for example, that internals tend to earn more money, gain more promotion and have higher job satisfaction than externals (see Spector, 1982, for a review).

Where do we now stand on personality theory? Most personality theories take an interactional approach (see Pervin, 1978, for a fuller discussion) accepting that, while behaviour is influenced by situations, there are underlying dispositions which we call personality. Indeed if there were not, as we have pointed out before, we would begin to doubt our own individuality. Personality can be considered to be like the weather, each area of the globe has its own weather pattern but with variations within it. Britain for example is, believe it or not, a temperate country and hence the ranges of temperature, rainfall etc. are fairly predictable over a period of a year of more. Within this general pattern there are however variations with which we have to come to terms. The crucial factor is that the variations within our climate are less than the differences between our climate and others e.g. desert, equatorial etc.

How can managers change the personality of one of their employees? The answer is that in practical terms they could not and in ethical terms they probably should not even try. What a manager can do however is to change behaviour; indeed it could be argued that behaviour is what the employee sells to the organization.

According to Skinner, people behave in certain ways because they have found that it produces rewards of various kinds. It is here that personality theory when expressed in terms of overt behaviour, overlaps with motivation - why do people behave in particular desirable/undesirable ways? For this reason we will defer consideration of behaviour change until the next chapter.

We have now considered some of the many theories of personality. Let us now consider how we might set about measuring personality.

Personality tests

Having personality dimensions, whether type or trait, is one thing; but to be of any use, for example in staff selection or choosing people who are to be part of a team, we need a method of measurement. One way in which to assess people is by observing their actual day-to-day behaviour. Many of you, while reading the personality descriptions given so far, will have been thinking of people you know to whom they apply. It becomes more difficult, however, to assess someone you do not know so well, and while you could say that Fred is extraverted compared to John, how do they compare with the average British male or successful salesperson or manager? How emotionally stable, for example, is the average airline pilot?

What is required to give us this information is a well standardized test that is both 'reliable' and 'valid'. These terms have specific meanings and apply to measuring instruments of any sort, from psychological tests to staff appraisal ratings. Because of this and their importance, a guide on what to look for when assessing a test and the meaning of reliability and validity is given in appendix 1. Inevitably we have to assess people's personalities from samples of their behaviours. The most widely used method is the interview, but the range of behaviour that can be obtained is limited, as interview situations are rather artificial, and the time available usually restricted. Research on selection interviewing, for example, shows us that it is first impressions which count for most in such situations and that decisions are made usually within the first four or five minutes. The main theories of personality which we have just considered, however, each have their own measuring instruments, or tests. In the case of Eysenck's theory the test is called the Eysenck Personality Questionnaire or EPQ (earlier versions are the EPI (the Eysenck Personality Inventory) and the MPI (the Maudsley Personality Inventory))

and Cattell's, as we have seen, is the 16PF. Each consists
of a series of questions (90 in the EPQ, 187 in the 16PF)
about how you are likely to behave in certain situations:
for example, do you find it easy to let yourself go at a
lively party? The answers to these questions are then
combined to give a score on the various dimensions.
Obviously some people may bias their answers so that they
'look good' but often such tests contain a lie scale to
check on those who might attempt such a bias towards socially desirable answers.

The reliability of all these tests is generally high. In
other words if a person completed the test one week and then
a few weeks or months later the scores would be very
similar. Thus, these tests are more reliable, for example,
than interviews, especially when conducted by an
inexperienced interviewer.

As far as the EPQ and 16PF tests are concerned, both
Eysenck and Cattell have carried out and reported a
considerable number of studies in which the tests have been
used on various occupational groups. The manual for the EPQ
lists the average extraversion, neuroticism, and
psychoticism scores for over 50 occupations ranging from
salesmen and company directors to telephonists and doctors.
Eysenck does not claim that a particular occupation requires
a certain personality; indeed within each of the occupations
for which he gives figures there is a wide range of scores,
but he does suggest that certain personality types will be
happier in some occupations than others. Men in the armed
forces for example tend to be stable extraverts. Teachers in
institutions of higher education are as a group about average on the stability scale but while the extraverts tend to
like contact with students the introverts prefer research.

Cattell, Eber and Tatsuoka (1970) report results for
people in a wide variety of occupations. They go further for
a small group of occupations, for which they were able to
obtain not only test results, but also a measure of each
person's performance at the job, for example the sales
volume of a particular group of salespersons. By considering
both sets of scores they have produced 'specification
equations', which give a mathematical formula into which a
person's scores on the relevant traits can be entered to
produce a figure which indicates how well they are likely to
perform. However, such findings may apply only to
particular, specific jobs and may not generalize even to
apparently similar jobs although recently Schmidt, Hunter,
Pearlman and Shane (1979) have suggested that there may be
more 'generalizability' than was previously thought.

Both Eysenck and Cattell have produced far more data
than we can adequately cover but, as we are concerned with
managers, let us consider the personality characteristics of
this group.

Eysenck (1967) used the EPI on a large group of
businessmen known (by their position and salaries) to be
successful. As a group they were more stable and more

introverted than the general population but while there was little difference within the group on stability there were variations in introversion. For example those who were in the areas of Finance, Research and Development, or Consultancy were significantly more introverted than the group as a whole. On the other hand, the most extraverted were those who said their job duties involved more than one area. (Perhaps this is a reflection of the extravert's desire for change and excitement.) Cattell (1970) using the 16PF also reports that a group of 'senior executives' were relatively stable and introverted, a finding which supports that of Eysenck, especially as Cattell used a different but equally reliable test.

There are some findings, using more specialist groups that do not support the findings about managers 'in general'. Lynn (1969) for example, found that a group of 'entrepreneurs' who had set up and run their own businesses were more neurotic and extraverted than managers in general. Henney (1975), while finding his group of managers to be stable also reported that they were more extraverted and Smithers (1968) found university Business Studies students (who might be considered potential managers) to be more neurotic and extraverted than managers. Both Lynn and Henney give some suggestions as to why the particular groups they studied should be different. In the case of the entrepreneurs, it is suggested that the high pressure and stress of owning and running a business (especially when there are other employees) is likely to lead to an increase in neuroticism. In addition there is a small relationship between neuroticism and creativity (e.g. artists) and it might be expected that entrepreneurs would need to be creative. For Henney as well the reasons are related to the nature of the job. The sample used were middle managers in a motor-car factory whose job involved a high degree of personal contact. This personal contact would most probably not suit introverts and hence they would tend not to apply for or be selected for such jobs.

In all the studies reported, however, there is no direct discussion of cause and effect. Do certain personalities choose certain jobs or do the jobs influence peoples' personalities? Notice, for example, that Lynn gives both reasons. Neurotics tend to be creative therefore they choose to become entrepreneurs. The job produces stress which causes an increase in neuroticism. Henney, on the other hand, suggests that the people in his group are stable because they would not be able to stand the stress if they were not. And finally what of the prospective managers, will the neurotic extravert students become stable introvert leaders of industry? Most probably, as Eysenck and Eysenck (1975) have shown there is a steady decline in both extraversion and neuroticism with age. It is likely however that the job itself also affects the individual's behaviour but to prove that would take a very long-term study.

Although such self-report questionnaires are perhaps the best known and most widely used method of assessment, there are others of which the reader should be aware. Most people have heard of the 'ink-blot' test in which the person to be assessed is shown figures which look rather like large multi-coloured ink-blots. The test is an example of a projective test, the essential feature of which is that the figure is capable of being seen in many different ways. In interpreting the ambiguous figure the person unknowingly 'projects' onto the picture aspects of their own personality, and the reports of the images they see can be interpreted by a skilled psychologist. Another example of this kind of test is the Thematic Apperception Test or TAT (widely used to measure nAch), in which the individual is asked to make up a story around a series of pictures, each of which is, again capable of being interpreted in many different ways. For example, in the case of nAch there may be a picture of a boy sitting at a table piled up with school books and homework. The person being tested is asked to make up a story, for example, 'what is the boy thinking?', 'what will he do next?', and so on. These tests however require very skilled administration and interpretation and indeed some psychologists are sceptical about both their reliability and validity.

Increasing use is being made in industry of various forms of the Repertory Grid Technique. Having its theoretical basis in the Individual Construct Theory of Kelly, (1963) Rep-Grid (as it is known) seeks to discover the important psychological constructs that an individual uses in order to understand the world. Thus, rather than measure someone's personality in terms of dimensions derived by someone else, construct theory attempts to understand a person's behaviour in terms of the dimensions that they themselves find important. Man is seen as a 'scientist' developing theories or constructs about how the world around him works (see Bannister and Fransella 1971). The nature of an individual's constructs will determine the way they react. Teasing out these dimensions is not just as simple as asking a person to describe or list them, but may involve increasingly subtle mathematical programmes to analyse their pattern of responses. The use of such sophisticated forms of analysis means that it may be possible to discover personal and unconscious dimensions that the individual is unable, or unwilling to express openly, for example, race prejudice.

A recent test development by Cattell using similar techniques to those used in constructing the 16PF has been the Motivation Analysis Test, which is particularly relevant to managers. Like the 16PF it produces scores on a number of traits (e.g. career sentiment, assertiveness) but it goes further than the 16PF in scoring not only conscious motives but also motives of which the individual may not be aware, i.e. unconscious motives, thus highlighting areas of tension where conscious and unconscious motives are in conflict. The test has not been widely used in this country largely because it has a particularly American question content and it has not been standardized using British managers.

Although we have not dealt with the role of the unconscious it is interesting to note that Cattell, one of the most mathematically sophisticated test constructors, has borrowed the concept of unconscious motivation from Freud, whose major critics point to his lack of experimental rigour. In fact, Cattell also uses some of Freud's terminology for his dimensions.

More recently there has been a movement towards longer and more specific exercises as a method of observing how a person behaves. By assessing traits in a situation which, it is hoped, is similar to the job to be filled a more accurate measure will be achieved than that obtained from self-report pencil and paper tests. This is the core of the Assessment Centre approach, involving not only individual abilities, but also how a person contributes to group or team work. The problem with assessing personality by such procedures is that different observers watching the same scene may often disagree quite considerably in their interpretation of a person's personality (technically called inter-rater reliability). In order to improve this reliability, observers are now not asked to rate for personality dimensions such as 'dominance', 'leadership', etc., but to record actual behaviour, for example the number of times a person spoke and the nature of their contribution. In this way, observers can later meet together and discuss assessments made on the basis of agreed observations of behaviour. It is interesting to note that in undertaking this procedure of breaking down behaviour patterns we are perhaps going in the opposite direction to most personality theories, which group patterns of behaviour together. It appears that it is easier to agree about what a person actually does than it is to agree about the underlying personality, just as it is easier to describe symptoms than diagnose a disease.

The problem of getting agreement between observers about a person's personality (inter-rater reliability) or indeed of getting someone to rate a person the same on two different occasions (test/retest reliability) is one that can be overcome by the use of more objective tests. In some cases it is not immediately apparent that the test is measuring a personality dimension. Examples of such tests are the Gibson Spiral Maze (1965), and the Randell Steady Lad test. The latter test for example requires subjects to trace their way out of a simple maze as quickly as possible but without touching the sides. The distance reached and the number of errors made within a certain time have been shown to be related to such factors as safety awareness in a factory (Makin and Randell, 1978).

The personality measures with which we have dealt have been concerned with a person's temperament. In addition we might also be interested in their INTERESTS or VALUES. Indeed a person's interests as expressed in hobbies for example, might also give an indication of their suitability for different occupations. This is not necessarily so, however; and, although there are many psychological tests for assessing occupational interests (e.g. Kuder Preference, Rothwell-Miller etc.), they are mainly used in vocational guidance and counselling. In certain circumstances such as career planning they may, however, be of some use to the organization. Managers, for example, tend to have three main areas of interest: computational, persuasive and administrative. In addition they usually have an interest which is relevant to their specific industry. For example hospital administrators often have an interest in 'social service' work.

Personality is concerned mainly with temperamental and interest factors, but we also need to consider aptitudes and abilities.

Abilities

Abilities can be subdivided into aptitudes and achievements. Aptitudes are a potential whilst achievements are the results of turning those aptitudes into skilled behaviour. Having potential does not necessarily mean it will be put to good use.

Most of us are familiar with achievement tests. In fact our lives are full of them: examinations, driving tests, and so on. The construction and use of such tests is important especially, for example, in assessing the results of training courses. Important as it is, space precludes us from dealing with it here and the main emphasis in this chapter is upon aptitudes. (A good introduction to the testing of industrial skills can be found in Jones and Whittaker, 1975.)

Aptitude tests can be classified according to their generality. Some seek to tap more general abilities such as 'critical thinking' while those at the other end of the scale seek to measure more specific ones such as the ability to rotate an object mentally. Perhaps the most general and widely known ability is that of intelligence.

Intelligence

Like personality, intelligence is a term which we frequently use without the necessity of a formal definition. Someone whom we describe as intelligent is likely to be quick at analysing and solving problems, especially when they are of a highly abstract nature. They often perform well at school and achieve high educational qualifications. Some tasks we consider to require a high level of intelligence, others not. Being good at snooker, for example, is not seen as requiring intelligence (although some snooker players may be highly intelligent), whereas we would normally expect a Nobel prize winner or a chess grand master to be intelligent. We appear therefore to have an initial idea about what being intelligent means, 'I can't define an elephant but I know one when I see one.'

We do not intend to define intelligence at this stage but leave it to the end for reasons which, we hope, will become obvious. You should be aware, however, that whatever we mean by 'intelligence', there is a continuing debate about the factors which influence it - the so-called nature versus nurture argument. The supporters of the 'nature' school would argue that intelligence is inherited and this sets an unalterable 'upper limit' on intellectual achievement. Supporters of the latter school however would argue that this upper limit is influenced far more by the intellectual environment to which the individual is exposed. Most psychologists accept that both are involved but the debate about their relative importance continues. And in case you think this argument is purely academic, remember that the work of Sir Cyril Burt, whose research has been heavily criticized recently and who stressed the importance of nature, was an important factor in the decision to select children at age 11 for grammar or secondary modern education.

General intelligence, or 'g' is usually broken down into two major sub-divisions 'v:ed' or verbal: educational and 'k:m' or kinaesthetic: motor. The v:ed questions in a test usually require you to give the meaning of a particular word, or to choose a word which is the same or opposite to it. The k:m questions, on the other hand, usually ask you to decide what time a clock would show if it were viewed in a mirror, or to imagine what shape a series of dots would make if they were joined together. Often included to measure the quantitative aspects of k:m are questions of a mathematical reasoning nature, for example finding the next number in a series. As we see in the section on the uses of such tests these two major subdivisions have different uses.

If you ask a psychologist for a definition of intelligence he may well answer that intelligence is what is measured by intelligence tests. This may appear a rather circular form of reasoning which does not get us very far, but in fact the concept and its measures are nevertheless useful. High scores on such tests are a reasonable indication of academic or intellectual success and indeed we can go further and show that high scorers on v:ed will tend to do well on verbal subjects (e.g. history, literature etc.) while those high on k:m will be better in areas like engineering. These two major subdivisions can however be further broken down into more specific aptitudes and it is to these that we now turn.

Specific aptitudes

We limit ourselves to those aptitudes which have particular importance for management. Except for the most repetitive manipulation tasks, any job consists of a range of requirements: and there are two different but overlapping approaches to identifying these with which we are concerned. The first consists of trying to analyse the particular job into a number of very specific ability requirements each of which can be measured independently by specific tests. These can range from tests of manual dexterity to spatial ability

80

but, by combining the scores in a way which reflects their relative importance in the task, we can arrive at a score which would indicate probable success in the job. The second approach is to develop tests of a practical nature which consist of a small sample of the actual job requirements. Trainability tests and some of the techniques used in assessment centres are examples of such an approach. We deal with both in this section.

Clerical aptitude

The main abilities required in clerical occupations are those of accurately checking and comparing verbal and numerical information, plus the ability to operate keyboards of various sorts. In addition, if preparation of reports is involved, some verbal facility is often desirable. Numerical and verbal ability, can often be assessed by standard academic examinations, but fast and accurate checking and keyboard working are often not part of formal examinations. For example the 'General Clerical Test' of The National Foundation for Education Research tests clerical speed and accuracy, numerical ability and verbal facility while the ACER 'Short Clerical Test' assesses the ability to perceive, remember and check written or printed matter. For those who have not worked with keyboards before there are various tests of finger dexterity such as the 'Flanagan Tapping Test'.

Mechanical aptitude

The aptitudes required for mechanical jobs can be divided in two: those involving physical manipulation and those involving mental manipulation. In the former category are tests designed to measure physical abilities often involving fine manipulation or speed of assembly. Examples include the Purdue Pegboard Test. These skills are obviously required in many fine assembly jobs and, for example, the setting up of lathes. Such tests are not only used for assessing unskilled or semi-skilled performance; there is a move towards introducing such tests for prospective dental students. Physical co-ordination tests are a standard part of selection techniques for pilots and astronauts.

The mental skills involved obviously vary according to the particular job requirements but may include speed and accuracy of checking, similar to clerical aptitudes, but involving physical objects rather than letters or numbers. This would, of course, be of importance on such jobs as quality control and inspection. Tests involving mechanical operations have also been widely used. In tests of this nature (e.g. the Bennett Mechanical Comprehension Test) the subject is presented with problems involving pulleys and gear trains which require an understanding of basic mechanical principles. Invariably included in any battery of tests for mechanical aptitude are tests of spatial ability. Spatial ability is a broad term covering a number of sub-divisions depending upon the actual mental task involved.

Thus, for example, a figure may have to be remembered and compared with other figures in the same or different orientation - this involves mentally turning the figure either in two or three dimensions, a skill which may be important for draughtsmen or design engineers.

More recently there has been a trend towards using job sample or trainability testing in selecting people for training. Each individual is given a brief period of instruction on the job to be performed and then, after an opportunity to ask questions, they are given certain simple tasks to accomplish. The speed at which they acquire the relevant skills is recorded and used as an assessment of their trainability. The technique has been used for occupations such as sewing machining, fork lift truck driving and bricklaying (e.g. Robertson and Mindel, 1980); and it appears to predict success at the end of training courses. In addition it is claimed to have certain advantages as far as the job applicants are concerned. First, even applicants who are rejected feel that they have at least been given a chance to display the appropriate skills, something which is not always apparent to someone completing a more traditional psychological test which attempts to measure certain underlying aptitudes. Second, it gives the applicants an opportunity to assess their own abilities against the job requirements, and studies show that they often self select by discovering that the job was not what they thought (see Downs, Farr and Colbeck, 1978). The usefulness of such tests appears to fade however with both time and job complexity. Studies with shipbuilding apprentices (Smith and Downs, 1975) appear to indicate that trainability tests are not as useful for skilled trades involving long training as they are with semi-skilled jobs.

Managerial aptitude

Although in some cases it may be desirable that managers are able to do all the jobs under their supervision, the main aptitudes required in a manager are mental, together with an ability to represent the results of such mental activity whether in writing or orally.

Formal qualifications are perhaps the most widely used assessment of these aptitudes. More than half of all university graduates do not become employed in an area in which they have qualified, and an increasing number are entering management. The university degree, rather than being used for example, to assess knowledge of History or French, is used as a three-year test of ability to work unaided, to analyse problems, to absorb knowledge and to express oneself clearly.

Slightly more specific are tests of various intellectual capacities. Tests of general intelligence are often used for managerial selection but, whilst intelligence is obviously required for managerial success, high levels of intelligence are not usually predictive of greater performance. More specific still are tests of concept attainment and critical thinking (e.g. the Watson Glaser Critical Thinking Test). Such tests often form part of managerial potential assessment and are tests not so much of speed of problem solving, but of depth and power of analysis.

As with mechanical aptitude however there has been a trend towards assessing managerial aptitudes or potential as they manifest themselves in a characteristic sample of the actual job. An example of such a test is the so-called 'in-basket' or 'in-tray' test in which the subject is presented with a full in-tray for the job he is about to take over. Among the items included are production reports, memoranda from other departmental heads, messages from customers and suppliers and so on. The subject's task is to decide how important each one is and take appropriate action - writing or telephoning various people or arranging meetings or appointments. An analysis of how the person perceives and deals with the problems with which he is faced, gives an indication of factors such as his ability to give the right priority to problems, or to take a broad view of matters (the so-called helicopter effect).

The in-basket and other decision-making exercises are often a part of a wider assessment method known as Assessment Centres. (Originally the assessment centre was the place where these tests and exercises were carried out, but the term is now used to refer to the techniques involved.) Decision-making ability is often assessed within the context of a simulated committee or 'leaderless group' and such group discussions and teamwork can form the basis for assessing a person's personality on such dimensions as sociability, leadership etc. Recent studies (e.g. Dulewicz and Fletcher, 1982) have shown that although assessment centre performance is not seriously affected by previous experience, it is related to the level of general intelligence of the participants. For this reason some companies have started using intelligence tests to screen possible candidates.

In the assessment centre therefore we see a trend that has been apparent in both personality and aptitude assessment, namely the move towards measurement in specific situations. But this is only possible where we know what the situation will be and, as we shall see, this is not always possible.

Personality and aptitude tests in use

In our consideration of some of the more important discussions of personality and aptitudes, we have seen how they might be associated with particular tasks and jobs and, from an organizational point of view, it is not surprising to find that their major usage is in selection and placement.

At first sight it might appear that all we have to do is decide what personality or aptitudes a particular job requires, select a test which measures them, (such tests may be traditional psychological test, job sample, interviews or any other method of assessment), test all the applicants, and select the one with the highest score. But things are rarely so simple. Let us consider some of the major problems at each of these stages.

First, how do we decide on the important personality or aptitudes required? Some may appear obvious. Salespersons for example should be extraverted ; a potential mechanic should score high on a test of mechanical aptitude. Even here however we come across problems: does a salesperson have to be an extravert? Might not some clients be discouraged or irritated by a bright and breezy approach? It could be agreed that both Churchill and Atlee were effective Prime Ministers but there were obvious differences in their personalities and styles of leadership. Then again, the term 'mechanic' covers a wide range of jobs. In some the main requirement might be an ability to analyse the likely consequences of certain adjustments; whilst in others fine manipulative skills may be more crucial. Analysing the job to be done does, however, give us an idea of the factors likely to be important, especially when the analysis is done with the help of a number of recently developed techniques.

Job analysis

Job analysis has, from a psychological point of view, recently gone through a 'lean patch' from which it is only just recovering and, although it is not our major concern, it is perhaps worth mentioning some recent developments.

Whereas the engineer when analysing a job will tend to concentrate upon the tasks that have to be done to produce the required output, the psychologist concentrates more on the behaviour of the worker. As we have seen with descriptions of personality, however, we have to reduce the massive number of possible descriptions to a more manageable number.

One of the best examples of such a worker-orientated approach is that of McCormick, Jeanneret and Mecham (1972). After considerable research they produced the position analysis questionnaire (PAQ). This consists of about 190 job activities which cluster into six major areas: information input (e.g. perception), mediation processes (e.g. reasoning), work output (e.g. bodily activity), interpersonal activities (e.g. personal contact), work situations (e.g. physical conditions) and miscellaneous.

In an interesting study using the PAQ, Arvey and Begalla (1975) analysed the job of the housewife and found that the major components were: being aware of body movement and balance, physically active, manipulating equipment with hands and feet, engaging in personally demanding situations, and working to an irregular schedule. As well as allowing us to analyse jobs, however, the PAQ can be used to compare jobs to see how alike they are. Indeed in the study just quoted, the researchers went on to discover which of 20 other jobs were most like that of the housewife. In increasing order of similarity these were: fireman, kitchen helper, airport maintenance chief, home economist and finally the most similar - police officer!

The PAQ is not the only system which can be used. Olsen, Fine, Myers and Jennings (1981) for example, use functional job analysis (FJA) which concentrates on things, data and people, while Jones, Main, Butler and Johnson (1982) have experimented with Narrative Job Descriptions where the analysis is based upon narrative descriptions of jobs. Their findings suggest that these relatively simple analyses can produce results comparable with more complicated procedures such as the PAQ.

Perhaps the most appropriate, from our point of view is the Trait Orientated technique developed by Primoff (1974) and refined by Lopez, Kesselman and Lopez (1981). The job concerned is analysed into five areas (physical, mental, learnt, motivational and social), these are sub-divided into 21 job functions: for example, physical exertion, attention, communication, limited mobility, interpersonal contact, etc. The functions are then further subdivided into 33 traits. Examples are vision, memory, oral expression, dependability and personal appearance.

Such analyses provide us with a basis for choosing the kinds of tests and other measures that will, we hope, help us predict successful job performance. They also have some additional benefits not directly related to selection. We have already looked at job sample tests and it is obvious that the type of job analysis that we have just described can be used as a basis for the construction of such tests. In addition the areas of training needs can be determined and evaluated. It is also perhaps worth mentioning that some studies have also been published (Taylor, 1978) which suggest that these job analyses may be useful for job evaluation (i.e. determining the pay rate for the job).

Predicting success

Having selected a number of tests, how do we decide which are likely to be best at predicting successful performance, i.e. which ones are valid? The best way would be to assess the test's predictive validity, but time and money usually rule this out so we use concurrent validity, that is, we measure our current employees' performance and then compare those with test results. This is an acceptable way of proceeding but you should beware of a major drawback. By using your current employees you are inevitably going to be selecting others in their image. Can you be sure that they are the best possible individuals for the particular job?

A major problem which confronts us at this stage, however, is that of obtaining reliable and accurate measures of job performance. The obvious choice, especially where output is concerned, is production figures or comparable criteria such as sales figures. Even these however are not as straightforward and clear-cut as we might think. First, over what period of time do we take them; and, second, how responsible can individuals be held for their own results?

For example, how do we assess a salesperson who sells nothing for 10 months and then lands a huge order (remember attribution theory)? In addition how far can we blame the individual for the first 10 months and praise him for the eleventh? Sales areas, like production machines, vary, and the influence of such factors, over which the individual has little or no control, can be considerable.

We have also been talking as if there is only one criterion of job performance, but this is obviously not the case. Most jobs include a number of important aspects; for example as well as selling, a salesperson will be expected to fill in reports, deal with administrative matters, and look after his car. Indeed the job analysis, which we have previously mentioned, can often be a source of dimensions for the appraisal of performance. Do we therefore have one overall rating or do we use a number of the more 'important' dimensions?

Often because of the problems associated with objective measures such as production figures or training school test results, what we end up with are subjective ratings. These ratings may be done by a person's superiors, subordinates, peers or even themselves (see Makin and Robertson, 1983). The ratings are usually on a series of scales, for example, initiative, attendance etc., and are most commonly filled in by a person's superior, either with or without the agreement of the person being rated. There are, however, certain common problems with these scales which mean that it is difficult to assess how much reliance can be placed on their accuracy.

The following list of sources of possible error is by no means exhaustive, but will give some indication of the range of problems:

* the halo effect: this is the tendency for a rater's judgement on one scale to be influenced by his judgement on others. The result is an overall judgement rather than accurate profile of relative strengths and weaknesses;

* central tendency: although statistical theory tells us that about one third of the people being rated should be either high or low on scales, the people doing the rating rarely, if ever, use anything but the central region;

* leniency effect: when someone rates someone else they do so from their own frame of reference, often rating highly people who are more like themselves;

* meaning of dimensions: different raters may interpret scales differently. For example initiative or dedication to work may mean different things to different people;

* scale usage: what do different parts of the scale mean? It may be that one rater reserves the top end of the scale as

something he would use to score only the best conceivable
employee, whilst another rater would be happy to rate his
best present subordinate in that position.

There are, however, a number of techniques that attempt
to overcome these problems. One technique attempts to overcome the central tendency and leniency effects by forcing
the rater to choose between subordinates for example, by
ranking them from best to worst on each dimension. Another,
and sometimes useful, method involves the use of peer
ratings being done by workmates, but there are obvious
dangers in such a scheme, especially when assessments are
used as a basis for promotion.

One technique that has received considerable attention
has been that of behaviourally anchored rating scales
(BARS). The essential feature of BARS is that the scales,
instead of having numbers (e.g. 1-7) or verbal descriptions
(e.g. good, very good, poor, etc.) have descriptions of the
behaviour that might be expected from someone who was rated
at that point on the scale. For example on a scale of Use of
Tools the description of someone who 'could be expected to
apply the correct tension to screw', was placed near the top
of the scale by training instructors, while 'could be expected to hammer smooth surfaces' was near the bottom. The
raters therefore have anchors to show what the different
points on the scale represent.

As well as having those anchors, however, BARS are also
different in the way they are constructed. Rather than
someone in the personnel department deciding what the
dimensions and anchors should be, the emphasis is upon
involving those who will be doing the actual ratings in the
process of constructing the scale they will use. It may well
be, therefore, that the group discussions help each of the
raters clarify their own ideas about what makes a good or
bad employee, and compare their ideas with their colleagues.
Research into the efficiency of BARS however, has not shown
them to be always better than other methods, and there is no
doubt that the cost, in terms of time taken, is large. There
are however spin-off uses for BARS which are similar to
those from job analysis, for example, identification of
training needs, etc. (for a review see Schwab, Heneman and
Decotiis, 1975).

Having done the necessary research to identify the most
useful tests (there will usually be more than one) and
having tested all the applicants, how do we choose between
them? The answer may appear obvious: select the person with
the highest overall score. Anyone who has been involved in
selection knows that rarely does one applicant rank first on
all the requirements for the post.

Individuals have strengths and weaknesses, one being
better on one dimension but doing less well on another.
Which therefore is the most important dimension? Can a high
score on one offset a low score on another? Sophisticated
statistical techniques such as multiple regression can help,

but inevitably the choice will come down to individual judgement. So what, you may ask, is the use of all the test results?

The use of tests is not to give us explicit and immediate answers but to reduce uncertainty and hence the possibility of making an error. The relationship between test scores and job performance is not like that between wavelength and frequency (one perfectly predicting the other) but at best is like that between weight and height. If you ask me a man's weight I am likely to make a more accurate assessment if I know his height. In addition the usefulness (utility) of a test is not only determined by how accurate (valid) it is but also how, and for what job it is used. In particular when your past techniques have not been very successful, and when there are a lot of applicants per job (i.e. a high selection ratio), and where there is a large difference between the average and the best (or worst) performer even a moderately accurate test can substantially improve the efficiency of the selection procedure.

It is worth pointing out something that has been implied, even if not openly stated, in the previous paragraph: it is that jobs, even those that have the same title, may not be the same. In addition, even a particular job may change over time, for example a visual display unit (VDU) may take the place of a typewriter. The point to be made is what indicates performance on one job may not do so for an apparently similar job, and what used to indicate performance some time ago may not do so now! The motto, therefore, is develop your selection procedure carefully and keep checking it at regular intervals.

Finally, because this book is about management, the emphasis has been upon selection and placement; but the same tests that give information to selectors can also be used to give guidance to the applicants. This is the area of career or vocational guidance/counselling and those who are interested may refer to Ruth Holdsworth's volume 'Psychology for Careers Counselling' (1982); but one important point is worth making. We have seen that even a moderately valid test can have a high utility from the organization's view-point, especially when there are a lot of applicants. When we are talking about a particular individual however, accuracy becomes an important consideration. In this situation, where it is the individual who is being considered, the test results should be used for guidance, as an indication of areas to be explored rather than scores merely to be used in making the final decision.

It should not be forgotten however that whilst organizations choose those to whom they will offer a job, the individual also chooses whether or not to apply or accept. The better and more specific the relevant information available to both parties therefore the better the likely 'match'. The best predictor of future performance in a particular job is past performance in that job, so perhaps the best system of selection is one of pre-entry 'screening' for important personality/aptitude dimensions coupled with an extended trial period. There should also be the opportunity, especially where promotion is involved, for a return to a more suitable post without loss of face, if things do not work out.

References

Allport, G.W. and Odbert, H.S. (1936)
Trait-names: a psycho-lexical study. Psychological Monographs 47, No. 211.

Andrisani, P.J. and Nestel, G. (1976)
Internal-external control as a contributor to and outcome of work experience. Journal of Applied Psychology, 61, 156-165.

Arvey, R.D. and Begalla, M.E. (1975)
Analysing the homemaker job using the PAQ. Journal of Applied Psychology, 60, 513-517.

Bannister, D. and Fransella, F. (1971)
Inquiring Man: The theory of personal constructs, London: Penguin.

Cattell, R.B., Eber, H.W. and Tatsuoka M.M. (1970)
Handbook for the Sixteen Personality Factor Questionnaire (16 PF). Windsor, Berks: NFER Publishing.

Deaux, K. (1976)
Sex: a perspective on the attitude process. In Harvey, J.H. Ickes, W.J. and Kidd, R.F. (eds), New Directions in Attribution Research, Vol. 1. Hillsdale, NJ: Erlbaum.

de Board, R. (1978)
The Psychoanalysis of Organisations. London: Tavistock.

Downs, S., Farr, R.M. and Colbeck, L. (1978)
Self-appraisal: A convergence of selection and guidance. Journal of Occupational Psychology, 51, 271-278.

Dulewicz, V. and Fletcher, C. (1982)
The relationship between previous experience, intelligence and background characteristics of participants and their performance in an assessment centre. Journal of Occupational Psychology, 55, 197-207.

Eysenck, H.J. (1967)
Personality patterns in various groups of businessmen. Occupational Psychology, 41, 249-250.

Eysenck, H.J. (1970)
The Structure of Human Personality. London: Methuen.

Eysenck, H.J. (1983)
Stress, disease, and personality: the inoculation effect. In C.L. Cooper (ed.), Stress Research: Issues for the 80s. London: Wiley.

Eysenck, H.J. and Eysenck, S.B.G. (1975)
The Manual of the Eysenck Personality Questionnaire. Sevenoaks, Kent: Hodder and Stoughton.

Freud, S. (1973)
New Introductory Lectures on Psychoanalysis. Harmondsworth: Penguin.

Friedman, M.D. and Rosenman, R.H. (1974)
Type A Behaviour and Your Heart. New York: Knopf.

Gibson, H.B. (1965)
Manual of the Gibson Spiral Maze. London: University of London.

Holdsworth, R. (1982)
Psychology for Careers Counselling. London: The British Psychological Society and Macmillan.

Henney, A.S. (1975)
Personality characteristics of a group of industrial managers. Journal of Occupational Psychology, 43, 65-67.

Jones, A. P., Main, D.S., Butler, M.C. and Johnson, L.A. (1982)
Narrative job descriptions as potential sources of job analysis ratings. Personnel Psychology, 35, 813-828.

Jones, E.E. and Nisbett, R.E. (1971)
The Actor and the Observer. Divergent Perceptions of the Causes of Behaviour. Morristown, NJ: General Learning Press.

Jones, P. and Whittaker, P. (1975)
Testing Industrial Skills. Epping, Essex: Gower.

Kahn, H.A. (1972)
The incidence of hypertension and associated factors: The Israel ischemic heart disease study. American Heart Journal, 84, 171-182.

Kelly, G.A. (1963)
A Theory of Personality. New York: Norton.

Loevinger, J. and Knoll, E. (1983)
Personality: stages, traits and the self. Annual Review of Psychology, 34, 195-222.

Lopez, F.M., Kesselman, G.A. and Lopez, F.E. (1981)
An empirical test of trait-orientated job analysis technique. Personnel Psychology, 34, 479-502.

Lorenz, K. (1966)
On Aggression. London: Methuen.

Lynn, R. (1969)
Personality characteristics of a group of entrepreneurs. Occupational Psychology, 43, 151-153.

Makin, P. J. and Randell, G.A. (1978)
Selection and Validation of Psychological Tests for the Prediction of Mechanic Performance. Bradford: University of Bradford Management Centre.

Makin, P.J. and Robertson, I.T. (1983)
Self assessment, realistic job previews and occupational decisions. Personnel Review, 12, (3), 21-25.

McCormick, E.J., Jeanneret, P. and Mecham, R.C. (1972)
A study of job characteristics and job dimensions as based on the position analysis questionnaires. Journal of Applied Psychology, 36, 347-368.

McClelland, D.C. (1961)
The Achieving Society. Princeton, NJ: Van Nostrand.

McClelland, D.C. and Winter, D.G. (1969)
Motivating Economic Achievement. New York: Free Press.

Mischel, E. (1968)
Personality and Assessment. New York: Wiley.
Olsen, H.C., Fine, S.A., Myers, D.C. and Jennings, M.C. (1981)
The use of Functional Job Analysis in establishing performance standards for heavy equipment operations. Personnel Psychology, 34, 351-364.
Pervin, L.A. (1978)
Current Controversies and Issues in Personality. New York: Wiley.
Pervin, L.A. (1980)
Personality: Theory, assessment and research. New York: Wiley.
Primoff, E.S. (1974)
How to Prepare and Conduct Job-element Examinations. Washington, DC: US Civil Service Commission. Personnel Research and Development Centre.
Robertson, I.T. and Mindel, R.M. (1980)
A study of trainability testing. Journal of Occupational Psychology, 53, 131-138.
Rorer, L.G. and Widiger, T.A. (1983)
Personality structure and assessment. Annual Review of Psychology, 34, 431-463.
Schmidt, F.L., Hunter, J.E., Pearlman, K. and Shane, G.S. (1979)
Further tests of the Schmidt-Hunter Bayesian validity generalization procedure. Personnel Psychology, 32, 257-281.
Schwab, D.P., Heneman, H.G. and Decotiis, T.A. (1975)
Behaviourally anchored Rating Scales: a review of the literature. Personnel Psychology, 28, 549-562.
Sheldon, W. H. (1954)
Atlas of Men: A guide for somatotyping the male at all ages. New York: Harper.
Skinner, B.F. (1974)
About Behaviourism. New York: Knopf.
Smith, M.C. and Downs, S. (1975)
Trainability assessments for apprentice selection in shipbuilding. Journal of Occupational Psychology, 43, 39-43.
Smithers, A.G. (1968)
Some characteristics of business students in a technological university: I. Personality patterns. Occupational Psychology, 42, 161-165.
Spector, P.E. (1982)
Behavior in organizations as a function of employees' locus of control. Psychological Bulletin, 91, 483-497.
Steers, R.M. and Spencer, D.G. (1977)
The role of achievement motivation in job design. Journal of Applied Psychology, 62, 472-479.
Stewart, V.J. and Stewart, A. (1981)
Business Applications of Repertory Grid. London: McGraw-Hill.

Storms, M.D. (1973)
Videotape and the attribution process: reversing actors' and observers' points of view. Journal of Personality and Social Psychology, 27, 165-175.

Taylor, L.R. (1978)
Empirically derived job families as a foundation for the study of validity generalization. Study 1. The construction of job families based upon the component and overall dimensions of the PAQ. Personnel Psychology, 31, 325-340.

Thibaut, J.W. and Riecken, H.W. (1955)
Some determinants and consequences of the perception of social causality. Journal of Personality, 24, 113-133.

Questions

1. What do we mean by personality?
2. To what extent can human behaviour be explained by instinct?
3. Is man by nature aggressive/lazy?
4. What is the relationship between body build and personality?
5. Are successful managers born, or are they made?
6. How relevant are Freud's theories to managers?
7. What is your most common reaction to frustration at work? What effect does it have upon your fellow workers?
8. What are defence mechanisms? Describe and give examples of two.
9. Discuss the strengths and weaknesses of type theories.
10. Are 16 traits enough to describe unique individuals?
11. The best way to assess someone's personality is to observe how they behave. Discuss with reference to Assessment Centres.
12. Compare the reliability and validity of interviews, psychological tests and work sample tests.
13. Is there an ideal managerial personality?
14. Our friends succeed because of their skills, our enemies because of luck. Discuss.
15. How stable is personality (a) over time? (b) from one situation to another?
16. Can a person's personality be changed?
17. Is our individual level of intelligence due to nature or nurture?
18. How useful are aptitude tests in selecting prospective managers?
19. Describe some of the problems that arise when you attempt to measure job performance.

Annotated reading

Anastasi, A. (1982). Psychological Testing. New York: Macmillan.

Invaluable for those who wish to read more deeply into the theory and practice of psychological testing.

Lindzey, G., Hall, C.S. and Manisevitz, M. (1973). Theories of Personality: Primary sources and research. New York: Wiley.

Extracts from the writings of the major personality theorists supplemented by research findings. A valuable source book.

Pervin, L.A. (1980). Personality: Theory, assessment and research. New York: Wiley.

Perhaps the best general textbook of personality theory.

Chapter 5

Motivation at work
Cary L. Cooper and Peter Makin

An individual's performance at any task is determined by three major factors. First, they must have the ability to do the task in question, an ability which itself is a combination of an aptitude which has been 'built on' by subsequent training. Second, and perhaps obviously, they must have the right tools for the job. Third, they must also have the drive or motivation to do the job.

Given that we have selected individuals well on the basis of aptitude, that we have supplemented this with successful and relevant training, and that we have properly equipped them, the main factor that will determine the level of performance is the level of motivation.

This relationship between performance and motivation has often been expressed as follows:

performance = ability x motivation

This is not meant, however, to be a mathematical formula for it is not possible to put figures into the equation and get an answer. What it is meant to indicate is the interactive nature of ability and motivation. For example, if there is zero ability, even a very high level of motivation will still produce zero performance. On the other hand, if there is a reasonable level of ability, the effect of even small increases in motivation will produce noticeably better performance. There is, however, a limit beyond which the equation ceases to work. According to the Yerkes-Dodson Law the relationship between performance and motivation is like an inverted-U, an increase in motivation leads to an increase in performance up to a certain point, after which any further increase actually leads to a decrease in performance. The suggested reason for this is that, beyond the optimum point, the methods used to increase motivation in fact produce anxiety which interferes with performance. In this chapter, however, we generally assume that we are not approaching this downward slope, but as you see in chapter 14 on stress, it is just those aspects of a manager's job that he finds rewarding which he also finds stressful when they go beyond certain levels.

The purpose of this chapter is to consider studies that have been carried out to test the various theories of motivation at work, and to demonstrate their relevance to and implications for management. In doing this we assume that you have already read the relevant section in chapter 2 so if you have not already done so, we would recommend that you refer back to it before reading further.

In considering the various theories, we deal with them in approximately chronological order. Theories, whether they be chemical, physical or psychological, are not always rejected because they do not fit the facts but because of the lack of a better theory. Each theory builds upon the strengths, and attempts to minimize the weaknesses of, previous theories. In addition, as we see, even those theories which are now considered inaccurate often have a kernel of truth which is retained by those which supplant them.

If you were asked what it was that characterized living organisms, one of the things that you would most probably list is the fact that they try to keep themselves alive. In the simplest terms, they have 'needs' for a particular environment in terms of temperature range, oxygen content, etc. These basic 'needs' are known as 'primary' needs but, by association, we learn that there are indirect ways of satisfying these needs through so called 'secondary' needs. The most obvious of these is concerned with money. Money in itself cannot satisfy hunger or thirst but, because we learn that it can be exchanged for food and water it acquires the status of a secondary need. During the first 30 years of this century, psychologists sought to list all the human needs, but this list became so long as to be unmanageable. To see the problems we have only to use our example of money. For misers, money appears to be a need in itself, independent of its usefulness for buying goods and indeed, even if they did buy goods what 'needs' could they be satisfying? You obviously have a need for food and drink, but do you have a 'need' for Chateaubriand washed down with a 1962 Chateau Latour? At one point indeed someone suggested that there appeared to be a need among psychologists to produce lists of needs. What was needed was some means of classifying needs and ordering them as to their importance.

Frederick Taylor

The first major influence on motivation as it applied specifically to work was that of Frederick Taylor (1911). Taylor concentrated upon just one secondary need - one we have already mentioned and the one which, if you asked people why they work, would be the most common answer - money! Taylor's technique, known as Scientific Management, was simple; he reorganized the working methods so as to produce the most efficient method of operation whilst at the same time ensuring that payment was dependent upon productivity, and hence that there was a financial incentive to work hard. Taylor called this the management of 'initiative and incentive'; if you want your employees to show initiative you must give them an incentive. In saying this,

Taylor acknowledges that he is merely stating what others already claim to do. There is, he says, 'a universal prejudice' in favour of the approach but it was in his practical applications that he went beyond others.

The famous example used to show the effect of scientific management was the study of loading pig iron into railway trucks at Bethlehem Street in the USA in the first decade of this century. By carefully designing the task and selecting the men, the amount of pig iron loaded per man per day rose from 12½ long tons to 47 long tons. The corresponding increase in pay was from $1.15 per man per day to $1.85. The selection of the men was crucial and was done on an individual basis, to quote Taylor (1911, p. 59):

> One of the first requirements for a man who is fit to handle pig iron as a regular occupation is that he shall be so stupid and so phlegmatic that he more nearly resembles in his mental make-up the ox than any other type.

Given this approach to motivation at work it is perhaps hardly surprising that the next important theory, perhaps as a reaction, was 'human relations' theory. Despite this apparently insensitive approach to man management, for which Taylor is often berated, we should not overlook the other aspects of his theory which have received less attention. Indeed, most of the criticism of Taylor concentrates on two of his four propositions, the first of which concerns a detailed task analysis and more particularly on the second, which concentrates on the selection, training and development of the workman. His third and fourth propositions however perhaps anticipate later developments and these we quote verbatum (Taylor, 1911, p. 36-37):

> Third. They heartily cooperate with the men so as to insure all of the work being done in accordance with the principles of the science which has been developed ... Fourth. There is an almost equal division of the work and responsibility between the management and the workmen.

Taylor's ideas fell, however, because in the particular case in question, the success of the scheme depended upon a supply of strong, stupid and most probably non-unionized men. In addition, social critics were demanding that more attention be paid to the individual worker than to treating them merely as a machine. Despite this, it is perhaps time that Taylor's ideas were looked at again and indeed Locke (1982) has recently undertaken such a reappraisal.

The Hawthorne studies
The next major revision of theory came from the studies carried out at the Hawthorne works of Western Electric in the 1920s and 1930s and reported by Roethlisberger and

Dickson (1939) and Mayo (1975). Although Mayo used these studies to support his own theories, many people mistakenly believe that he was an active member of the research team. As Smith (1975), in his foreword to Mayo (1975) points out however, the studies were 'neither designed nor directed by Mayo' (p. xiv). Initially, the researchers were trying to establish the relationship between various physical conditions, for example temperature, lighting and productivity. They found however that, although the productivity in the groups they were studying increased, the level of lighting had no consistent effect. Indeed productivity went up in the control group where the level of lighting was not even changed and, even more surprising, it stayed high in the experimental group when the level was reduced to that of moonlight. The researchers concluded from this that other 'psychological' factors were at work.

In order to test their hypotheses they set up various small group experiments and concluded that motivation at work could be explained in terms of 'social relationships'. The reason for the increase in productivity in their initial groups was that the members felt that the researchers were taking an interest in them. Indeed the 'Hawthorne effect' has entered the sociological and psychological vocabulary as meaning the effect you observe merely as the result of observing; for people respond favourably to being taken notice of.

Although the studies took place over 50 years ago, the results are still a matter of discussion and controversy. Most researchers now accept that the Hawthorne studies were poorly constructed and controlled and that results can be explained in ways other than purely 'social'. For example, some of the members in the group were replaced by 'more friendly' workers. In addition, they worked shorter hours, had more frequent rest pauses and were allowed other privileges. Despite this, however, they have, like Taylor, left their mark on motivational theory by drawing attention to the social and psychological aspects of behaviour at work.

We have seen now how the answer to the question 'what motivates people at work?' has been answered by two theories, one stressing money, the other stressing social relationships, both formal and informal. It is apparent however that neither by themselves, nor indeed both together, are adequate to explain the complexity of motivation at work. Consider for example the often told story of Bette Davis who had written into her contract with the movie studios that she would receive a salary of $1 more than any other star. Obviously the money itself was irrelevant, what was important was its indication to everyone of her status.

A recent study by Warr (1982) has demonstrated that money is not the sole reason for working. A large sample of British men and women were asked if they would carry on working if it were not financially necessary: 69 per cent of men and 65 per cent of women said they would. The percentage is also relatively stable across social classes, although the figure for the middle class is higher than for working class: for men the respective figures are 76 per cent and 63 per cent and for women, 72 per cent and 55 per cent. Although Warr does not explore the reasons for a desire to continue work, studies of unemployment show that people's self-esteem suffers, a fact which is hardly surprising in a society where our work role gives us so much of our self-identity.

Maslow

There are, it would appear, a whole range of 'needs' that each of us has, but is there any pattern to these? Are some more or less important than others? Maslow's theory (see chapter 2) is an attempt to answer these questions. To recapitulate briefly, the theory suggests that needs can be classified into one of six categories arranged into a hierarchy. Before a particular class of needs becomes important those below it in the hierarchy must be satisfied. For example, when threatened with redundancy our need for self-actualization at work suddenly melts into insignificance as the implications of loss of work on physical and social well-being are realized. When examined in this way, Maslow's theory has an initial intuitive appeal but research so far has not tended to support it (see Wahba and Bridwell, 1976, for a review). Not only do the lower levels not have to be satisfied before the higher ones become important but the particular 'needs', when mathematically analysed, do not fit neatly into the six classifications. Maslow, however, might claim that the research does not do justice to the theory. First, there are considerable difficulties in developing reliable methods of measuring the strengths of various needs; indeed different studies use different measures and the results cannot therefore be properly compared. Second, most of the studies use so called 'cross-sectional' methods which look at the hierarchy at one particular point in time rather than see how 'needs' develop within the individual. This would need a 'longitudinal' study. Finally, it has been applied to large groups of people so that the results can be statistically analysed, whereas Maslow (who was a clinical rather than an occupational psychologist) intended the theory as a method of examining how an individual develops. If we accept Maslow's theory, however, what implications does it have for management?

What Maslow's theory does is to provide us with a method of classifying an individual's needs, finding out which, at the present time, are most important (i.e. unsatisfied) and hence determining what rewards will be most valued. Thus, if people have enough pay to satisfy their physical and security needs, money will lose some of its importance, and rewards that satisfy social needs will be more effective as motivators. Likewise, when social needs are satisfied, ego needs such as group esteem become important. In a company for which one of the authors worked, most salesmen valued a four-door (as opposed to a two-door) company car far more than a corresponding increase in salary because of its status value.

Alderfer (1969) has proposed a theory that reduces Maslow's classification to three: existency needs, relationship needs and growth needs (hence called the ERG theory). In addition, Alderfer differs from Maslow in the way he suggests that people move up the hierarchy of needs. If a particular need level is satisfied, Maslow suggests that it is the next need higher that requires satisfying and that further satisfaction of the lower level will have no effect. Alderfer, on the other hand, suggests that extra reward at lower levels can compensate for a lack at higher levels. In this he is most probably proposing a slightly more optimistic view as far as management is concerned: if you can't give them job satisfaction more pay will do!

Although these theories are not, despite their initial appeal, generally accepted as a view of how everyone is motivated, they do highlight a general feature about what people will find rewarding. As we see, rewards are arranged in a hierarchy, some being more important than others, but the nature of this hierarchy will differ from one person to another and even within a particular person at different times.

Herzberg

Maslow's theory suggests that the reason a pay rise which at first we find rewarding, soon loses its initial effect, is that the 'need' has been largely satisfied. Herzberg (1966), on the other hand, suggests that the reason is that money, like other externally controlled 'hygiene' factors, will only reduce dissatisfaction. An increase in satisfaction can only be obtained by using the internally based 'motivators'. This theory is covered in chapter 2 by Payne, but one or two further points might usefully be made.

As regards the initial studies, it is worth pointing out that the evidence used by Herzberg to support his two distinct dimensions (hygiene and motivators) is often far from clear-cut. For example, although opinions about salary levels contributed to low job attitude in about 18 per cent of cases, they also appeared at a similar percentage in its contribution to high job attitude. In addition, support for Herzberg's theory has generally only come from studies which used similar samples of people (normally professionals) and a similar method of investigation (asking people to report on their own performance and attitudes). The use of such self-report techniques may be criticized on two grounds. First, people may be unable or unwilling to make accurate assessments of their own performance (see Makin and Robertson, 1983). Second, and perhaps more important, it might be that Herzberg's analysis merely shows a more general human characteristic in apportioning blame and praise. When things go wrong we tend to 'blame things out to 'blame things out there', for example poor management, low pay, poor equipment and so on, but when things go right it is because 'of our own abilities'.

Whatever the validity of Herzberg's theory, however, there is little doubt that it has had a significant influence in the area of job design as part of what has become known as the QWL, or Quality of Working Life, movement (for example, see Hackman and Suttle (1977)).

Job enrichment and job enlargement

The nature of the job affects the way we feel and this in turn has effects upon absenteeism, time lost through 'illness', quality of work, and industrial disputes, etc. There are two ways, it is suggested, in which jobs can be made more interesting. Job enrichment concentrates on increasing the range or the size of the job 'vertically'. For example job enrichment for someone who fastened one part onto a car engine would mean that he would become responsible for the total construction of the engine from its component parts. Another method of changing the task is job enlargement, and this is horizontal rather than vertical. Job enlargement typically consists of adding more tasks to a short, repetitive cycle.

Herzberg considers that job enlargement should be avoided and that, by enriching a job by including more responsibility and authority, the motivational properties of the job can be increased. Other writers have found evidence that job enlargement can also increase satisfaction by increasing the variety of tasks performed. Other approaches have concentrated on the individual in groups by creating leaderless, autonomous working groups which have responsibility for their own working procedures (see Wall, 1978).

The most comprehensive model of the effect of the job on work-related attitudes and behaviour is the Job Characteristics Model of Hackman and Oldham (1976), a model which has received general support (e.g. Wall, Clegg and Jackson, 1978). The model is drawn in figure 1 but as can be seen, Hackman and Oldham suggest that the effects of the job on personal and work outcomes are moderated by an individual's GNS (growth needs strength). The effects of an enriched or enlarged job, they recognize, will only have an effect on those people who have a high need for job autonomy and responsibility. Unlike Herzberg, therefore, they accept that there are individual differences between people. Some would not find additional responsibility desirable at all.

Although it is likely that unsuccessful attempts at increasing motivation through job redesign go unreported, some studies have shown encouraging results. Paul and Robertson (1970), for example, report the results of a redesign of the work of sales representatives. Individual autonomy and responsibility were increased by allowing the salesmen to determine how often they called on each customer and whether a formal record of the visit was required. In addition, they were given some financial discretion in determining the selling price and in being able to offer some financial recompense in cases of complaint. Compared with a similar group whose job was not enriched, they showed improved attitudes and their performance increased by 19 per cent. Given that over the same period the other group's performance fell by 5 per cent, the results are impressive.

Figure 1

**The job characteristics model of work motivation
Hackman and Oldham (1976)**

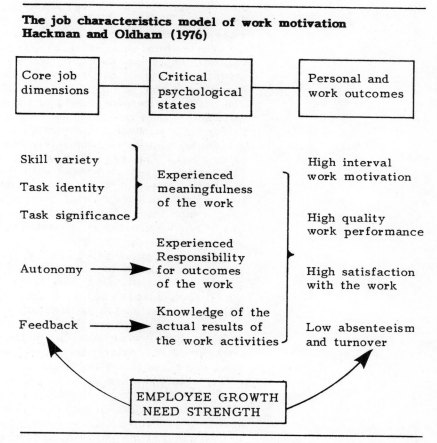

One of the major problems both for implementing and evaluating job redesign, however, is that many factors are involved. Often, when such schemes are implemented, other changes take place within the organization at the same time; so it is difficult to identify the precise cause of any particular change. For example, payment schemes are likely to alter as people take on new responsibilities. Indeed, even if changes in job design do produce desirable results, it would be useful to know precisely what aspect of the changes produced the desired effect. It might be that the same, or very similar outcome could be achieved at a lesser cost. Unfortunately, the more our research gets like 'real life' the more complicated it becomes and the more difficult it is to control all the relevant variables.

Job satisfaction

It is useful at this point to consider briefly the role of a job-related attitude which we encountered in the discussion of Herzberg's theory and which has become part of everyday language: job satisfaction. Job satisfaction is sometimes considered as just one measure but more often various different aspects of the job are measured. The job description inventory (or JDI) for example (see Smith, Kendall and Hulin, 1969), considers five separate aspects: work content, co-workers, supervision, pay and promotion. The worker opinion survey (WOS) often used for shop-floor studies (see Soutar and Weaver, 1982), includes all of these but also measures satisfaction with the organization as a whole.

These items present an oversimplified view of the various components of a job, for we can all think of certain aspects of our job that we enjoy and others that we do not. But what is the effect of job satisfaction on performance? The general consensus among researchers is that job satisfaction does not lead, by itself, to increased performance. Indeed, if anything, the view is now that it is performance, when appropriately rewarded, that leads to satisfaction. This general view that increased job satisfaction is not associated with increased performance has been contradicted in some studies and it would appear that a link can be shown in cases where the people involved have a high level of commitment to their work. In addition, the relationship between job satisfaction and other non-performance measures appears to be more encouraging. Job satisfaction appears to be related more to aspects such as absenteeism, lateness and quality of output rather than quantity of output. Does this mean that job satisfaction as a goal should be ignored by management? Most probably not, although increased job satisfaction may not lead to increased performance, the ground-swell of public opinion over the last few decades for increasing satisfaction from work would be difficult to ignore. People expect it. In addition, there is evidence that work attitudes and experiences influence other non-work activities. It may be that job satisfaction is desirable not from the point of view of a particular organization but as a contributor to a healthy society.

So far you may have noticed that all the theories have concentrated upon the 'things' that motivate people rather than 'how' they motivate. For this reason they are called 'content' theories. More recently however, attention has tended to concentrate on theories which, whilst obviously being concerned with what motivates individuals, examine the way in which motivation takes place. These are the so-called 'process' theories. (In chapter 2 Payne uses different methods of classifying these theories, but there are often different methods of grouping theories together, each of which can be useful. For example, cars can be classified by their make, engine size, colour, front-wheel or rear-wheel drive, etc. The particular way you choose depends upon which is most useful and meaningful to you.)

Equity theory

One of the most intuitively appealing processes by which our motivation can be affected is by a comparison between the effort which we put into our jobs and the rewards we get and the efforts and rewards of others. This process of comparison has been called 'social referent' or 'equity' theory and is outlined on page 31. It is based on an assumption of 'fairness': that equal work will be equally rewarded. If the ratio of our perceived inputs and outputs is seen as out of step with others, in that we are being either under-rewarded or over-rewarded we will take steps to restore the equity. The way in which the balance is restored will vary, depending upon the rewarding conditions. For example, for those who feel they are being under-rewarded the way in which they will reduce their input will depend upon whether they are paid on a piecework system or not. Those who are on a piecework rate will not want to reduce their quantity of output as this would mean a cut in wages, so instead they reduce the quality. For an hourly paid worker, on the other hand, quantity will be reduced. For those who feel they are over-rewarded the opposite will happen.

Laboratory experiments with students have provided some support for the theory but field experiments in 'real life' situations have been less supportive. Once again, however, the problem may not lie with the theory but with the difficulty of controlling all the necessary variables and having accurate measures with which to assess them. What evidence there is suggests that the theory is better at explaining the effects of perceived under-reward rather than over-reward. (Hands up those who are over-paid!)

Despite the lack of support from research studies, most people would accept that a feeling that we are being fairly rewarded as compared with other people in a similar situation is an important factor which will influence job-related attitudes and behaviour. A similar concept exists in sociology: that of 'relative deprivation'. We feel deprived as a result of judging our own conditions against others within our own society, not by comparing ourselves with those in the third world.

Goal setting and management by objectives

We will now deal with two approaches to motivation that arose and developed separately, but appear at least initially, to have a considerable degree of similarity. These are goal setting (Locke, 1976) and management by objectives or MBO (Drucker, 1954).

As you will have read in Payne's chapter, according to Locke it is the setting of the goal and the striving in attempting to achieve it that is the motivating force, not the rewards that accrue from success. Indeed, Locke has shown that setting specific rather than very general goals leads to an increase in performance and that this improvement is enhanced if moderately difficult rather than easy targets are set, especially when the person involved accepts them. The effects of participation in goal setting are, according to Mitchell (1979), less clear. Although participation leads to general satisfaction it does not by itself lead to greater performance. It may, however, be valuable in that participation may lead to the acceptance of difficult goals.

Those who have had experience of MBO will recognize the similarities between it and goal setting. The joint setting of specific, rather difficult but realistic goals, often by discussion with the boss, is characteristic; but there are also additional aspects. Most systems of MBO also include, either formally or informally, a continual system of appraisal which involves giving feedback as to progress. Also there is often some incentive scheme associated with it. It is here that the difference between goal setting as seen by Locke and MBO become apparent. For Locke it is the act of setting and striving that motivates, the incentives are immaterial, whereas MBO usually involves a whole package of changes.

While there is some research evidence to support Locke's theory, the evidence to support the effectiveness of MBO is substantial but usually anecdotal. As Howell and Dipboye (1982) state, MBO is considered as desirable as 'the flag, motherhood and apple pie'. Even if only some of the evidence can be adequately substantiated, however, it is apparent that MBO can have beneficial effects but, as we saw with job design, the problem is identifying the particular aspects of the MBO 'package' that are most effective. Is it the setting of goals as Locke would suggest, or is it purely the incentives? We should also not forget that there are other changes involved which may have some effect, for example, on the introduction of regular, participative meetings with the boss to review progress jointly and to set new targets. It is likely all these aspects will have some effect but we need to know which are most effective, under what circumstances and with what sorts of people. There is evidence (Ivanecevich, 1977) that the effect of goal setting reduces with time, and perhaps not only for the individual. MBO schemes, like any others, gradually change because the initial enthusiasm wears off and aspects of the scheme fall into disuse. If we could identify the most effective parts of such schemes we could then concentrate our energies on ensuring that those endured.

One particular factor that is involved in goal setting and MBO has, like job satisfaction, become part of everyday language and that is participation. Indeed, most of the evidence suggests that greater participation leads to greater satisfaction but, like satisfaction it does not, by itself, lead to better performance. Participation may indeed lead to greater commitment and acceptance of goals but, like job satisfaction, it may not be effective in all situations. While some may consider participation in decision making desirable, there are other groups for whom participation may be less attractive. For example, where the group's task is highly structured, that is determined by the equipment, and unambiguous, that is provides little room for discretion, starting a participation scheme may be seen by the group as a half-hearted 'nod' towards the latest management 'fad'.

Expectancy valence theory

The most influential theory at present, at least to academic researchers, is expectancy-valence theory (p. 29). The reason for this interest is that it recognizes that an individual's behaviour is to a considerable degree influenced by that individual's expectations of what will happen in the future. In addition, later developments of the theory provide a framework within which many of the theories we have so far discussed can be fitted. As such it is an 'over-arching' theory and this is not only one of its strengths and attractions, but also its major weakness. The elaboration on Vroom's (1964) original theory that we consider is that of Porter and Lawler (1968) shown in figure 2.

Figure 2

Diagram of the Theoretical Model of Porter and Lawler (1968)

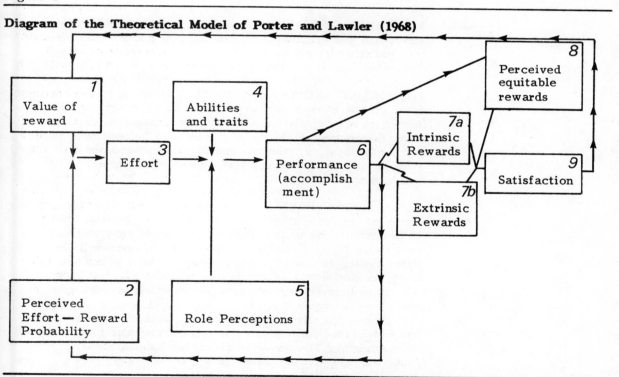

Let us work round the model considering each numbered box in turn and looking at the implications for management.

1. VALUE OF REWARD. The reward can be anything that the job can provide: pay, promotion, car parking space, etc. The important thing to notice is that it is the value of the

reward as perceived by the individual. What is rewarding to
you may not be for your boss or subordinates. For some,
being sent on a management training programme is a reward,
to others it is a punishment. Note also that the present
value of rewards will have been determined to a large extent
by the satisfaction they have given us in the past (hence
the arrow from box 9). One of us has a 12-year-old daughter,
who values a 'credit' from her English teacher '10 times
(said with emphasis) more' than a credit from maths because
she 'really has to work' to earn that credit.

2. PERCEIVED EFFORT-REWARD PROBABILITY. Notice again
the use of the word 'perceived'. It is what people believe
that is important. You may believe that your subordinates
can reach their targets if they try, but they may see them
as totally out of reach. Notice also the feedback from box 6
(accomplishment); our past successes (and failures) will
influence our beliefs. The so-called 'success spiral' can be
assisted by ensuring that, at least at the beginning of a
person's career, these perceptions can be made favourable by
ensuring early success.

3. EFFORT. There exists a distinction in this model between
effort and performance. We are all aware that effort has to
be correctly channelled to be effective, and this is largely
dependent upon the next two factors.

4. ABILITIES AND TRAITS. We have discussed this item in some
detail in the chapter on personality and it is apparent that
individual characteristics place an upper limit on the level
of a person's performance. A person may believe (box 2)
because of past experience (box 6), that no matter how much
effort is put in, it is out of the question to paint a
reasonable portrait.

5. ROLE PERCEPTIONS. Role perceptions are the other major
factor which determines whether effort will lead to
performance, and unlike abilities and traits they can be
altered. In the authors' view this is often a reason for
effort failing to result in achievement. Many of us have
often not performed as our bosses would wish, not because of
lack of willingness but because we were unaware of what it
was we were required to do. In such circumstances we may
well expend our effort in appropriate ways. For example, we
may not have done a particular job because the boss seems to
enjoy doing it. The boss, on the other hand, may be
wondering why the subordinates are so lazy that he has to do
some of their work.

6. PERFORMANCE. The final results of effort as moderated by
abilities, traits and role perceptions.

7. REWARDS. These are the outcomes that a person receives as
a result of personal performance. Once again these can only

be defined subjectively; that is, if people receive something for performing well that they do not value, it is not a reward. We consider this further when we deal with reinforcement theory and behaviour modification. Porter and Lawler also make a distinction between intrinsic and extrinsic rewards which are very similar to Herzberg's hygiene and motivation categories.

7a. INTRINSIC. These are internal to the individual and derive from feelings of satisfaction and accomplishment. They include the higher levels of Maslow's hierarchy.

7b. EXTRINSIC. These are the physical rewards such as pay and promotion that the organization can give.

The lines linking these two boxes with performance are jagged. This is to indicate that the link is rarely as straightforward, even where it might be thought to be so (e.g. piecework payments). Later we also consider this problem in more detail.

8. PERCEIVED EQUITABLE REWARDS. This is Equity Theory (see p. 29).

9. SATISFACTION. The extent to which the received rewards are felt to be appropriate to the level of performance.

As we stated earlier (p. 105) the theory is very comprehensive; but this means that it is extremely difficult to test. Indeed most studies have concentrated on small parts of the model. The findings from these studies have not always been encouraging and have been better at predicting effort than performance. Once again, there have also been considerable problems in developing adequate measures, but the theory still attracts considerable attention; and, from a manager's point of view, it is extremely useful as a method of highlighting the various factors he needs to consider when assessing his own work force and organization.

Behaviour Modification

There are obviously many different ways of affecting people's behaviour at work, but we deal in this section with techniques which developed from the ideas of Pavlov and Skinner. This technique is known as Behaviour Modification, and it has been successfully used in clinical psychology and in education. Within the last 10-15 years it has become apparent that the technique can usefully be extended to the influencing of behaviour at work and, although you need to understand the basic theory, it is with the practical applications that we are mainly concerned.

The theory underlying behaviour modification can be stated in many different and often long-winded ways but it rests upon three major propositions which can be simply stated as follows:

* behaviour is learnt;

* behaviour that is rewarded will occur more frequently;

* behaviour that is either punished or not rewarded will
  occur less frequently.

When stated like this, behaviour modification appears to
be merely common sense but as Bertrand Russell once
remarked, 'common sense is rarely common'. We all use the
techniques in everyday life, but because we do not have the
theoretical background, we use them inconsistently,
unsystematically and hence ineffectively. A knowledge of the
theory gives us the prescription for analysing and changing
a wide range of behavioural problems, so let us now examine
each of the above propositions in more detail.

Behaviour is learnt. The proposition consists of two major
parts 'behaviour' and 'learnt', each of which is of crucial
importance. By 'behaviour' we mean anything a person does
that can be observed by another, for example, kicking a
football, driving a car, or swearing at the foreman, and so
on. We can also include physiological functions that we can
observe with the help of instruments; for example blood
pressure, sweating, or heart rate. What we cannot include
are purely mental phenomena such as attitudes or
personality. This is not to say that attitudes or
personality are not important, merely that we are only
concerned with the behaviour that results from them. We
cannot observe attitudes or personality until they manifest
themselves as behaviour: voting Conservative, kicking the
cat, telling saucy jokes. The emphasis on observable behaviour is essential if we are to use behaviour modification
effectively, and the more precise the description the
better. Descriptions such as 'lacks motivation' or 'doesn't
have the right attitude' are not specific enough. If we are
to change behaviour we need to know exactly what the
behaviour is, that is what people do and what they say. The
second part of the proposition emphasizes that behaviour is
learnt; and this has important implications. If behaviour is
learnt, it can also be unlearnt and new, and, it is hoped,
more appropriate behaviour learnt in its place.
     The first person to study learning systematically by
association (known as conditioning) was the Russian, Ivan
Pavlov, (1927) and the subjects of his experiments were
dogs. Pavlov knew that any dog, when hungry, will salivate
at the sight of food. This response by the dog, to the
stimulus of a plate of food does not have to be learnt, it
is wired in to the dog's nervous system and hence is termed
'unconditioned'. Thus the unconditioned stimulus (food)
leads to an unconditioned response on the part of the dog
(salivation).
     So far no learning (or conditioning) has been involved
but what happens, for example, if we now start ringing a

bell just before we present the food to the dog? Normally ringing a bell would not produce much of a response from the dog, except maybe a little apprehensive behaviour the first time it happened; it certainly would not cause the dog to salivate. If, however, we continue to ring the bell just before the food is presented, the dog will become conditioned to the fact that the bell 'means' that food is on the way, and will begin to salivate in anticipation. In other words, the conditioned (or learnt) stimulus of the sound of the bell will lead to a conditioned response (salivation) which is almost the same as the salivation that occurs when the food itself is presented (the unconditioned response). We say 'almost the same' because there is usually slightly less salivation to the bell than to the food. This process, by which an initially neutral stimulus comes to have almost the same effect as a stimulus which produces an automatic physiological response, is called classical or Pavlovian conditioning.

Obviously, most of our behaviour is not 'built-in' and automatic but is voluntary. We respond to the environment and operate upon it: hence learning which is concerned with such behaviour is called 'operant conditioning' or 'Skinnerian conditioning' after B .F. Skinner (1976) who is its major advocate.

Skinner maintains that it is the outside environment which influences which behaviours will be repeated and which will not by the way it rewards behaviour. Consider, for example, a hungry man placed in a panelled room. He will most probably explore the room in a random manner until, by accident, he presses a particular panel and some food appears. He may not immediately associate pressing the panel with the arrival of the food but, when he gets hungry again, it is likely that he will repeat what he was doing about the time the food first appeared and, after several attempts, he will most probably 'learn' that pressing a particular panel leads to a reward, in this case food. In technical terms the pressing of the particular panel has been 'reinforced' by the reward, while the pressing of any of the other panels has been ignored - these responses have been 'exting-uished'. This then brings us back to our second and third postulates, namely 'behaviour that is either punished or not rewarded will occur less frequently'.

In our hypothetical experiment it was possible to reinforce the pressing of the panel every time, but 'real life' is rarely so predictable. So what is the effect of reinforcing only occasionally? We could, for example, reinforce the panel pushing every tenth time it occurred. This is called 'fixed ratio reinforcement'. Imagine how you would react to such a reinforcement schedule - in all likelihood you would press away at a fairly constant rate, perhaps speeding up as you neared the tenth. This fixed ratio scale would therefore produce a fairly steady performance rate, but what if the food suddenly failed to appear at the tenth push? You would most probably persist for a while (it could just be a random fault) but you would give up within a relative short time. The pressing would have been 'extinguished' fairly quickly.

Now let us try 'fixed interval' reinforcement; for example, reinforcing the behaviour at intervals of one minute, irrespective of the number of pushes. Probably none of us would bother pressing at all for the first 45 seconds or so but, without the benefit of a clock, we would start pushing quicker and quicker as the expected time approached. This indeed is what we observe in experimental situations. As with the variable ratio schedule, however, the responses are quickly extinguished.

As well as using a 'fixed' schedule of reinforcement we can also try varying the ratio or intervals. For example we may reinforce on average every tenth push. On some occasions this may be immediately after a push that has already been reinforced or it may be 30 or more pushes later. This would be a 'variable ratio' schedule, and similarly if we used the same system but used an average time this would be 'variable interval'. Once again, how do you think you would react? Because of the uncertainty involved you would not be able to predict exactly when the next reinforcement would come, for it could be the next one or quite a few hence. The effect of this uncertainty leads to a relatively high and consistent level of response and this again is what we find. In addition, because it is just as difficult to predict when reinforcement has stopped, responses which have been variably reinforced are very resistant to extinction. These variable reinforcements prove to be the most powerful in influencing behaviour, indeed you only have to look at fruit machines - which use variable ratio reinforcement, to see just how powerful they can be.

Having mentioned gambling as an excellent example of partial reinforcement we might mention here the role of 'modelling' or 'vicarious reinforcement'. In the examples we have used the individual is personally reinforced but we can also learn by copying behaviour for which we have seen others receiving rewards (vicariously). For example, many people who have never won on the football pools continue to invest in them because they know that other people have been rewarded. They learn, therefore, not by being reinforced themselves, but modelling their behaviour on those who have.

So far we have been considering behaviour that was either rewarded (i.e. the person was given something they valued) or ignored. In trying to influence behaviour, however, we also use other techniques such as taking away something that is valued (e.g. stopping overtime) or actually punishing undesirable behaviour. What are the effects and uses of these different methods? We can classify all these techniques as follows. Whether the behaviour results in something being given or taken away, and whether it is liked or disliked. This results in four different categories.

* something that is liked is given: this is like a reward and is known as positive reinforcement;

* something that is disliked is taken away: this is known as negative reinforcement. An example might be that the foreman continues to stare at you (which presumably you do not like) until you start work. In this example you 'escape' by starting work.

The reason that both these conditions are known as re-inforcement is that both lead to an increase in the desired behaviour. In the next two cases the intention is to suppress undesired behaviour.

* something that is liked is taken away: this is a form of punishment known as 'omission training'. The example given about the withdrawal of overtime is one of such training.

* something that is disliked is given: this is what we normally recognize as punishment.

You may remember that we mentioned ignoring behaviour as a method of reducing or 'extinguishing' undesired behaviour, and you may perhaps be wondering whether it is better to extinguish or to punish undesirable behaviour. All the research evidence shows that extinguishing behaviour is far more effective than punishment. Punishment merely suppresses: it does not lead to 'unlearning' and so the behaviour will tend to re-occur. One of the reasons why this is so is that the imposition of punishment often leads to an adverse emotional reaction. However 'mild' punishment can be effective especially when it is done to inform (for example, 'don't do that it's dangerous') and, in addition, where the alternative behaviour is rewarded.

To summarize, therefore, desired behaviour can be increased by reinforcement and undesired behaviour decreased by extinction or mild punishment. But what events or actions act as reinforcers? The answer is that the range of re-inforcers will vary, and that the strength of something as a reinforcer will vary from one person to another. The most obvious reinforcer in the work situation is money, but it is not the only one; for example, recognition, a key to the executive toilet, a numbered parking space and many others may be included. Some are obviously applicable to most people (for example, money) but others may be specific to particular individuals. The crucial thing is to realize that what one person may find rewarding (for example, visiting clients) may not be so for others in the same group. Even for a particular individual there is a hierarchy of rewards, for example designing a new information retrieval system may be more rewarding than dealing with the week's payroll. Once the particular reinforcers have been identified we are in a position to start changing behaviour.

The stages involved can be described as follows:

* identify the undesirable behaviour and state it as precisely as possible. For example 'Fred is lazy' will not be good enough. Why is Fred lazy? Does he arrive late every day, or is it that he starts preparing to go home 10 minutes before everyone else?

* identify the rewards that are keeping the behaviour going - both reinforcers and punishment; remember that even occasional reinforcement is more powerful than frequent punishments;

* specify as precisely as possible the behaviour you want to encourage - the 'target behaviour'; remember, if you do not know where you want to get to, you will not know when you arrive;

* work out a reinforcement schedule and implement it;

* keep checking that it is working and, if it is not, go back to the first stage and repeat the procedure.

At the risk of being repetitious, the question that behaviour modification says we should ask is not 'why is Fred so lazy, aggressive and unco-operative', but 'what are the reinforcers in the environment that are causing Fred to be late for work, or shout at the foreman, or refuse to do overtime?'

When first introduced to behaviour modification many people consider it to be a covert and manipulative way of changing a person's behaviour, but it often works better when it is undertaken with the co-operation of the person or persons involved and to measure their sense of self-control. In addition we can use it on ourselves.

We have mentioned that individuals have a hierarchy of rewards, some more valuable than others. You might therefore try drawing up a hierarchy of rewards for yourself. At the top for example might be 'dealing with new projects' while much lower down might be 'doing the monthly report'. Once you have your hierarchy, use it! Do the monthly report and reward yourself by spending the afternoon on new projects. Make doing something you like a reward for doing those jobs you have been putting off. You will be amazed at how well it works!

So far we have been mainly concerned with the behaviour of individuals but how does it work on groups of people? Although we have constantly been stressing that individuals differ in what they consider rewarding, there are common potential reinforcers, especially within groups of people from similar backgrounds. Also the emphasis has been upon rewarding people as individuals, not as members of groups. In general, personal reinforcement is preferable. Rewarding a group as a whole may work but only where the individuals within the group find its approval rewarding and its disapproval punishing, and this is not always the case.

There are many studies reported and these can be followed up by using the reading list at the end of the chapter, but here we use one example which, we think, highlights a number of important points.

Before describing the techniques used, however, it is useful to state the problem so that you may give some thought as to how you might tackle it. The situation was a noisy weaving shed where, according to health regulations, all employees were required to wear wax earplugs to protect their hearing. Despite a number of safety campaigns and the imposition of various sanctions, including suspension, when spot checks were made only about 30 per cent of workers were wearing earplugs. Your job is to devise a procedure to produce an earplug usage of over 90 per cent at a very small cost. (The final cost for the technique actually used averaged only $15 for each of the 180 employees). The full details of the study can be found in Zohar and Fussfeld (1981). Let us go through the steps we have previously described using their study as an example.

* identify and state the undesirable behaviour: in this case it is fairly easy to do - not wearing earplugs all the time whilst in the weaving shed.

* identify what is keeping the behaviour going: since punishment in the past has not worked, the wearing of earplugs is obviously not being rewarded. Indeed as with many aspects of safety, although they are accepted as desirable in the long run, they are initially un- comfortable. If this initial period of adjustment can be overcome people will tend to continue because the feeling of safety is itself rewarding.

* specify the desired behaviour: once again this is fairly easy - it is the wearing of earplugs by all the employees, all the time they are in the weaving shed. (We can accept that 90 per cent do so at any one moment.)

* work out a reinforcement schedule and implement it: as we have seen reinforcement works best when it is variable ratio or interval and when the rewards are valued. The best way to determine if rewards are valued is to ask those who are the subjects of the experiment, and this was indeed done. The rewards were a range of consumer goods, each of which had a price expressed in 'tokens'. For a period of one month random visits were made to the weaving shop and those employees wearing earplugs received a token. At the end of this period, it was made plain that continued wearing of earplugs was expected and that now not wearing would be punished.

* check that it is working: the system proved very successful, earplug usage rising from the baseline of 30 per cent to well over 90 per cent, even in a follow-up six months later. Indeed, despite an annual labour turnover rate of over 20 per cent, all the newcomers conformed, most probably because their own use of earplugs was 'reinforced' by their new work colleagues whose approval they valued.

If it had not worked, a return to stage one would have been required. On occasions the goal may have been wrongly defined. For example, during the campaign to eradicate smallpox a reward scheme was introduced for health visitors in a remote part of India. The goal was of course 'no more smallpox' and the health visitors were rewarded for the lack of smallpox in their area, but still the disease kept re-occurring. Finally, it was realized that although the final goal was 'no smallpox' the way in which this was achieved was by the intermediate goal of 'identify and treat'. The reward system was then changed so that health visitors were rewarded for each case of the disease they discovered and smallpox was eradicated.

Finally, in a lot of situations where safety is involved, it is only the initial period of adjustment that has to be overcome and hence the reinforcement techniques need only be used for a relatively short time. In situations which are not inherently rewarding - for example, production quantity or quality - the reinforcement may have to continue indefinitely.

Conclusion

What can we conclude from these various theories of motivation?

We can summarize as follows:

* set clear and moderately difficult goals that are accepted by the person concerned;

* make valued rewards upon achievement of goals; and

* make rewards through an explicit and fair system.

All of these terms will depend upon subjective judge-ments and hence the only source of objective information is the people concerned, and perhaps the only way of obtaining the correct information is by asking them. Never assume that people's perceptions of the same thing are the same - just ask a wages clerk and a shop-floor worker how the piecework system works! Participation is perhaps desirable therefore because more than anything else it is a source of information for all parties.

Let us conclude with an example from the authors' own experience. A key group of workers had a high level of

absenteeism compared with their colleagues who worked in the
same small group. The absence of these key workers was
immediately apparent to supervisors as work could not
commence without them. If they arrived late, therefore, this
was immediately noticed and led to disciplinary procedures
(even though the supervisors, when asked said that they
would rather have them arrive later rather than not at all).
It took only a few minutes talk with one or two of these
workers to discover the cause of their absenteeism. If they
were late - discipline; but if they were off for the full
day 'ill' - no discipline. In addition, if they were off one
day - loss of pay; but if for three or more days - sickpay
backdated. The result was that, if you were going to be late
you were better to have three days off!

References

Alderfer, C.P. (1969)
An empirical test of a theory of human needs.
Organizational Behaviour and Human Performance, 4, 142-175.

Drucker, P.F. (1954)
The Practice of Management. New York: Harper.

Hackman, J.R. and Oldham, G.R. (1976)
Motivation through the design of work. Test of a theory.
Organizational Behaviour and Human Performance, 16, 250-279.

Hackman, J.R. and Suttle, J.L. (1977)
Improving Life at Work. Santa Monica, Ca.: Goodyear.

Herzberg, F. (1966)
Work and the Nature of Man. Cleveland, Ohio: World
Publishing.

Howell, W,C, and Dipboye, R.L. (1982)
Essentials of Industrial and Organizational Psychology.
Homewood: Dorsey.

Ivanecevich, J.M. (1977)
Different goal setting treatments and their effects on
performance and job satisfaction. Academy of Management
Journal, 20, 406-419.

Locke, E.A. (1976)
The nature and causes of job satisfaction. In M.D.
Dunnette (ed.) (1976), Handbook of Industrial and
Organizational Psychology. Chicago Ill.: Rand McNally.

Locke, E.A. (1982)
The Ideas of Frederick W. Taylor: An Evaluation. Academy
of Management Review, 7, 14-24.

Makin, P.J. and Robertson, I.T. (1983)
Self assessments, realistic job previews and
occupational decisions. Personnel Review, 12, (3),
21-25.

Mayo, E. (1975)
The Social Problems of an Industrial Civilization.
London: Routledge & Kegan Paul.

Mitchell, T.R. (1979)
Organizational behaviour. Annual Review of Psychology, 30, 243-281.

Paul, W.J. and Robertson K.B. (1970)
Job Enrichment and Employee Motivation. London: Gower.

Pavlov, I.P. (1927)
Conditioned Reflexes. London: Oxford University.

Porter, L.W. and Lawler, E.E. (1968)
Managerial Attitudes and Performance. Homewood: Irwin-Dorsey.

Roethlisberger, F.J. and Dickson, W.J. (1939)
Management and the Worker. Boston, Mass.: Harvard University.

Skinner, B.F. (1976)
About Behaviorism. New York: Vintage Books.

Smith, J.H. (1975)
Foreword in Mayo (1975)

Smith, P.C., Kendall, L.M. and Hulin, C.L. (1969)
The Measurement of Satisfaction in Work and Retirement. Chicago. Ill.: Rand-McNally.

Soutar, G.N. and Weaver, J.R. (1982)
The measurement of shop-floor job satisfaction. The convergent and discriminant validity of the worker opinion survey. Journal of Occupational Psychology, 55, 27-33.

Taylor, F.W. (1911)
Scientific Management. New York: Harper.

Vroom, V.H. (1964)
Work and Motivation. New York: Wiley.

Wahba, M.A. and Bridwell, L.B. (1976)
Maslow reconsidered: a review of research on the need hierarchy theory. Organizational and Human Performance, 15, 212-240.

Wall, T.D. (1978)
Job redesign and employee participation. In P.B. Warr (ed.), Psychology at Work. Harmondsworth: Penguin.

Wall, T.D., Clegg, C.W. and Jackson, P.R. (1978)
An evaluation of the job characteristics model. Journal of Occupational Psychology, 51, 183-196.

Warr, P. (1982)
A national study of non-financial employment commitment. Journal of Occupational Psychology, 55, 297-312.

Zohar, D. and Fussfeld, N. (1981)
A systems approach to organizational behaviour modification: theoretical considerations and empirical evidence. International Review of Applied Psychology, 30, 491-505.

Questions

1. How far do you think motivation at work can be explained in terms of 'universal' needs?
2. What motivates politicians? (Avoid libel if possible).
3. How relevant do you think Taylor's 'Scientific Management' is in the 1980s?

4. 'Man does not live by bread alone'. Discuss, with reference to need hierarchy theories (Maslow and Alderfer).
5. Can money motivate people, or does it merely stop them being dissatisfied?
6. Consider ways in which your own job could be enlarged or enriched. What effect do you think it would have upon your job satisfaction and performance?
7. 'The other man's grass is always greener'. How could Equity Theory suggest we would react to such a state of affairs at work?
8. Discuss the strengths and weaknesses of Management by Objectives.
9. How important are peoples' expectations in influencing their work performance?
10. Behaviour modification is manipulation. How far is this true?
11. Reinforcement theory is too simplistic to be able to explain all human behaviour. Discuss.

Annotated reading

Steers, R.M. and Porter L.W. (1979). Motivation and Work Behavior. New York: McGraw Hill.
> A comprehensive set of readings, presenting the major theories together with associated research and criticism.

Luthans, F. and Kreitner, R. (1975). Organizational behaviour modification. Glenview Ill: Scott, Foresman.
> The best available text for those who wish to take a closer look at behaviour modification.

Cummings, L.L. and Schwab, D.P. (1973). Performance in Organizations. Glenview Ill: Scott, Foresman.
> Takes a broad look at motivation together with appraisal systems.

Warr, P.E. (ed.) (1976). Personal Goals and Work Design. Chichester: Wiley.

Hackman, J.R. and Suttle, J.L. (eds.) (1977). Improving Life at Work. Santa Monica, Ca.: Goodyear.

> Both books with contributions from important authors in the job design/quality of working life field.

Chapter 6
Learning and teaching
David Fontana

Learning can be defined as a relatively persistent change in an individual's possible behaviour due to experience. It is thus clearly distinguished from those changes in behaviour which come about as a consequence of maturation (i.e. as a consequence of the individual's physical growth and development). Learning can take place either as a result of informal circumstances (e.g. parent-child relationships, interaction with friends and with the mass media), or as a result of the formal efforts of society to educate its members through schools and academic institutions. Though both are important our main concern is with the latter: that is, with the ways in which the teacher or the tutor can best monitor and assist learning within the class or lecture room.

Bruner (1973) considers that in dealing with learning activities the teacher must take account of three important variables, namely the nature of the learner, the nature of the knowledge to be learnt and the nature of the learning process. Accordingly we adopt this threefold division as a way of structuring the present chapter, taking each of the variables in turn and examining the major factors associated with them.

The nature of the learner

There are a number of factors within individual learners that influence their ability to learn. Best known of these are cognitive factors such as intelligence and creativity, but there are many others of equal relevance. These include affective factors, motivation, age and sex, study habits and, above all perhaps, memory.

Affective factors
Psychologists take the term 'affective' to cover all aspects of personality. One of these aspects which has particular importance for learning is anxiety. From general experience the teacher soon discovers that a mild degree of anxiety in a pupil can be a useful aid to learning, but that too much anxiety has an inhibiting effect (particularly if the learning task is a complex one). We see this particularly in a student preparing for an important examination, or in a student fearful of the anger or ridicule that failure in a particular task may invite from unsympathetic tutors or

classmates. The anxiety consequent upon these stressful situations interferes with both learning and performance, and results are produced way below the individual's potential. Closely linked to anxiety as an affective factor is the individual's self-esteem. Research studies show that individuals with low self-esteem (i.e. with a low regard for their personal worth and abilities) consistently set themselves artificially depressed learning and attainment goals, and consistently perform less well than individuals of similar intelligence and background who enjoy high levels of self-esteem. It appears that low self-esteem subjects are so fearful of further blows to their self-regard that they set themselves low goals in order to avoid the chances of failure.

High and low self-esteem can be referred to as a dimension of personality. Another such dimension that has implications for learning is that of extraversion-introversion. Typically the extravert is an individual who enjoys change and variety and is orientated towards the external world of people and experiences, while the introvert is more concerned with stability and the inner world of thoughts and feelings. All of us find our place at some point on this dimension, and the evidence suggests that those who incline towards the two extremes learn best in different kinds of learning environments. The extravert tends to favour groups and social activities, with plenty of variety and fresh stimuli, while the introvert generally prefers more ordered individual activity. Thus a particular learning failure may be due less to any lack of ability on the part of the learner than to the fact that the working environment is not really suited to relevant aspects of that learner's personality. On occasions teachers or tutors may also tend to favour pupils whose personalities approximate to their own, with the extravert complaining that an introverted pupil is too quiet, and the introvert complaining that an extraverted pupil is too noisy.

Motivation

Satisfactory learning is unlikely to take place in the absence of sufficient motivation to learn. We have already mentioned one possible source of motivation, namely a degree of anxiety, but there are many others. For convenience we can divide these into intrinsic forms of motivation, which come from within the individual, and extrinsic which are imposed by the environment. Taking intrinsic first, it is axiomatic that people work generally harder at learning tasks that interest them than at those that do not. If we had to say why a particular thing captures a person's interest we would probably argue that it has some direct relevance to the individual's daily life. It either diverts or amuses in some way (and thus makes the person feel better) or it enables him to cope more effectively with the problems and achieve the ambitions in his daily life. No matter what the subject, however, there is often the danger that learners are asked to tackle theoretical issues whose practical application escapes them, or to work towards goals that are too remote or not of their own choosing. Whilst of course students cannot be the arbiters of what they should or should not learn, it is important that tutors who wish to appeal to intrinsic motivation should be fully aware of the concerns and aspirations of their students, and should demonstrate clearly the way in which the proposed learning relates to them.

Nevertheless, however stimulating the teacher, there will always be occasions when intrinsic motivation is insufficient and recourse has to be made to motivation of an extrinsic kind. Such motivation usually consists of marks, grades, examinations, and of course tutor praise and approval. Success in these areas builds up prestige in the student's own eyes and standing is enhanced in the eyes of others. Students find that success is rewarding. It builds up expectations which they have to work harder and more purposefully to fulfil. Thus extrinsic motivation can be highly effective, but it raises a number of important considerations (quite apart from the obvious fear that it may raise anxiety to an inhibiting level).

* Instead of success, some individuals experience only failure. This tends to produce either the low self-esteem to which we have already made reference, or a rejection of everything to do with the formal learning tasks offered through educational institutions. Such rejection is a defensive attempt to protect self-esteem by insisting that it is these tasks that are at fault rather than the individuals themselves (i.e. it is a way of saying 'I could do it if it was worth doing'). To combat the harmful effects of consistent failure the wise tutor provides students with opportunities for success at however low a level. Through such opportunities students gradually build up new self-images and new attitudes to work, and are encouraged progressively to set their sights higher.
* Sometimes motivation suffers because students are not supplied with prompt knowledge of results. The longer the gap between performance and the provision of this knowledge, the greater the chance that students will lose interest in the whole exercise.
* Competition between students is a useful extrinsic motivator provided they are all of a similar level of ability and can all experience a fair degree of success. Co-operation, where students adopt group norms and work together to achieve them, can be of even more benefit.
* Wherever the pressures of extrinsic motivation are too strong students may resort to strategies like feigned illness (or even cheating) to avoid the consequences of failure.

Age and sex
The ability to tackle complex learning tasks increases throughout childhood. Both Piaget (cf. Inhelder and Piaget,

1958) and Bruner (1966) have demonstrated that children appear to go through a number of stages in the development of their powers of thinking, and that unless learning tasks are presented to them in the form appropriate to their particular stage they may be unable to understand what is required of them. For example, before children reach what Piaget calls the stage of formal operations (usually at approximately age 12) they are strictly limited in their ability to engage in abstract thinking, and can only handle concepts when they have experienced them in some practical sense (e.g. they can deal with weight and number, which can be practically experienced, but not with density and volume, which require to be defined more theoretically). On the basis of this kind of evidence it seems that the individual's powers of thinking reach maturity during adolescence, and we know that measured intelligence and memorizing abilities also appear to have reached their peak by the end of this period. Much less is known about the subsequent decline of these powers and therefore of the ability to learn. There certainly appears to be a general slowing of the rate at which the individual can learn many mental and physical skills throughout adult life, and this decline may have reached significant proportions in people not involved in academic work by the mid- and late-twenties. In those constantly using academic skills, however, the decline may be more gradual, and may be amply offset by greater self-discipline, higher motivation, and the increased ability to organize learning that comes through experience.

Just as the ability to learn is influenced by age variables, so is it influenced by sex. Girls are generally more verbal than boys at school age, and have fewer reading, speech, and general behaviour problems (Davie, Butler and Goldsmith, 1972), while boys are more advanced in number skills. These differences tend to disappear by the age of 16, however, and boys between five and ten years of age appear twice as likely to show an increase in measured intelligence as girls (Kagan, Sontag, Baker and Nelson, 1958). Throughout school life, however, girls tend to be better all-rounders, while boys are better at the subjects they enjoy and spurn those they do not. These sex-related differences could be in part genetic and in part related to the home (where girls are generally taught to be more dependent and more concerned for adult approval), but recent research in the USA suggests that they could also be due to the fact that most early school teaching is done by women, and boys therefore come to associate school with feminine values. Where such teaching is done by men, the higher rate of backwardness and school rejection shown by boys tends to disappear. Sadly, at all ages, girls tend to show lower self-esteem than boys, and may artificially depress their level of performance in conformity with an outmoded and unfortunate social conception of the inferiority of the female role.

Memory

Clearly, learning depends intimately on memory. At the
practical level psychologists recognize the existence of two
main kinds of memory, short-term and long-term. All information received by the senses and to which we pay attention
seems to enter short-term memory, but it can be held there
briefly and is either then forgotten (as when we look up a
telephone number and forget it the moment we have dialled
it) or translated to long-term memory where it can be held
more permanently (though it is still, of course, subject to
forgetting). Obviously this transfer is vital for effective
learning. Available evidence suggests it involves some form
of consolidation, typically a short pause during which the
information is held consciously in the mind. Even after an
interesting lesson or lecture students often remember
little, probably because each piece of information is so
quickly followed by the next that there is no time for
consolidation. However, a number of strategies exist for
helping consolidation and for increasing the efficiency of
long-term memory generally.

*   By pausing, repeating and questioning, the lecturer can
    prompt students to dwell sufficiently upon material for
    transfer from short- to long-term to take place.
*   By putting material to immediate practical use consoli-
    dation is also greatly helped. Material that is inter-
    esting, and that is properly understood, is also more
    likely to be remembered than is material which is
    perceived as dull or irrelevant.
*   By practising overlearning, material is made parti-
    cularly resistant to forgetting. Overlearning implies
    the continued revision of a learning task even after it
    appears to have been perfected, and is particularly
    valuable where the material has to be remembered in a
    stressful situation (e.g. in the examination room or on
    the concert platform).
*   By associating new material with something that is
    already familiar, or with something that is particularly
    striking or novel in itself, the chances of its being
    remembered are greatly improved. Through the association
    with something that is already familiar the material is
    placed within context, and can be recalled readily when
    cued in by this material in future; through the associ-
    ation with something striking the material tends to be
    remembered when this striking stimulus is called to
    mind. This is particularly true if the stimulus is a
    visual one: hence the importance of visual aids. Such
    aids need not necessarily be closely linked in terms of
    meaning with the material to be learnt (witness the
    highly successful advertisements on commercial tele-
    vision), but they must be presented concurrently with
    this material so that a strong association is built up.

In discussing memory, it is important to stress that there

appears to be a functional difference between recognition (where we spot as familiar some stimulus physically presented to us) and recall (where we have to retrieve some word or fact from memory itself). Recognition appears to come more readily than recall (e.g. it is easier to recognize a face than to recall a name, to recognize a work in a foreign language than to recall it from memory), and in consequence, unless we are deliberately setting out to test recall, it is of value to provide appropriate cues that bring recognition to the aid of recall.

So much for the factors that aid long-term memory. Now for those that appear to interfere with it. One of these, anxiety, has already been touched upon. Material that can readily be recalled in a relaxed state may prove elusive when one is under stress. Two others of importance are known as retroactive and proactive interference respectively. Retroactive interference occurs when recently learnt material appears to inhibit the recall of that learnt earlier. The phenomenon appears to take place at all levels of learning, and is apparent, for example, in students who cram for an examination and find that the facts they learnt the night before keep coming back when attempts are made to recall those studied earlier in the week. Proactive interference, on the other hand, occurs when earlier learning seems to block the recall of later, as when students start learning a second foreign language and find themselves unable to remember the word they want because the equivalent in the first language keeps coming to mind. We discuss ways of minimizing retroactive inhibition when we deal with study habits below, but proactive inhibition is only likely to be a problem when the two subjects being studied share certain similarities, and it tends to disappear as the new material becomes more familiar and overlearning takes place.

Finally, we come to the subject of memory training. It is often assumed that the memory can be trained, like a muscle, if we exercise it (e.g. by learning large chunks of poetry). There is no evidence, however, that this assumption is correct. The memory is improved by learning how to memorize rather than by the simple act of memorizing itself. We have already listed some of the skills relevant to this task, and reference is made to others in the next section, but we should perhaps mention here the value of mnemonic devices. These are devices created specifically to aid recall, and range from simple tricks like tying a knot in a handkerchief and short jingles like 'thirty days hath September ...' to the elaborate devices used by stage 'memory men'. One such device is the so-called peg-word system, where the digits 1-10 (or more) are each associated with a rhyming word (e.g. 1 is bun, 2 is shoe, 3 is a tree, etc.). These simple associations are learnt, and then the facts to be memorized are associated with them in turn, preferably using visual imagery. Thus, for example, if we wished to learn the agricultural produce exported by New Zealand we could visualize first butter spread on a bun,

second a lamb wearing shoes and so on. Such devices are
remarkably effective in the learning of long lists of facts,
though their use beyond this is limited.

Study habits

Much of the effectiveness of learning depends upon good
study habits, particularly in older students who have to
take more responsiblity for their own work. Some of these
habits, like working in an environment free from distrac-
tion, are obvious while others, like overlearning, have
already been covered. We can summarize the remainder as
outlined below.

* REALISTIC WORK TARGETS. Realistic work targets,
  which the student plans in detail, are far more effective than impossibly ambitious or vague commitments.
  Ideally these targets should be expressed publicly (so
  that prestige is at stake if the student fails to stick
  to them!).
* REWARDS. Small rewards, built into the student's work
  schedule, can be very effective in helping sustain
  effort. These can take the form of a cup of coffee, for
  example, or a five-minute break at the end of each hour
  of solid work, with the purchase perhaps of an inexpensive though coveted treat each time weekly or monthly
  targets are met.
* PUNCTUALITY. Work should be started promptly at the
  appointed hour. This forestalls the elaborate (and
  plausible) strategies we each develop to delay actually
  sitting down at our desks and getting on with it.
* WHOLE AND PART LEARNING. A new learning task
  should be read through first in its entirety to get the
  general drift of it before being broken down into small
  units and learnt methodically.
* ORGANIZING MATERIAL. Often textbooks (and lectures)
  do not present material in a way which accords best with
  the learner's own experience and understanding. Time
  spent reorganizing the material into notes that render
  it generally more comprehensible and assimilable is time
  well spent.
* REVISION. A programme of phased revision throughout
  the duration of a course is of far more value than an
  attempt to cram everything in during the final weeks
  before an exam. Retroactive inhibition (and increased
  anxiety) are the almost inevitable consequences of such
  cramming. Phased revision, however, leads to a growing
  mastery of the whole course as students work their way
  through it, with each new piece of knowledge being
  placed in its proper context. When it comes to final
  examination preparation the student is therefore looking
  back over material that has already been overlearnt.
  Revision is best done before material has actually been
  forgotten. This is known as maintenance revision.

The nature of knowledge to be learnt

Obviously in any learning activity we have to consider not only the abilities of the learner but the nature of the new material. Equally obviously, this material must be organized in such a way that learning is facilitated, and in such a way that we can assess afterwards whether the desired learning has taken place or not. In considering such matters we have first of all to decide the level at which we wish learning to take place. Do we want the learner simply to learn facts, or do we want him to operate at higher levels and understand these facts, and be able to put them to use? Bloom (1956) has presented us with a comprehensive list of the various levels at which learning can take place, and this list is an indispensable aid in all matters relating to the planning and assessment of learning. The list arranges the various levels in hierarchical order, from the simplest to the most complex. Each of the higher levels subsumes those inferior to it (e.g. learning at level 3 involves learning at level 1 and 2 as well), and we can summarize them in ascending order. It will be noted that this taxonomy, as it is called, relates only to thinking skills (or skills in the cognitive domain). Other taxonomies exist which cover aspects of personality (the affective domain: see Krathwohl, 1964) and physical skills (the psychomotor domain: see Simpson, 1972), but these are of less immediate relevance for our purpose.

Levels of learning in the cognitive domain (after Bloom et al, 1956)

* Knowledge (i.e. simple knowledge of facts, of terms, of theories, etc.).
* Comprehension (i.e. an understanding of the meaning of this knowledge).
* Application (i.e. the ability to apply this knowledge and comprehension in new and concrete situations).
* Analysis (i.e. the ability to break material down into its constituent parts and to see the relationship between them).
* Synthesis (i.e. the ability to re-assemble these parts into a new and meaningful relationship, thus forming a new whole).
* Evaluation (i.e. the ability to judge the value of material using explicit and coherent criteria, either of one's own devising or derived from the work of others).

Having decided the level at which we intend to work, the next step (both for the tutor and for the student planning his own study programme) is to define the precise outcomes (or objectives) that our learning is intended to achieve. This is often one of the hardest parts of the exercise. Frequently learning objectives make the mistake of simply outlining what is to be done rather than concentrating upon why it is done. The best way to avoid this error is to remember that a learning objective should state the behaviour expected from a student as the result of a lesson. Thus, for example, we would not write that our objective is 'to demonstrate a particular skill (whatever it may happen to be) to the class', but rather that at the end of the lesson the students should be able to do one or more of the following (depending upon the level at which we intend learning to take place):

* to recognize and identify the elements involved in the skill (these elements would then be specified - this is an objective at the knowledge level);.
* to define these elements and to know the part they play in the skill (an objective at the comprehension level);
* to practise the skill itself (an objective at the application level);
* to describe what is happening - and why - during this practice (an objective at the analysis level);
* to utilize elements of this skill in solving a particular novel problem (an objective at the synthesis level);
* to assess the degree of success achieved in this solution and to propose improvements (an objective at the evaluation level).

It can be readily appreciated that, once a clear objective (or objectives) has (or have) been stated at the beginning of the lesson plan, the tutor is in a much better position to determine the lesson content and to keep it practical and relevant. It is also easier to assess whether learning has taken place or not at the end of the lesson, since it is specified in advance that student behaviour will provide evidence of that learning. An assessment is a major topic in itself, as we now turn to it in more detail.

Assessment

Much assessment takes place simply observing student behaviours, or by directing questions at students, but often the tutor wishes to provide a class with specially devised opportunities to demonstrate whether their behaviour has changed in the desired direction or not. The tutor's choice of which opportunities to offer (i.e. of which assessment techniques to use) will be influenced by the level (in terms of the taxonomy discussed above) at which it is intended learning should take place. All too frequently, particularly in arts and social science subjects, assessment simply takes the form of a written essay, which may be appropriate for gauging progress at the more complex cognitive levels but which samples only a very limited range of knowledge and comprehension. The main alternative to the essay is the so-called objective test, each of whose items carries only a single right answer. Such items are usually of the multiple choice variety, with the student being asked which of a range of possible answers is the correct one: for example, 'The Theory of Association was first advanced by; Herbart/ William James/Francis Galton/none of these'. It will be noted that multiple choice questions test recognition; if it was desired to test recall, the question would be allowed to stand on its own without the addition of the possible answers.

It is often claimed that objective tests take the tutor longer to construct than tests of the essay type. There is no gainsaying this, but on the other hand they are quicker to mark, and teachers are left with the satisfaction of knowing that they have adequately tested the knowledge that they set out to test. Further, students are motivated to acquire this knowledge since they know that it is to be comprehensively tested, rather than fractionally sampled as in an essay. They are also left with the reassurance that good marks really do mean that they know the field and are equipped with the basic grammar of the subject.

The nature of the learning process

Having looked at the learner and at the knowledge to be learnt we now come to the last major variable, namely the process (or methods or techniques) by means of which learning actually takes place. Gagné (1974) suggests that the learning act involves a chain of eight events, some internal to the learner and others external. These events are, in their usual order of occurrence:

* motivation (or expectancy);
* apprehending (the subject perceives the material and distinguishes it from the other stimuli competing for his attention);
* acquisition (the subject codes the knowledge - i.e. makes sense of it, relates it to what is already known);
* retention (the subject stores the knowledge in short- or long-term memory);
* recall (the subject retrieves the material from memory);
* generalization (the material is transferred to new situations, thus allowing the subject to develop strategies for dealing with them);
* performance (these strategies are put into practice);
* feedback (the subject obtains knowledge of results).

Where there is a failure to learn, Gagné argues, it will take place at one of these eight levels, and it is thus the task of tutors to ascertain which. It may be that the learning has failed to capture the pupils' attention, or it makes no sense to them, or they have failed to transfer it to long-term memory, or they are unable to recall it from their memory. Analysing learning failure in this way renders tutors much better able to help the pupil since it enables them to concentrate upon the specific point at which the pupil appears to be going wrong. Frequently, too, they may discover that the fault lies not simply with the pupil but with the way in which the learning task has been presented - and explained - to the pupil.

The manner in which this presentation should be effected depends again upon the level (in terms of Bloom's taxonomy) at which we intend learning to take place. Where we are concerned with levels 1-3 (knowledge, comprehension, and application) then the strategy derived from the experimental findings of Skinner (e.g. Skinner, 1969) is of most help. Skinner's work indicates that factual knowledge and its comprehension and application is normally absorbed most efficiently if it is presented to the learner in small steps, each of them within his competence; if he is then required to demonstrate this learning in some way; and if he is given immediate knowledge of results on whether his demonstration was correct or not. In the event of failure, the whole procedure is repeated. This strategy cannot only be put to efficient use by teachers in their direct dealings with pupils, it also lies at the heart of what has come to be known as programmed learning. Programmed learning uses either specially written textbooks or rolls of paper mounted in simple learning devices to present each unit of learning in turn to individual learners, to question them on it, and to inform them whether or not their answers to questions are correct. An example of an item from a programme on electrical wiring illustrates this clearly.

Stage 1 (information): In wiring a 13 amp plug the brown wire is connected to the live terminal.
Stage 2 (question): Which colour wire is connected to the live terminal of a 13 amp plug?
Stage 3 (answer): A. the blue; B. the brown; C. the green and yellow.
Stage 4 (results): The brown wire is connected to the live terminal of a 13 amp plug.

This example tests recognition in Stage 3 by offering the three possible right answers, but of course these could be omitted if we wished to test recall.

This learning procedure involves what Skinner calls operant conditioning in that at each point it involves, after the presentation of the information to be learnt, a stimulus (the question), an item of behaviour (the student's answer), and a reward or reinforcement (the knowledge of results). This operant conditioning (or S-B-R) model lies behind all learning, claims Skinner, and where there is learning failure this is normally because we have omitted to present the appropriate stimulus or, more frequently, the appropriate reinforcement. For many pupils immediate and accurate knowledge of successful results (remember that Skinner advocates presenting material to pupils in small steps, each one within their competence) is sufficient reinforcement, but for others teacher approval, good marks and grades, and even small physical rewards (e.g. where the child is retarded or handicapped and cannot understand the significance of marks and grades) may have to be used. Similarly, where incorrect learning has taken place, Skinner claims this can also be due to misapplied reinforcement. The parents or teachers, for example, fail to realize that the very fact of their attention (whether angry or not) is a powerful reinforcement for some children. Thus the more scolding the adult directs at the child's misbehaviour the more persistent it may tend to become. The correct procedure would be to ignore children when they produce this behaviour and reward them with attention when they show behaviour of the opposite, desirable kind. This approach is part of a range of strategies based upon conditioning theories (and known collectively as behaviour modification techniques) which are attracting increasing attention in educational and clinical circles.

Many psychologists, however, though granting the effectiveness of Skinner's approach at the first three levels in Bloom's taxonomy, consider it an inadequate basis for prompting learning at the higher levels. Learning at these levels involves more than a mere knowledge of the facts and formulae produced by other people (the so-called middle language of the subject); it involves the ability to discover the fundamental logic underlying the subject. Bruner (1966) argues that to help students achieve such discovery we must present them with problems and challenges, with questions that contain an element of controversy and contradiction. Such questions, known as springboard questions, introduce material which does not quite fit in with the student's accepted knowledge and beliefs. A 'level 1' question, such as 'What is the population of Britain?' or 'What is the formula for water?' demands nothing from the student beyond a single answer delivered in the form in which it was first heard. A springboard question, on the other hand, such as 'The poles are equidistant from the equator, yet the south is colder than the north; why?' or 'Christianity teaches you that you should love your enemies, yet men have committed terrible massacres in its name; why?' prompts students to reflect on the subtle ways in which their subject works, on the relationship between cause and effect, on methods of procedure and enquiry. The same is true of simulation exercises, which present learners with imaginary problems designed to mimic those faced in real life by social workers, nurses and economists, for example, and ask them to produce solutions. These solutions are then compared with genuine case histories, and comparisons and contrasts are drawn which promote debate, understanding, and the efficient workings of memory.

References

Bloom, B.S. (1956)
Taxonomy of Educational Objectives. Handbook 1: The cognitive domain. London: Longmans Green.

Bruner, J.S. (1966)
Towards a Theory of Instruction. Cambridge, Mass.: Harvard University Press.

Bruner, J.S. (1973)
The Relevance of Education. New York: Norton.

Davie, R., Butler, N. and Goldsmith, H. (1972)
From Birth to Seven. London: Longmans.

Gagné, R.M. (1974)
Essentials of Learning for Instruction. Hinsdale, Ill.:
Dryden Press.

Inhelder, B. and Piaget, J. (1958)
The Growth of Logical Thinking from Childhood to
Adolescence. London: Routledge & Kegan Paul.

Kagan, J., Sontag, L., Baker, C. and Nelson, V. (1958)
Personality and IQ change. Journal of Abnormal and
Social Psychology, 56, 261-266.

Krathwohl, D.R. (1964)
Taxonomy of Educational Objectives. Handbook II: The
affective domain. New York: David McKay.

Simpson, E.J. (1972)
The classification of educational objectives in the
psychomotor domain. The Psychomotor Domain, Volume III.
Washington: Gryphon House.

Skinner, B.F. (1969)
Contingencies of Reinforcement: A theoretical analysis.
New York: Appleton-Century-Crofts.

Questions

1. Sometimes anxiety is an aid to learning and sometimes
   the reverse. Why is this? Do we think we are ever right
   to encourage even mild anxiety?
2. Outline the kinds of learning environment likely to
   appeal to the marked extravert. How does this
   environment differ from that suitable for the marked
   introvert?
3. Make lists of the intrinsic and extrinsic motivators
   which have respectively been of most importance to you
   in your own learning experiences.
4. Why is it that the experience of consistent failure is
   so damaging to a person's readiness to learn?
5. List some of the factors both in the home and in the
   school which you feel may influence the respective rates
   at which boys and girls learn.
6. Define short- and long-term memory respectively. What
   are some of the strategies that aid transfer from one to
   the other?
7. Write down as many examples as you can of well-known
   mnemonics. Construct a mnemonic for aiding memory in an
   important area of your own subject.
8. Construct a simple multiple-choice test designed to
   establish whether a student has correctly learnt the
   principles and/or the facts behind one or more of the
   following: (i) propagating plants by means of softwood
   cuttings; (ii) starting a motor car and drawing safely
   away from the kerb; (iii) swimming the crawl; (iv) the
   symbols on a map (or on a weather map).
9. What are the eight events in a learning chain according
   to Gagne?
10. Construct a simulation designed to help students face
    common problems in their practical work. Suggest ways of
    evaluating their responses.

Annotated reading

Bigge, L. (1976) Learning Theories for Teachers (3rd edn). New York: Harper & Row.
> One of the best and most comprehensive surveys of learning theories and their application to teaching.

Fontana, D. (1977) Personality and Education. London: Open Books.
> A more general discussion, with an examination of the implications for the teacher.

Gagné, R.M. (1975) Essentials of Learning for Instruction. Hinsdale, Illinois: Dryden Press.

Gagné, R. M. (1977) The Conditions of Learning (3rd edn). London: Holt, Rinehart & Winston.
> Good introductions to Gagne's work.

Gronlund, N.E. (1978). Stating Objectives of Classroom Instruction (2nd edn). London: Collier Macmillan.
> One of the best short books on the writing of educational objectives. It also has something useful to say on the construction of objective tests.

Hintzman, L. (1978) The Psychology of Learning and Memory. San Francisco: Freeman.
> A good choice for those who want to take their study of learning theories rather further, and examine their relationship to memory.

Hunter, I.M.L. (1964) Memory (rev. edn). Harmondsworth: Pelican.
> Difficult to beat as an examination of all aspects of memory.

Jones, R.M. (1972) Fantasy and Feeling in Education. Harmondsworth: Penguin.
> A good discussion of Bruner's ideas within the practical classroom context.

Klatsky, R.L. (1975) Human Memory. San Francisco: Freeman.
> Gives a more up-to-date picture than Hunter's book.

Marjoribanks, K. (1979) Families and Their Learning Environments. London: Routledge & Kegan Paul.
> A thorough and scholarly survey of the research into the relationship between intelligence, personality, family variables and learning.

Rowntree, D. (1974) Educational Technology in Curriculum Development. London: Harper & Row.
> The best approach to programmed learning and the whole field of educational technology.

Rowntree, D. (1976) Learn How to Study. Harmondsworth: Pelican.

Mace, C.A. (1968) The Psychology of Study (rev. edn).
London: MacDonald.
> Both of these are among the good books currently
> available on study habits, and are highly recommended.

Taylor, J.L. and Walford, R. (1972) Simulation in the
Classroom. Harmondsworth: Penguin.
> Simulation exercises are comprehensively explained, with
> examples.

Vernon, P.E. (1964) An Introduction to Objective-type
Examinations. London: Schools Council Examinations Bulletin
No. 4.
> One of the most valuable short introductions to the
> subject.

Chapter 7

Transition: understanding and managing personal change

Barrie Hopson

In the ongoing flux of life, (the person) undergoes many changes. Arriving, departing, growing, declining, achieving, failing - every change involves a loss and a gain. The old environment must be given up, the new accepted. People come and go; one job is lost, another begun; territory and possessions are acquired or sold; new skills are learnt, old abandoned; expectations are fulfilled or hopes dashed - in all these situations the individual is faced with the need to give up one mode of life and accept another (Parkes, 1972).

Today, more than at any other time in our history, people have to cope with an often bewildering variety of transitions: from home to school; from school to work; from being single to being married and - increasingly - divorced; from job to job; from job to loss of employment; retraining and re-education; from place to place and friend to friend; to parenthood and then to children leaving home; and finally to bereavements and death. Alongside these and other major life events people are having to learn to cope with the passage from one stage of personal development to another: adolescence, early adulthood, stabilization, mid-life transition and restabilization.

What is a transition?

We define a transition as a discontinuity in a person's life space (Adams, Hayes and Hopson, 1976). Sometimes the discontinuity is defined by social consensus as to what constitutes a discontinuity within the culture. Holmes and Rahe (1967) provide evidence to show the extent of cultural similarity in perceptions of what are important discontinuities, in the research they conducted to produce their social readjustment rating scale. The life changes represented here (see table 1), along with their weighted scores, were found to be remarkably consistent from culture to culture: Japan, Hawaii, Central America, Peru, Spain, France, Belgium, Switzerland and Scandinavia. For example, death of a spouse requires about twice as much change in adjustment worldwide as marriage, and ten times as much as a traffic violation. The correlation between the items ranged from 0.65 to 0.98 across all the cultures.

Another way of defining a discontinuity is not by general consensus but by the person's own perception. These two may not always coincide: for example, adolescence is considered to be an important time of transition in most western cultures, whereas in other cultures like Sàmoa it is not considered to be a time of stressful identity crisis. Also, in a common culture some children experience adolescence as a transition while others do not. Consequently it cannot be assumed that everyone experiences a transitional event (e.g. a change of job) in the same way.

Table 1

The Holmes and Rahe social readjustment rating scale

LIFE EVENT	Mean value
1. Death of a spouse	100
2. Divorce	73
3. Marital separation from mate	65
4. Detention in jail or other institution	63
5. Death of a close family member	63
6. Major personal injury or illness	53
7. Marriage	50
8. Being fired at work	47
9. Marital reconciliation with mate	45
10. Retirement from work	45
11. Major change in the health or behaviour of a family member	44
12. Pregnancy	40
13. Sexual difficulties	39
14. Gaining a new family member (e.g. through birth, adoption, oldster moving in, etc.)	39
15. Major business readjustment (e.g. merger, reorganization, bankruptcy, etc.)	39
16. Major change in financial state (e.g. a lot worse off or a lot better off than usual)	38
17. Death of a close friend	37
18. Changing to a different line of work	36
19. Major changes in the number of arguments with spouse (e.g. either a lot more or a lot less than usual regarding childbearing, personal habits, etc.)	35
20. Taking on a mortgage greater than $10,000 (e.g. purchasing a home, business, etc.)	31
21. Foreclosure on a mortgage or loan	30
22. Major change in responsibilities at work (e.g. promotion, demotion, lateral transfer)	29

23.	Son or daughter leaving home (e.g. marriage, attending college, etc.)	29
24.	In-law troubles	29
25.	Outstanding personal achievement	28
26.	Wife beginning or ceasing work outside the home	26
27.	Beginning or ceasing formal schooling	26
28.	Major change in living conditions (e.g. building a new home, remodelling, deterioration of home or neighborhood)	25
29.	Revision of personal habits (dress, manners, associations, etc.)	24
30.	Trouble with the boss	23
31.	Major change in working hours or conditions	20
32.	Change in residence	20
33.	Changing to a new school	20
34.	Major change in usual type and/or amount of recreation	19
35.	Major change in church activities (e.g. a lot more or a lot less than usual)	19
36.	Major change in social activities (e.g. clubs, dancing, movies, visiting, etc.)	18
37.	Taking on a mortgage or loan less than $10,000 (e.g. purchasing a car, TV, freezer, etc.)	17
38.	Major change in sleeping habits (a lot more or a lot less sleep, or change in part of day when asleep)	16
39.	Major change in number of family get-togethers (e.g. a lot more or a lot less than usual)	15
40.	Major change in eating habits (a lot more or a lot less food intake, or very different meal hours or surroundings)	15
41.	Vacation	13
42.	Christmas	12
43.	Minor violations of the law (e.g. traffic tickets, jaywalking, disturbing the peace, etc.)	11

For an experience to be classed as transitional there should be:

* personal awareness of a discontinuity in one's life space;
* new behavioural responses required because the situation is new, or the required behaviours are novel, or both.

A person can sometimes undergo a transitional experience without being aware of the extent of the discontinuity or

PFM-J

that new behavioural responses are required. This at some point will probably cause the person or others adaptation problems. For example, following the death of her husband, the widow may not be experiencing strain - she might even be pleased that he is dead - but suddenly she becomes aware that no house repairs have been done, and a new dimension or loss becomes evident along with the awareness of new behavioural responses required.

Why is an understanding of transitional experience important?

Life in post-industrial society is likely to bring more and more transitions for people in all arenas of living. Any transition will result in people being subjected to some degree of stress and strain. They will be more or less aware of this depending upon the novelty of the event and the demands it makes upon their behavioural repertoires. Thus, there is likely to be a rise in the number of people experiencing an increased amount of stress and strain in the course of their daily lives.

Many practitioners in the helping professions are dealing directly with clients who are in transition. It is vital for them to understand how people are likely to react during transition, and to recognize the symptoms of transitional stress. Professionals also need helping techniques to ensure that individuals cope more effectively with their transitions, and to make organizations and social groups more aware of what they can do to help people in transition.

Is there a general model of transitions?

As we began to discover other work on different transitions, a general picture increasingly began to emerge. It appeared that irrespective of the nature of the transition, an overall pattern seemed to exist. There were differences, of course, especially between those transitions that were usually experienced as being positive (e.g. marriage and desired promotion) and those usually experienced negatively (e.g. bereavement and divorce). But these differences appeared to reflect differences of emphasis rather than require a totally different model.

The major point to be made in understanding transitions is that whether a change in one's daily routine is an intentional change, a sudden surprise that gets thrust upon one, or a growing awareness that one is moving into a life stage characterized by increasing or decreasing stability, it will trigger a cycle of reactions and feelings that is predictable. The cycle has seven phases, and the identification of these seven phases has come about through content analysis of reports from over 100 people who have attended transition workshops for the purpose of understanding and learning to cope more effectively with transitions they were experiencing and through extending the findings reported above.

Immobilization

The first phase is a kind of immobilization or a sense of being overwhelmed; of being unable to make plans, unable to reason, and unable to understand. In other words, the initial phase of a transition is experienced by many people as a feeling of being frozen up. It appears that the intensity with which people experience this first phase is a function of the unfamiliarity of the transition state and of the negative expectations one holds. If the transition is not high in novelty and if the person holds positive expectations, the immobilization is felt less intensely or perhaps not at all. Marriage can be a good example of the latter.

Minimization

The way of getting out of this immobilization, essentially, is by movement to the second phase of the cycle, which is characterized by minimization of the change or disruption, even to trivialize it. Very often, the person will deny that the change even exists. Sometimes, too, the person projects a euphoric feeling. Those readers who recall seeing Alfred Hitchcock's film 'Psycho' will remember that Tony Perkins spent considerable time shrieking at his mother in the house on the hill. It is not until the end of the film that one learns the mother has been dead for some time, and it is her semi-mummified body with which he has been carrying on his 'dialogue'. That is an extreme example of denying or minimizing the reality of a major change in one's life. Denial can have a positive function. It is more often a necessary phase in the process of adjustment. 'Denial is a normal and necessary human reaction to a crisis which is too immediately overwhelming to face head-on. Denial provides time for a temporary retreat from reality while our internal forces regroup and regain the strength to comprehend the new life our loss has forced upon us' (Krantzler, 1973).

Depression

Eventually, for most people - though not for Tony Perkins in 'Psycho' - the realities of the change and of the resulting stresses begin to become apparent. As people become aware that they must make some changes in the way they are living, as they become aware of the realities involved, they sometimes begin to get depressed: the third phase of the transition cycle. Depression is usually the consequence of feelings of powerlessness, of aspects of life out of one's control. This is often made worse by the fear of loss of control over one's own emotions. The depression stage has occasional high energy periods often characterized by anger, before sliding back into a feeling of hopelessness. They become depressed because they are just beginning to face up to the fact that there has been a change. Even if they have voluntarily created this change themselves, there is likely to be this dip in feelings. They become frustrated because it becomes difficult to know how best to cope with the new life requirements, the ways of being, the new relationships that have been established or whatever other changes may be necessary.

Letting go

As people move further into becoming aware of reality, they can move into the fourth phase, which is accepting reality for what it is. Through the first three phases, there has been a kind of attachment, whether it has been conscious or not, to the past (pre-transition) situation. To move from phase three to phase four involves a process of unhooking from the past and of saying 'Well, here I am now; here is what I have; I know I can survive; I may not be sure of what I want yet but I will be OK; there is life out there waiting for me.' As this is accepted as the new reality, the person's feelings begin to rise once more, and optimism becomes possible. A clear 'letting go' is necessary.

Testing

This provides a bridge to phase five, where people become much more active and start testing themselves vis-a-vis the new situation, trying out new behaviours, new life styles, and new ways of coping with the transition. There is a tendency also at this point for people to stereotype, to have categories and classifications of the ways things and people should or should not be relative to the new situation. There is much personal energy available during this phase and, as they begin to deal with the new reality, it is not unlikely that those in transition will easily become angry and irritable.

Search for meaning

Following this burst of activity and self-testing, there is a more gradual shifting towards becoming concerned with understanding and for seeking meanings for how things are different and why they are different. This sixth phase is a cognitive process in which people try to understand what all of the activity, anger, stereotyping and so on have meant. It is not until people can get out of the activity and withdraw somewhat from it that they can begin to understand deeply the meaning of the change in their lives.

Internalization

This conceptualizing, in turn, allows people to move into the final phase of internalizing these meanings and incorporating them into their behaviour. Overall, the seven transition phases represent a cycle of experiencing a disruption, gradually acknowledging its reality, testing oneself, understanding oneself, and incorporating changes in one's behaviour. The level of one's morale varies across these phases and appears to follow a predictable path. Identifying the seven phases along such a morale curve often gives one a better understanding of the nature of the transition cycle. This is shown in figure 1.

Figure 1

Self-esteem changes during transitions

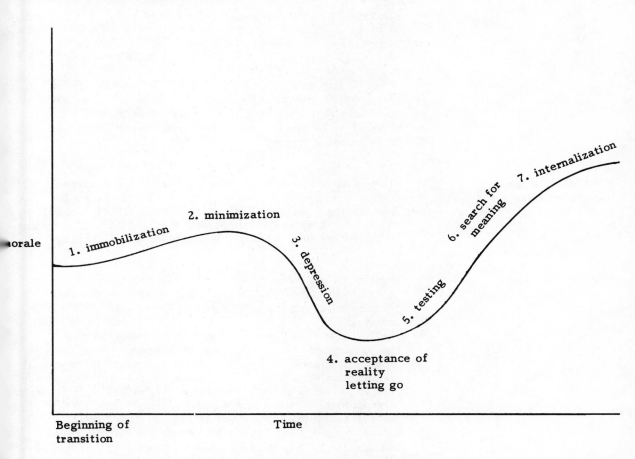

Interestingly, the Menninger Foundation's research on Peace Corps volunteers' reactions to entering and experiencing training (a transition for each person) produced a very similar curve. More recently, Kubler-Ross and those who joined her death and dying seminars have also charted a very similar curve of the reaction cycle people go through upon learning they are terminally ill, which is the ultimate transition.

Before proceeding, it is necessary to make it clear that seldom, if ever, does a person move neatly from one phase to another as has been described above. It can help someone in distress, however, to be made aware that what they are experiencing is not uncommon, that it will pass, and that they have a great deal they can do in determining how quickly it will pass.

It is also important to point out that each person's experience is unique and that any given individual's progressions and regressions are unique to their unique circumstances. For example, one person may never get beyond denial or minimization. Another may end it all during depression. Yet another might experience a major failure just as things begin to look up, and slip back to a less active, more withdrawn posture.

What is important is the potential for growth arising from any major disruption or calamity. One realizes this potential and moves toward it when one lets go and fully accepts the situation for what it is; one dies a 'little death' to become larger.

What effects do transitions have on people?

It is important to note here that all transitions involve some stress, including those considered by society to be positive changes, such as being left large sums of money, parenthood or marriage (Holmes and Rahe, 1967). Our own studies investigating this relationship show the following results:

* transitions are most stressful if they are unpredictable, involuntary, unfamiliar, of high magnitude (degree of change), and high intensity (rate of change);
* the incidence of illness is positively correlated with the amount of life change one undergoes;
* lack of feedback on the success of attempts to cope with strain-inducing events causes more severe stress-related diseases than when relevant feedback is present;
* interpersonal warmth and support during stressful periods seems to reduce the impact of the stress;
* viruses alone do not cause illnesses. The incidence of bad emotional experiences seems to upset the body and allow the viruses to take over;
* hypertension occurs more often in environments characterized by high stressors and few ways of responding to those stressors;
* the more major the life changes the higher the risk of coronary heart disease.

Every transition contains 'opportunity value' for the mover

However undesirable a particular transition may be for the mover, there is always opportunity for personal growth and development contained within it. If one takes a severe example such as death of a spouse, for the majority of those bereaved nothing will compensate for that loss. On the other hand, given that the loss is out of their control, what is under their control is what they decide to do with their lives from there on. There are opportunities for new relationships, travel, career change, new interests, etc. Obviously, during the grief process - which is essential -

the opportunities are difficult and often obnoxious to contemplate but part of the 'letting go' stage involves doing exactly that. The Chinese have two symbols for the concept of 'crisis': one means 'danger' while the other signifies 'opportunity'.

What are the coping tasks relevant to all transitional events?

We believe that there are common elements in any transition, which enable us to talk generally about transitional behaviour. We also assert that in dealing with any transitional event a person has two tasks to perform as he moves through the phases of the model:

* MANAGEMENT OF STRAIN: to manage the degree of strain generated by the stress in such a way that the individual can engage with the external problems caused by the transition.
* COGNITIVE COPING TASKS: a transition will always necessitate adjustment. Any adjustment requires decisions to be made about the appropriateness of new and old behaviour patterns. The individual will be asking questions such as: (i) how can I accept this situation?; (ii) what behaviour is expected of me?; and (iii) what do I want from this situation?

How successfully these two tasks are managed determines the speed with which the transition is completed.

What are the coping skills relevant to transitions?

At the Counselling and Career Development Unit at Leeds University we have been working for a number of years on developing training programmes to help adults in transition and to teach transition coping skills to young people in schools and colleges.

We have developed a questionnaire to be used to help people identify the transition coping skills they already possess and which simultaneously highlights the deficits in their coping repertory. Table 2 reproduces the questionnaire designed for use with adults. People are asked to answer 'yes' or 'no' to all the questions. Each time they reply 'no', it suggests an area where they are lacking in some theoretical understanding of the nature of transitions, or deficient in cognitive or behavioural skills. Each of the items is dealt with briefly below, along with some teaching points we make to participants. In a workshop, this learning would take place experientially and participants would have an opportunity to develop and practise their skills. The language used is written to convey the flavour of the work-shop approach. The text which follows should be read in conjunction with the questionnaire below.

Table 2
_____

Coping skills questionnaire

1. KNOW YOURSELF
a. Would I have chosen for this to have happened?
b. Am I proactive in new situations: do I take initiatives, have a purpose as opposed to sitting back and waiting on events?
c. Do I know what I want from this new situation?
d. Do I know what I don't want from this new situation?
e. If I feel under stress do I know what I can do to help myself?
f. Do I know how to use my feelings as indicators of where I am?

2. KNOW YOUR NEW SITUATION
a. Can I describe the transition?
b. Do I know how I'm expected to behave?
c. Can I try out the new situation in advance?

3. KNOW OTHER PEOPLE WHO CAN HELP: do I have other people:
a. To depend on in a crisis?
b. To discuss concerns?
c. To feel close to - a friend?
d. Who can make me feel competent and valued?
e. Who can give me important information?
f. Who will challenge me to sit up and take a good look at myself?
g. With whom I can share good news and good feelings?
h. Who will give me constructive feedback?

4. LEARN FROM THE PAST
a. Is there anything similar that has happened to me?
b. Can I identify what I did which helped me get through that experience?
c. Can I identify what I would have done differently?

5. LOOK AFTER YOURSELF
a. Do I know how to use supportive self-talk?
b. Do I get regular exercise or have a personal fitness programme?
c. Am I eating regularly and wisely?
d. Do I know how to relax?
e. Am I keeping to a regular schedule?
f. Do I know my 'personal anchor points'?
g. Do I give myself 'treats' when under stress?
h. Do I have other people who will take care of me?
i. Can I survive?
j. Do I know when my low points are likely to be?

6. LET GO OF THE PAST
a. Do I easily let go of old situations?

b. Do I continually feel that this should not happen to me?

c. Do I know how to vent my anger constructively?

7. SET GOALS AND MAKE ACTION PLANS

a. Do I know how to set goals?

b. Do I know what my goals are for this transition and for my life generally?

c. Do I know how to make and implement action plans?

d. Do I know how to set priorities?

e. Do I know how to make effective decisions?

f. Do I know how to generate alternatives, because there is always an alternative?

8. LOOK FOR THE GAINS YOU HAVE MADE

a. Can I find one thing which is positive about this experience?

b. Can I list a variety of new opportunities that did not exist before or that I would not have thought of previously?

c. Have I learnt something new about myself?

Know yourself

1. WOULD I HAVE CHOSEN FOR THIS TO HAVE HAPPENED? You may not have chosen this situation. This could make it more difficult for you to accept the transition. But it has happened. You now have three options:

(A) accept it and put up with it

(B) refuse to accept

(C) accept it and try to benefit from it

(A) will help you to survive. (B) will bring you nothing but bad feelings and worse; you will be less able to cope with the tasks facing you in the new situation. (C) will help you to grow in addition to merely surviving.

Given the inevitable, ask yourself the key question: 'What is the worst thing that could happen?' Having identified it, ask yourself if you can cope. Is it really so terrible?

It is essential to remember that problematic situations constitute a normal aspect of living. It is also useful to recall the variety of transitions that you have encountered and survived up until now. Through having survived you will probably have developed some skills. If, on looking back, you feel dissatisfied with how you managed a transition, it is important to ask yourself whether you had all the skills needed to deal effectively with that situation. More than likely you did not. Do not berate yourself for not having these skills. Instead be glad that you have identified the need for additional skills, for that in itself is the first stage of skill development.

2. AM I PROACTIVE IN NEW SITUATIONS: DO I TAKE INITIATIVES, HAVE A PURPOSE, AS OPPOSED TO SITTING BACK AND WAITING ON EVENTS? To be proactive involves a certain sequence of behaviour:

* knowing what you want;
* knowing alternative ways of achieving this;
* choosing one alternative;
* evaluating the results against your original objective.

The essence of proactive behaviour is that there is a reason for it, even if the end result involves no action. The reason, however, must stem from what Maslow (1968) calls a 'growth' need as opposed to a 'deficiency' need. Deciding not to give a public talk (objective), and knowing various ways of avoiding this (knowing alternatives), choosing one, and thereby achieving the objective at first glance seems to fit the description of 'proactive behaviour'. However, if the reason is based on fear of making a fool of oneself, this would not be classed as proactive. If it were due to over-commitment, or the feeling that you are not the best equipped person to do it, that would be proactive.

3. DO I KNOW WHAT I WANT FROM THIS NEW SITUATION?

4. DO I KNOW WHAT I DO NOT WANT FROM THIS NEW SITUATION? If you are unclear as to what you want or do not want from a new situation this usually signifies a lack of knowledge about your own values or about what the new situation has to offer. There is an entire educational technology designed to help young people and adults to crystallize their needs and values. It has been developed in the USA and is known generically as 'values clarification' (Simon, Howe and Kirschenbaum, 1972; Simon, 1974; Howe and Howe, 1975; Kirschenbaum, 1977). Obtaining more information about the new situation is dealt with in the next section.

5. IF I FEEL UNDER STRESS DO I KNOW WHAT I CAN DO TO HELP MYSELF? Avoid situations where you might over-react. If you have recently separated from your spouse and it is still painful, do not accept an invitation to an event where you know you will encounter your spouse again. Make as few decisions as possible as you will not be thinking clearly enough. Do not make more than one transition at a time. It is amazing how often people choose one transition to be the stimulus for a host of others. If you have changed your job, do not change your spouse, residence and/or life style all at the same time. A new broom can sometimes sweep you over!

    Look after yourself (see below).

    Do not waste time blaming yourself (see below).

    Remember that time itself will not eliminate the stress or heal you, it is what you do with that time. There are a variety of cognitive shielding techniques that you can use to minimize the strain. These all involve controlling the amount of stimulation in the environment. Some examples are:

* time management: making priorities;
* making lists;
* queuing: delaying decisions during a difficult period by queuing them up, dealing with them one at a time, and not thinking about future decisions until the time to make them arrives. Writing down a decision in a diary to be made at a future date is a good way of queuing.
* temporary drop-out: refusing to resolve decisions until after a recuperation period. This can appear initially as reactive; however, it is correctly termed proactive as the mover is deliberately opting out of the situation temporarily as part of a strategy to move in later and thereby more effectively.

There are now some excellent resources available for techniques of preventing and managing stress (e.g. Lamott, 1975; Sharpe and Lewis, 1977; Forbes, 1979).

6. DO I KNOW HOW TO USE MY FEELINGS AS INDICATORS OF WHERE I AM? Many people, especially men, as a result of their upbringing are emotionally illiterate: that is, they have not developed the skills of 'reading' their own emotions. One's 'gut' feelings are the surest indicator of how one is coping at any particular time. The skill is in learning to recognize the changes in feelings when they occur and then having an emotional vocabulary to be able to label them correctly. Often when people are asked what they are feeling they will answer you in terms of only what they are thinking (see Johnson, 1972; Hopson and Scally, 1980a).

Know your new situation
1. CAN I DESCRIBE THE TRANSITION? An essential prerequisite to successful transition coping is to know that you are in one. It is essential to be aware of when the transition began, where you are in relation to it and what are all the variables involved. For example, considering changing your job might involve geographical change, relationship changes, financial implications, holiday plans for this year, and so on.

2. DO I KNOW HOW I AM EXPECTED TO BEHAVE? Transitions are naturally accompanied by stress even if they are desired. Anxiety certainly increases the less information you have about your new situation. Collect as much data as you can about what others expect of you, what society expects and how you are to behave. You may decide not to live up to or down to those expectations, but again you need the initial data before you can make that decision. You also need to know the consequences of any decision before you make it.

You can ask people who have made a similar transition or indeed are presently going through the same transition. A variety of self-help and special interest groups have developed in recent years to provide mutual support and information to people undergoing similar transitions: ante-natal classes, induction courses, orientation programmes, women's and men's 'rap' groups for people redefining their sex roles, widows' clubs, singles' clubs, one-parent family groups, and so on.

It is important to remember that other people often forget, or in some cases are not even aware, that this is a new situation for you. They may need reminding. For example, one new day at the end of your first week at a new job con-stitutes 20 per cent of the time you have worked there. For people who have been here for five years, one new day rep-resents less than 0.4 per cent of the time they have been there. Consequently, their feelings about that day are like-ly to be quite different from your feelings about the same day.

3.   CAN I TRY OUT THE NEW SITUATION IN ADVANCE?
Some transitions can be 'sampled' in advance, for example, starting a new job, moving to another country; even a divorce or death can sometimes be anticipated. Reading books about anticipated transitions can be valuable, as can talk-ing to others who have experienced it, while remembering that no one will experience it just like you. Where appro-priate you can visit places, meet people, watch films, etc., prior to your transition.

Knowing other people who can help
There is now considerable evidence to show the beneficial effects on stress reduction of talking problems through with people: friends, colleagues, even strangers.

We often make the mistake of expecting too few people, typically a spouse and children, to satisfy too great a proportion of our needs. Check the list in the question-naire. How many categories of person do you have available to you in your life? Are there any gaps? How many different people make up your 'support' group? How dependent are you on one or two?

We are also better at developing some forms of support at the expense of others. For example, people are often better at developing friendships than relationships with people who challenge us. The challengers in most people's support systems are about as abrasive as a marshmallow. Yet sometimes challengers are exactly what we require to shift us out of stereotyped thinking. Who are the challengers in your support systems? Remember, you may not even like them

Learn from the past
Our past is an important part of our present. Our past is the history of our successes and our failures and is thereby a record of our learning. As such, we can continue to learn

from our past experiences. 'Mistakes' are another way of labelling 'opportunities for learning'. If we can identify times in the past when we have had similar feelings or experienced similar transitions, we have an opportunity to monitor those chapters of our history and evaluate our performances against the criteria of our own choosing. What did we do that really did not help the situation? What would we avoid if we were to have that experience again? Can we learn from that experience and generalize it to the new transition? A sense of one's own history is a prerequisite to a fully functioning present and a portent for one's range of possible futures.

Look after yourself

1. DO I KNOW HOW TO USE SUPPORTIVE SELF-TALK? Many of the problems we create for ourselves and much of the support that we give ourselves derives from the same source: our internal dialogue with ourselves. This dialogue continues throughout most of our waking hours. These 'cognitions' are vital to our survival and growth. They enable us to adapt to new situations, to learn, to feel and to enact cognitively a variety of scenarios without having to perform any of them. Ellis, with his Rational-Emotive Therapy, for years has claimed that the way we think determines what we feel, with the corollary that if we can change how we think we can also change how we feel (Ellis and Harper, 1975). His therapeutic method involves retraining people to talk internally to themselves to minimize the negative emotions which they otherwise would create. Ellis claims that most people carry a variety of 'irrational beliefs' in their heads unfounded in reality, but which result in their creating bad feelings for themselves as a result of 'shoulds' and 'oughts' which they believe are infallible. These beliefs usually belong to one of three categories, which Ellis calls the 'Irrational Trinity' on the road to 'mustabation':

*   A belief that I should be a certain sort of person, or a success, or perfect, or loved by everyone, and if I'm not, I'm a failure and worthless;
*   a belief that you, or other people, should do as I want them to do: love me, work for me, understand me, etc., and if they do not, it is terrible, and I deserve to be miserable or they should be made to suffer;
*   a belief that things should be different; there should not be racial hatred, this organization should run better, our parents should not have to die, etc., and if things are not as I want them to be it is awful and either I cannot cope and deserve to be miserable, or I have every right to be furious.

Since it takes years to develop our patterns of self-talk, changing them involves practice. There are a variety of programmes now available for helping people to restructure their self-talk into more supportive statements. Mahoney and Mahoney (1976) call this process 'cognitive ecology': cleaning up what you say to yourself.

2. DO I GET REGULAR EXERCISE OR HAVE A PERSONAL FITNESS PROGRAMME? Physical fitness is related to one's ability to cope with stress. It has also been shown to be related to the ability to create effective interpersonal relationships (Aspy and Roebuck, 1977) which in turn is related to stress reduction.

You need to be fit to cope effectively with transitions. Yet, of course, it is often when we are most in need of fitness that we are often least inclined to make time for it. There are a number of well-researched fitness programmes available (Health Education Council, 1976; Carruthers and Murray, 1977; Cooper, 1977; Royal Canadian Air Force, 1978).

3. AM I EATING REGULARLY AND WISELY? Now is not the time for a crash diet. Your body needs all the help it can get. People in transition often have neither the time nor inclination to eat wisely. There is sometimes a reliance on quick junk foods, take-away meals or eating out. Remember to eat something every day from the four major food groups: meat, fish, poultry; dairy products; fruits and vegetables; bread and cereals.

Do not replace food with alcohol or smoking. Obviously there may be times when alcohol will help you get through a lonely evening. You need a holiday from self-work as much as from any other kind of work. The danger signs are when alcohol or a cigarette is used as a substitute for meals.

Be wary of developing a dependence on drugs at this time. Sleeping tablets can sometimes be helpful during a crisis, but get off them quickly. They can serve to prevent you from developing healthier coping strategies.

It is a good idea to acquire an easy to read book on diet but one that is critical of food fads. The Health Education Council's booklet, 'Look After Yourself' (1976), contains a simple introduction to good nutrition, and Breckon's 'You Are What You Eat' (1976) is a fascinating survey of dietary facts and fiction, arguing strongly against overdosing oneself with vitamins and dealing in a balanced way with the hysteria over additives.

4. DO I KNOW HOW TO RELAX? There are two ways of reducing stress. One is to organize your life to minimize the number of stressors working on you. The other concerns how to reduce the effect of stress when it hits you. The latter is typically the biggest problem when coping with a transition. Unfortunately, the very people who are most prone to stress illnesses often exacerbate the problem by packing their lives with transitions.

There are numerous relaxation methods, each of which have their advocates. A brief guide follows.

* Learn a relaxation technique. Progressive relaxation is simple and easy to learn. It is described in Hopson and Hough (1973) as a classroom exercise. Transcendental meditation is now well researched and strong claims are made for it as a technique which directly affects the body's physiology. Most cities have a TM centre. You could also read Russel (1977). For those who do not enjoy the ritual cliquishness that accompanies TM, read Benson (1977).

* Direct body work to encourage relaxation: massage. The basics can be learnt quickly on a course. If there is a Personal Growth centre near you, make contact as they might run courses. Read Downing (1972). You will need to keep an open mind regarding some of the sweeping generalizations made on behalf of some of these techniques.

5. AM I KEEPING TO A REGULAR SCHEDULE? If your internal world is in crisis, keep your external world in order. Keeping irregular hours, eating at strange times, going to lots of new places, meeting new people; all these can be disorientating.

6. DO I KNOW MY 'PERSONAL ANCHOR POINTS'? Toffler (1970) described this concept as one antidote to 'future shock'. When all around us things are changing we need an anchor point to hold on to. For some people it is their home, for others a relationship, children, a job, a daily routine, a favourite place or a hobby. Anchor points are plentiful, and it is vital to have at least one. In the midst of instability a stable base offers confirmation of identity, disengagement from the problem, and maybe even relaxation.

7. DO I GIVE MYSELF 'TREATS' WHEN UNDER STRESS? This list of tips has been packed with work. But play is vital too. If you are feeling low, or under stress, how about simply giving yourself a treat? It might even be a reward for accomplishing a difficult test or situation, but it does not have to be.

Draw up a list of treats. Try to become an expert on self-indulgence: a theatre trip, a massage, a book, see friends, make love, have a disgustingly 'bad for you' meal, take a holiday, or pamper yourself.

The only warning about treats is: do not spend so much time treating yourself that you use these as a diversion from coping directly with the transition.

8. DO I HAVE OTHER PEOPLE WHO WILL TAKE CARE OF ME? It is all right to be taken care of sometimes. Allow a friend, lover or colleague to look after you. If they do not offer, be proactive, ask them. Be brave enough to accept help from others. Recall what you feel when others close to you ask for help. There are pay-offs for helpers as well as those who receive help.

9. CAN I SURVIVE? Of course you can. You may doubt it at the moment. Perhaps it will help to remind yourself that what you are feeling now is normal for someone having experienced what you are experiencing. It is also necessary before you can move on to the next stage of finding out more about you and what this transition can do for you instead of to you.

Do not worry about feelings of suicide. Sometimes survival does not seem like such a good idea. If these feelings really seem to be getting out of hand see a counsellor, ring a Samaritan, or consult a doctor; you will probably get more librium than counselling, but that can take off the pressure until you have regrouped your resources.

The feeling will pass. Talk to people, keep a regular routine, treat yourself; at the end of each day recall one good experience, then you can match it with a bad one, then another good experience followed by a bad one, etc., or contract with a friend to call you at certain times.

10. DO I KNOW WHEN MY LOW POINTS ARE LIKELY TO BE? These can usually be predicted quite easily; after a phone call to your children (in the case of a divorced parent), seeing your ex-spouse with a new partner, just seeing your ex-spouse, discovering a personal belonging of your dead spouse, seeing an old workmate (redundancy, retirement), and so on.

Keep a diary or a journal. This will help you to clarify your thoughts and feelings as well as to identify times, places and people to avoid. If you are experiencing the loss of a love it is usually advisable to fill your Sundays, bank holidays and Saturday nights!

Let go of the past
1. DO I EASILY LET GO OF OLD SITUATIONS? Sometimes people cannot let go because they try too hard to hold on. It is permissible to grieve. Grief shows that you are alive. Think about what you are missing, feel it. Ask people if you can talk to them about it. They will often be too embarrassed to mention it or worry that it will 'upset' you. Cry, rage, scream, recognize the loss, do not deny the pain. Wounds hurt when you dress them, but you know that is the first stage of the wound getting better. It is permissible to feel anger too.

2. DO I CONTINUALLY FEEL THAT THIS SHOULD NOT HAPPEN TO ME? Then you are guilty of making yourself unhappy by hitting yourself over the head with 'shoulds' and 'oughts'. You need to look again at the section on supportive self-talk.

3. DO I KNOW HOW TO VENT MY ANGER CONSTRUCTIVELY? Allow yourself to feel the anger. If it is kept inside it will only hurt you. Feel angry at the person who

left you, at the person who took something from you, at the world that let you down or at friends who cannot be trusted. Hit a pillow, scream aloud (in a closed car this is very effective; just like an echo chamber) or play a hectic sport. Do not hurt anyone, including yourself.

Anger is only a feeling. It cannot hurt anyone. Only behaviour hurts. Once the anger is cleared away, you are then freer to begin to evaluate, make plans and decide.

Set goals and make action plans

1. DO I KNOW HOW TO SET GOALS? Some people fail to manage their transitions effectively because they have not identified a desirable outcome. 'If you don't know where you're going, you'll probably end up somewhere else' (Campbell, 1974).

It is essential to identify what you want to achieve in terms which are as behaviourally specific as possible, such as 'I want a new job worth £8,000 per annum where I have overall responsibility for financial operations of a medium-scale department.' 'In six months I want to be able to go out on my own, to visit friends by myself, and to have developed one new interest' (this was an objective of a recent widow in one of my workshops).

2. DO I KNOW WHAT MY GOALS ARE FOR THIS TRANSITION AND FOR MY LIFE GENERALLY? This requires the specific skill of knowing how to set, define, and refine objectives.

3. DO I KNOW HOW TO MAKE AND IMPLEMENT ACTION PLANS? Once the objectives are clear the action steps follow next. There are a variety of resources available with guidelines on making effective action plans. Carkhuff's two books (1974a, b) are useful. An action plan needs to be behaviourally specific: 'I will make an appointment to see the solicitor tomorrow morning'. It needs to be in terms of 'what I will do now', not in terms of 'what I will do sometime', or 'what we will do eventually'. An action plan should read like a computer programme, with each step so clearly defined that someone else would know how to carry it out.

4. DO I KNOW HOW TO SET PRIORITIES? Having a variety of goals is one thing, having the time to achieve them all is another. Skills of time management are required along with a systematic way of measuring the desirability of one goal with another.

5. DO I KNOW HOW TO MAKE EFFECTIVE DECISIONS? Katz (1968) has talked about the importance, not so much of making wise decisions but of making decisions wisely. There are a variety of teaching programmes now available to help people become more proficient at making choices (Hopson and Hough, 1973; Watts and Elsom, 1975).

6. DO I KNOW HOW TO GENERATE ALTERNATIVES, BECAUSE THERE IS ALWAYS AN ALTERNATIVE? Often people do not make as good a decision as they might have simply because they have not generated enough alternatives. The techniques of 'brainstorming', 'morphological forced connections' and 'synectics' (all described in Adams, 1974) are ways of doing this. The key quite often, however, is the belief that no matter now hopeless the situation, how constrained one feels, there is always an alternative, no matter how unpalatable it may initially appear, and that you can choose. This is the central concept in the model of the 'self empowered person' described by Hopson and Scally (1980b).

Look for the gains you have made
If gains are not immediately apparent, review the section again under 'Know yourself'. Have you had to cope with something with which you have not had to cope before? If so, this will have shed light on a new facet of your personality. What is it? Do you like it? Can you use it to any advantage in the future?

Quick check-list on client's transition coping skills

1. DOES HE KNOW WHAT HE WANTS FROM THE NEW SITUATION? If not, you must help him to define what he wants; getting him to be as specific as possible. He may not be used to thinking in terms of objectives. You will have to teach him. Write down options on a blackboard, flip chart, or a note-book. Help him to evaluate the costs and benefits of different alternatives. Give him homework on this to be discussed at a future session.

2. DOES HE TEND TO BE PROACTIVE IN NEW SITUATIONS OR TO SIT BACK AND WAIT FOR THINGS TO HAPPEN? If he appears to be proactive, check out that it really is proactivity and not just acting to minimize anxiety, for instance jumping into something to alleviate ambiguity. If he is reactive you will need to point out that this will minimize his chances of getting what he wants and you will need to give him a task which is small enough for him to complete successfully (e.g. doing some homework) in order to develop his confidence in the ability to make things happen. Give him a suitable book to read (see the section on self-help books) which is simultaneously instructive and a task to be completed.

3. DOES HE HAVE OTHER PEOPLE HE CAN RELY ON FOR HELP? Get him to specify who and what they can do for him. If he is deficient in help, steer him towards an appropriate self-help group.

4. HAS ANYTHING LIKE THIS HAPPENED TO HIM BEFORE? Look for links with previous experiences. Help him to discover what he did then which helped, and what in retrospect he would now choose to do differently.

5. HOW WELL CAN HE LOOK AFTER HIMSELF? Is he physically fit and eating sensibly? If not, advise him of the importance of this. Similarly, help him to discover the 'anchor points' in his life and persuade him to keep to a regular schedule. Encourage him to give himself a treat from time to time. Help him to identify when the low points are likely to be and to plan to minimize the impact of these: for example, always have something planned for Sunday when you are newly divorced.

6. CAN HE LET GO OF THE PAST? If not, encourage him to experience the grief and the anger as a way of discharging it and accepting that these feelings are normal and acceptable. They only become a problem if we can never let go of them.

7. CAN HE SET GOALS AND MAKE ACTION PLANS? Persuade him to begin thinking about specific goals as outlined under point 1. Help him define priorities, generate alternatives, and weigh them up.

8. CAN HE SEE POSSIBLE GAINS FROM HIS NEW SITUATION? Gently pressure him to begin to look for gains. The timing of this is vital. If he has not sufficiently let go of the past your intervention can appear heartless. Empathy is essential, but also you are trying to get him to see that however much he may not have chosen for an event to happen, that there will be something to gain.

Is it possible to train people to cope more effectively with transitions?

This has had to be empirically tested. Our general hypothesis is that people experiencing transitions will have similar tasks to cope with, namely, managing strain and dealing with cognitive tasks presented by the transition. We are assuming that to a considerable extent people's reactions to being in transition are learnt as opposed to being inherited. To the extent that individuals' reactions are learnt, we should be able to develop preventive, educative and re-educative strategies to help them manage their affairs and relationships more effectively at lower psychological costs, and derive greater benefits from the opportunity values embedded in every major transition.

This means that training programmes could be generated to help develop more effective coping styles for a number of people either (i) experiencing different transitional events, or who are anticipating transitional events, or (ii) as general training for any presently unknown future transitions.

We have already conducted a variety of transitions workshops in the UK, the USA and Scandinavia with populations including managers, trade unionists, counsellors, organization development specialists, social workers, case workers, teachers and youth workers. These have been primarily designed for participants who in turn will have to deal with individuals in transition. We believe that it is only possible to do such work when one has a clear understanding not just of a theoretical orientation, a collection of coping skills and teaching techniques, but also of one's own transitional experiences, skills and deficits, joys, confusion and sadness.

The final question is always 'why'? Why spend the energy, use the time, deplete the resources, all of which could be directed to something else?

We can only give our answer. A transition simultaneously carries the seeds of our yesterdays, the hopes and fears of our futures, and the pressing sensations of the present which is our confirmation of being alive. There is danger and opportunity, ecstasy and despair, development and stagnation, but above all there is movement. Nothing and no one stays the same. Nature abhors vacuums and stability. A stable state is merely a stopping point on a journey from one place to another. Stop too long and your journey is ended. Stay and enjoy but with the realization that more is to come. You may not be able to stop the journey, but you can fly the plane.

References

Adams, J.L. (1974)
  Conceptual Blockbusting. San Francisco: Freeman.
Adams, J.D., Hayes, J. and Hopson, B. (1976)
  Transition: Understanding and managing personal change. London: Martin Robertson.
Aspy, D.N. and Roebuck, F.N. (1977)
  Kids Don't Learn From People They Don't Like. Amherst, Mass.: Human Resource Development Press.
Benson, H. (1977)
  The Relaxation Response. London: Fountain Well Press.
Breckon, W. (1976)
  You Are What You Eat. London: BBC Publications.
Campbell, D. (1974)
  If You Don't Know Where You're Going You'll Probably End Up Somewhere Else. Hoddesdon, Herts.: Argus Publications.
Carkhuff, R.R. (1974a)
  The Art of Problem Solving. Amherst, Mass.: Human Resource Development Press.
Carkhuff, R.R. (1974b)
  How To Help Yourself. Amherst, Mass.: Human Resource Development Press.
Carruthers, M. and Murray, A. (1977)
  F/40: Fitness on forty minutes a week. London: Futura.
Cooper, K. (1977)
  The New Aerobics. New York: Bantam.
Downing, G. (1972)
  The Massage Book. New York: Random House.
Ellis, A. and Harper, R. (1975)
  A New Guide to Rational Living. Hollywood, Ca: Wilshire Books.

Forbes, R. (1979)
Life Stress. New York: Doubleday.

Health Education Council (1976)
Look After Yourself. London: Health Education Council.

Holmes, T.H. and Rahe, R.H. (1967)
The social readjustment rating scale. Journal of
Psychosomatic Research, 11, 213–218.

Hopson, B. and Hough, P. (1973)
Exercises in Personal and Career Development. Cambridge:
Hobsons Press.

Hopson, B. and Scally, M. (1980a)
How to cope with and gain from life transitions. In B.
Hopson and M. Scally, Lifeskills Teaching Programmes
No. 1. Leeds: Lifeskills Associates.

Hopson, B. and Scally, M. (1980b)
Lifeskills Teaching: Education for self-empowerment.
London: McGraw-Hill.

Howe, L.W. and Howe, M.M. (1975)
Personalizing Education: Values clarification and
beyond. New York: Hart.

Johnson. D.W. (1972)
Reaching Out. Englewood Cliffs, NJ: Prentice-Hall.

Katz, M.R. (1968)
Can computers make guidance decisions for students?
College Board Review, No. 72.

Kirschenbaum, H. (1977)
Advanced Value Clarification. La Jolla, Ca: University
Associates.

Krantzler, M. (1973)
Creative Divorce. New York: M. Evans.

Lamott, K. (1975)
Escape from Stress. New York: Berkley.

Mahoney, M.J. and Mahoney, J. (1976)
Permanent Weight Control. New York: W.W. Norton.

Maslow, A. (1968)
Towards a Psychology of Being (2nd edn). New York: Van
Nostrand.

Parkes, C. M. (1972)
Bereavement: Studies of grief in adult life. London:
Tavistock.

Royal Canadian Air Force (1978)
Physical Fitness. Harmondsworth: Penguin.

Russel, P. (1977)
The Transcendental Meditation Technique. London:
Routledge & Kegan Paul.

Sharpe, R. and Lewis, D. (1977)
Thrive on Stress. London: Souvenir Press.

Simon, S. (1974)
Meeting Yourself Halfway. Hoddesdon, Herts.: Argus
Publications.

Simon, S., Howe, L.W. and Kirschenbaum, H. (1972)
Value Clarification. New York: Hart.

Toffler, A. (1970)
Future Shock. London: Bodley Head.

Watts, A.G. and Elsom, D. (1975)
Deciding. Cambridge: Hobsons Press.

Questions

1. Why is an understanding of the psychological processes associated with transitions important in your life?
2. What are the major types of transition and how are they related?
3. How would you set about rating the impact of life events on people?
4. Critically evaluate the Hopson-Adams model of transitions.
5. What effects do transitions have on people?
6. What are the coping tasks relevant to all transitions?
7. Describe the coping skills which are relevant to transitions.
8. Which will be the most important influence in ensuring a successful transition and why? Is it the coping skills of the mover or the structure and practices of the organization, institution or social norms?
9. Describe a life transition in terms of the stages the person might go through and what that person could do to maximize the chances of coping with it effectively and gaining from the experience.
10. How effectively can we train people to improve their transition coping skills?

Annotated reading

Adams, J.D., Hayes, J. and Hopson, B. (1976) Transition: Understanding and managing personal change. London: Martin Robertson.
 This is the first attempt to provide a conceptual framework to describe the psychological sequence of a transition. It is primarily a theoretical book, although some guidelines for the practitioner are available.

Hopson, B. and Scally, M. (1980) How to cope with and gain from life transitions. In B. Hopson and M. Scally, Lifeskills Teaching Programmes No. 1. Leeds: Lifeskills Associates.
 This is for a classroom teacher of young people and consists of a series of carefully described group exercises to teach young people about transitions and how to cope more effectively with them.

Parkes, C. M. (1975) Bereavement: Studies of grief in adult life. Harmondsworth: Penguin.
 This book is about more than bereavement, although this topic is discussed at great length. Parkes generalizes from bereavement to other aspects of separation and loss in people's lives.

Part three

Dealing with others

Chapter 8

Introduction to Part 3
Cary L. Cooper and Peter Makin

A large proportion of a manager's time is spent in dealing with other people, either on a 'one-to-one' basis or in committees. Indeed, it is quite common to find that the higher someone rises in the managerial structure, the more they have to deal with people rather than 'things' and 'social' becomes more important than 'technical'.

Unlike technical expertise, however, we all have a wealth of experience of social interaction; it is part of everyday life, both in work and leisure. The extent of our experience in social interaction may be dangerously misleading in that we may be lulled into the view that there is little that we can be taught that we do not already know. In the chapters that follow we hope to throw some new light on common occurrences such as the interview. Indeed, the comment made by Edward Teller the nuclear physicist might be appropriate for this section. When asked what he considered the objectives of teaching to be he replied, that it was 'to make things simple which people think difficult and to make difficult what they think simple'. After reading this section, you should appreciate some of the complexities of social interaction.

In the first chapter, Argyle gives us an insight into some of the many facets of social behaviour. In particular he draws attention to the fact that the factors which influence such behaviour are 'motor' skills which can, like other skills, be improved by appropriate training. In addition he also makes the distinction between verbal and non-verbal methods of communication, a distinction which has been made popular by a spate of books on 'body language'. (Beware, however, most of these popular books are based on speculation and the contents are often suspect.) Argyle's books on the other hand are excellently researched. As Argyle points out, many aspects of non-verbal communication are not realized by either sender or receiver but, it should be pointed out, others are. For example we all realize that our feelings may be unwittingly revealed by facial expressions or hand movements, and hence we consciously control them in certain situations. We are not so conscious, however, of the movements of our feet and it can be very illuminating to observe the movement of people's feet in committee meetings: indeed the most worn part of the carpet in the Council

Chamber at UMIST, where we work, is that beneath the seat of the Chairman.

We make no apologies for including two chapters on interviewing because it can be considered to be the basic building block of our dealings with others. Often, however, interviewing is only looked at as one of the techniques used in personnel selection; but if we consider the interview as a 'conversation with a purpose', its importance becomes apparent. Indeed, viewed in such terms, we can see that it covers such diverse activities as a session with a psychotherapist, and a detective interrogating a suspect. Few managers would like to be in the position of having colleagues and subordinates who either told them all their innermost thoughts or who, at the other end of the scale, were determined not to divulge any information at all. Nevertheless a manager will need a flexible range of interviewing skills and need to be capable of dealing with assessment interviews, goal setting, problem solving, disciplining, etc. As Randell, Packard, Shaw and Slater (1974) point out, the appraisal interview can be an important step in improving an individual's performance. For a manager the interview is most probably the most important research tool in so far as it involves the efficient gathering of information. In addition, however, it often involves the giving as well as receiving of information and of reaching decisions which are, it is hoped, mutually acceptable.

The emphasis upon decision making is reflected in the final chapter on bargaining and negotiation. As we have mentioned before, interviews at work are rarely at the extreme ends of the scale; more likely they lie towards the centre of the scale. There is unlikely to be total agreement on every occasion in even the best working relationships, and inevitably one or both of the parties have to be persuaded, cajoled or coerced into making some concessions in order to reach an agreement. The important elements in this process are discussed and evaluated by Morley.

References

Randell, G.A., Packard, P.M.A., Shaw, R.L. and Slater, A.J. (1974)
Staff Appraisal. London: Institute of Personnel Management.

Chapter 9

Social behaviour
Michael Argyle

We start by presenting the social skill model of social
behaviour, and an account of sequences of social interaction. This model is relevant to our later discussion of
social skills and how these can be trained. The chapter
then goes on to discuss the elements of social behaviour,
both verbal and non-verbal, and emphasizes the importance
and different functions of non-verbal signals. The receivers
of these signals have to decode them, and do so in terms of
emotions and impressions of personality; we discuss some of
the processes and some of the main errors of person perception. Senders can manipulate the impressions they create
by means of 'self-presentation'. The processes of social
behaviour, and the skills involved, are quite different in
different social situations, and we discuss recent attempts
to analyse these situations in terms of their main features,
such as rules and goals.

We move on to a number of specific social skills.
Research on the processes leading to friendship and love
makes it possible to train and advise people who have difficulty with these relationships. Research on persuasion
shows how people can be trained to be more assertive. And
research on small social groups and leadership of these
groups makes it possible to give an account of the most
successful skills for handling social groups.

Social competence is defined in terms of the successful
attainment of goals, and it can be assessed by a variety of
techniques such as self-rating and observation of role-
played performance. The most successful method of improving social skills is role-playing, combined with modelling,
coaching, videotape-recorder (VTR) playback, and 'homework'.
Results of follow-up studies with a variety of populations
show that this form of social skills training (SST) is very
successful.

Harré and Secord (1972) have argued persuasively that
much human social behaviour is the result of conscious
planning, often in words, with full regard for the complex
meanings of behaviour and the rules of the situations. This
is an important correction to earlier social psychological
views, which often failed to recognize the complexity of
individual planning and the different meanings which may be
given to stimuli, for example in laboratory experiments.

However, it must be recognized that much social behaviour is not planned in this way: the smaller elements of behaviour and longer automatic sequences are outside conscious awareness, though it is possible to attend, for example, to patterns of gaze, shifts of orientation, or the latent meanings of utterances. The social skills model, in emphasizing the hierarchical structure of social performance, can incorporate both kinds of behaviour.

The social skills model also emphasizes feedback processes. A person driving a car sees at once when it is going in the wrong direction, and takes corrective action with the steering wheel. Social interactors do likewise; if another person is talking too much they interrupt, ask closed questions or no questions, and look less interested in what is being said. Feedback requires perception, looking at and listening to the other person. Skilled performance requires the ability to take the appropriate corrective action referred to as 'translation' in the model: not everyone knows that open-ended questions make people talk more and closed questions make them talk less. And it depends on a number of two-step sequences of social behaviour whereby certain social acts have reliable effects on another. Let us look at social behaviour as a skilled performance similar to motor skills like driving a car (see figure 1).

Figure 1

The motor skill model (from Argyle, 1969)

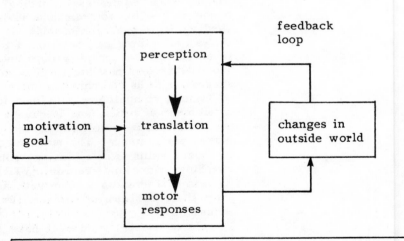

In each case the performer is pursuing certain goals, makes continuous response to feedback, and emits hierarchically-organized motor responses. This model has been heuristically very useful in drawing attention to the importance of feedback, and hence to gaze; it also suggests a number of different ways in which social performances can fail, and suggests the training procedures that may be effective, through analogy with motor skills training (Argyle and Kendon, 1967; Argyle, 1969).

The model emphasizes the motivation, goals and plans of interactors. It is postulated that every interactor is try-ing to achieve some goal, whether or not there is awareness of that. These goals may be, for example, to be liked by another person, to obtain or convey information, to modify the other's emotional state, and so on. Such goals may be linked to more basic motivational systems. Goals have sub-goals; for example, doctors must diagnose patients before they can be treated. Patterns of response are directed towards goals and sub-goals, and have a hierarchical struc-ture: large units of behaviour are composed of smaller ones, and at the lowest levels these are habitual and automatic.

The role of reinforcement

This is one of the key processes in social skills sequences. When interactor A does what B wants done, B is pleased and sends immediate and spontaneous reinforcements: smile, gaze, approving noises, and so on, and modifies A's be-haviour, probably by operant conditioning; for example, modifying the content of subsequent utterances. At the same time A is modifying B's behaviour in exactly the same way. These effects appear to be mainly outside the focus of conscious attention, and take place very rapidly. It follows that anyone who gives strong rewards and punishments in the course of interaction will be able to modify the behaviour of others in the desired direction. In addition, the strong-er the rewards that A issues, the more strongly other people will be attracted to A.

The role of gaze in social skills

The social skills model suggests that the monitoring of another's reactions is an essential part of social perfor-mance. The other's verbal signals are mainly heard, but non-verbal signals are mainly seen; the exceptions being the non-verbal aspects of speech and touch. It was this implication of the social skills model which directed us towards the study of gaze in social interaction. In dyadic interaction each person looks about 50 per cent of the time, mutual gaze occupies 25 per cent of the time, looking while listening is about twice the level of looking while talking, glances are about three seconds, and mutual glances about one second, with wide variations due to distance, sex combination, and personality (Argyle and Cook, 1976). However, there are several important differences between social behaviour and motor skills.

* Rules: the moves which interactors may make are governed by rules; they must respond properly to what has gone before. Similarly, rules govern the other's responses and can be used to influence behaviour; for example, questions lead to answers.
* Taking the role of the other: it is important to

perceive accurately the reactions of others. It is also necessary to perceive the perceptions of others; that is, to take account of their points of view. This appears to be a cognitive ability which develops with age (Flavell, 1968), but which may fail to develop properly. Those who are able to do this have been found to be more effective at a number of social tasks, and more altruistic. Meldman (1967) found that psychiatric patients are more egocentric (i.e. talked about themselves more than controls), and it has been our experience that socially unskilled patients have great difficulty in taking the role of the other.

* The independent initiative of the other sequences of interaction: social situations inevitably contain at least one other person, who will be pursuing personal goals and using social skills. How can we analyse the resulting sequences of behaviour? For a sequence to constitute an acceptable piece of social behaviour, the moves must fit together in order. Social psychologists have by no means discovered all the principles or 'grammar' underlying these sequences, but some of the principles are known, and can explain common forms of interaction failure.

Verbal and non-verbal communication

Verbal communication

There are several different kinds of verbal utterance.

* Egocentric speech: this is directed to the self, is found in infants and has the effect of directing behaviour.
* Orders, instructions: these are used to influence the behaviour of others; they can be gently persuasive or authoritarian.
* Questions: these are intended to elicit verbal information; they can be open-ended or closed, personal or impersonal.
* Information: may be given in response to a question, or as part of a lecture or during problem-solving discussion.

(The last three points are the basic classes of utterance.)

* Informal speech: consists of casual chat, jokes, gossip, and contains little information, but helps to establish and sustain social relationships.
* Expression of emotions and interpersonal attitudes: this is a special kind of information; however, this information is usually conveyed, and is conveyed more effectively, non-verbally.
* Performative utterances: these include 'illocutions' where saying the utterance performs something (voting, judging, naming, etc.), and 'perlocutions', where a goal

is intended but may not be achieved (persuading, intimidating, etc.).
* Social routines: these include standard sequences like thanking, apologizing, greeting, and so on.
* Latent messages: in these, the more important meaning is made subordinate ('As I was saying to the Prime Minister ...').

There are many category schemes for reducing utterances to a limited number of classes of social acts. One of the best known is that of Bales (1950), who introduced the 12 classes shown in figure 2.

Non-verbal signals accompanying speech
Non-verbal signals play an important part in speech and conversation. They have three main roles:

* completing and elaborating on verbal utterances: utterances are accompanied by vocal emphasis, gestures and facial expressions, which add to the meaning and indicate whether it is a question, intended to be serious or funny, and so on;
* managing synchronizing: this is achieved by head-nods, gaze-shifts, and other signals. For example, to keep the floor a speaker does not look up at the end of an utterance, keeps a hand in mid-gesture, and increases the volume of his speech if the other interrupts;
* sending feedback signals: listeners keep up a continuous, and mainly unwitting, commentary on the speaker's utterances, showing by mouth and eyebrow positions whether they agree, understand, are surprised, and so on (Argyle, 1975).

Other functions of non-verbal communication (NVC)
NVC consists of facial expression, tone of voice, gaze, gestures, postures, physical proximity and appearance. We have already described how NVC is linked with speech; it also functions in several other ways, especially in the communication of emotions and attitudes to other people.

A sender is in a certain state, or possesses some information; this is encoded into a message which is then decoded by a receiver.

sender ⟶ encodes ⟶ message ⟶ decodes ⟶ receiver

Encoding research is done by putting subjects into some state and studying the non-verbal messages which are emitted. For example Mehrabian (1972), in a role-playing experiment, asked subjects to address a hat-stand, imagining it to be a person. Men who liked the hat-stand looked at it more, did not have hands on hips and stood closer.

Figure 2

The Bales categories (from Bales, 1950)

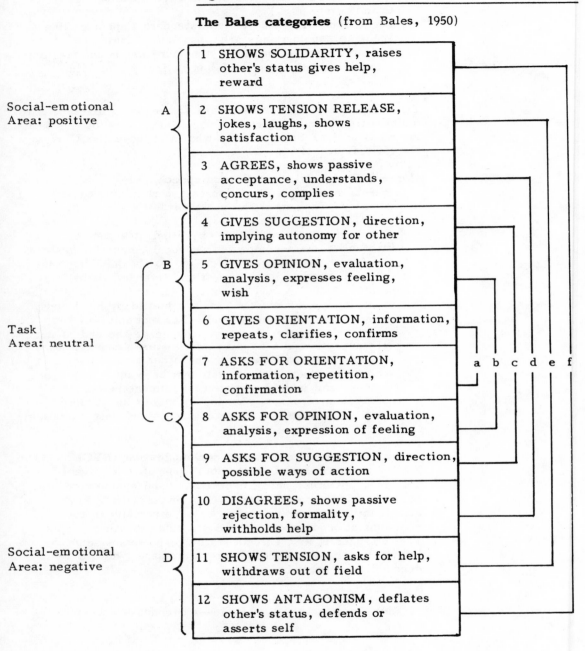

KEY

a problems of communication

b problems of evaluation

c problems of control

d problems of decision

e problems of tension reduction

f problems of reintegration

A positive reactions

B attempted answers

C questions

D negative reactions

Non-verbal signals are often 'unconscious': that is, they are outside the focus of attention. A few signals are unconsciously sent and received, like dilated pupils, signifying sexual attraction, but there are a number of other possibilities as shown in table 1.

Table 1

Awareness of non-verbal signals

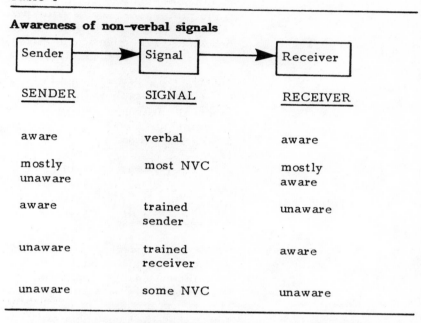

SENDER	SIGNAL	RECEIVER
aware	verbal	aware
mostly unaware	most NVC	mostly aware
aware	trained sender	unaware
unaware	trained receiver	aware
unaware	some NVC	unaware

Strictly speaking pupil dilation is not communication at all, but only a physiological response. 'Communication' is usually taken to imply some intention to affect another; one criterion of successful communication is that it makes a difference whether the other person is present and in a position to receive the signal; another is that the signal is repeated, varied or amplified if it has no immediate effect. These criteria are independent of conscious intention to communicate, which is often absent.

* Interpersonal attitudes: interactors indicate how much they like or dislike one another, and whether they think they are more or less important, mainly non-verbally. We have compared verbal and non-verbal signals and found that non-verbal cues like facial expression and tone of voice have far more impact than verbal ones (Argyle, Salter, Nicholson, Williams and Burgess, 1970).
* Emotional states: anger, depression, anxiety, joy, surprise, fear and disgust/contempt, are also communicated more clearly by non-verbal signals, such as facial expression, tone of voice, posture, gestures and gaze. Interactors may try to conceal their true emotions, but these are often revealed by 'leakage' via cues which are difficult to control.

Person perception

In order to respond effectively to the behaviour of others it is necessary to perceive them correctly. The social skills model emphasizes the importance of perception and feedback; to drive a car one must watch the traffic outside and the instruments inside. Such perception involves selecting certain cues, and being able to interpret them correctly. There is evidence of poor person perception in mental patients and other socially unskilled individuals, while professional social skills performers need to be sensitive to special aspects of other people and their behaviour. For selection interviewers and clinical psychologists the appraisal of others is a central part of the job.

We form impressions of other people all the time, mainly in order to predict their future behaviour, and so that we can deal with them effectively. We categorize others in terms of our favourite cognitive constructs, of which the most widely used are:

* extraversion, sociability;
* agreeableness, likeability;
* emotional stability;
* intelligence;
* assertiveness.

There are, however, wide individual differences in the constructs used, and 'complex' people use a larger number of such dimensions. We have found that the constructs used vary greatly with the situation: for example, work-related constructs are not used in purely social situations. We also found that the constructs used vary with the target group, such as children versus psychologists (Argyle, Furnham and Graham, 1981).

A number of widespread errors are made in forming impressions of others which should be particularly avoided by those whose job it is to assess people:

* assuming that a person's behaviour is mainly a product of personality, whereas it may be more a function of situation: at a noisy party, in church, and so on;
* assuming that behaviour is due to the person rather than the person's role; for example, as a hospital nurse, as a patient or as a visitor;
* attaching too much importance to physical cues, like beards, clothes, and physical attractiveness;
* being affected by stereotypes about the characteristics of members of certain races, social classes, etc.

During social interaction it is also necessary to perceive the emotional states of others: for example, to tell if they are depressed or angry. There are wide individual differences in the ability to judge emotions correctly (Davitz, 1964). As we have seen, emotions are mainly conveyed by non-verbal signals, especially by facial expression and tone of voice. The interpretation of emotions is also based on perception of the situation the other person is in. Lalljee at Oxford found that smiles are not necessarily decoded as happy, whereas unhappy faces are usually regarded as authentic.

Similar considerations apply to the perception of interpersonal attitudes, for instance who likes whom, which is also mainly based on non-verbal signals, such as proximity, gaze and facial expression. Again use is made of context to decode these signals: a glance at a stranger may be interpreted as a threat, an appeal for help or a friendly invitation. There are some interesting errors due to pressures towards cognitive consistency: if A likes B, then A thinks that B likes A more than B on average actually does: if A likes both B and C, A assumes that they both like each other more than, on average, they do.

It is necessary to perceive the on-going flow of interaction in order to know what is happening and to participate in it effectively. People seem to agree on the main episodes and sub-episodes of an encounter, but they may produce rather different accounts of why those present behaved as they did. One source of variation, and indeed error, is that people attribute the causes of others' behaviour to their personality ('He fell over because he is clumsy'), but their own behaviour to the situation ('I fell over because it was slippery'), whereas both factors operate in each case (Jones and Nisbett, 1972). Interpretations also depend on the ideas and knowledge an individual possesses: just as an expert on cars could understand better why a car was behaving in a peculiar way, so also can an expert on social behaviour understand why patterns of social behaviour occur.

Situations, their rules and other features

We know that people behave very differently in different situations; in order to predict behaviour, or to advise people on social skills in specific situations, it is necessary to analyse the situations in question. This can be done in terms of a number of fundamental features.

Goals

In all situations there are certain goals which are commonly obtainable. It is often fairly obvious what these are, but socially inadequate people may simply not know what parties are for, for example, or may think that the purpose of a selection interview is vocational guidance.

We have studied the main goals in a number of common situations, by asking samples of people to rate the importance of various goals, and then carrying out factor analysis. The main goals are usually:

* social acceptance, etc.;
* food, drink and other bodily needs;
* task goals specific to the situation.

We have also studied the relations between goals, within and between persons, in terms of conflict and instrumentality.

This makes it possible to study the 'goal structure' of situations (cf. Argyle et al, 1981).

Rules

All situations have rules about what may or may not be done in them. Socially inexperienced people are often ignorant or mistaken about the rules. It would obviously be impossible to play a game without knowing the rules and the same applies to social situations.

We have studied the rules of a number of everyday situations. There appear to be several universal rules; to be polite, friendly, and not embarrass people. There are also rules which are specific to situations, or groups of situations, and these can be interpreted as functional, since they enable situational goals to be met. For example, when seeing the doctor one should be clean and tell the truth; when going to a party one should dress smartly and keep to cheerful topics of conversation.

Special skills

Many social situations require special social skills, as in the case of various kinds of public speaking and interviewing, but also such everyday situations as dates and parties. A person with little experience of a particular situation may find that he lacks the special skills needed for it (cf. Argyle et al, 1981).

Repertoire of elements

Every situation defines certain moves as relevant. For example, at a seminar it is relevant to show slides, make long speeches, draw on the blackboard, etc. If moves appropriate to a cricket match or a Scottish ball were made, they would be ignored or regarded as totally bizarre. We have found 65-90 main elements used in several situations, like going to the doctor. We have also found that the semiotic structure varies between situations: we found that questions about work and about private life were sharply contrasted in an office situation, but not on a date.

Roles

Every situation has a limited number of roles: for example, a classroom has the roles of teacher, pupil, janitor, and school inspector. These roles carry different degrees of power, and the occupant has goals peculiar to that role.

Cognitive structure

We found that the members of a research group classified each other in terms of the concepts extraverted and enjoyable companion for social occasions, but in terms of dominant, creative and supportive for seminars. There are also concepts related to the task, such as 'amendment', 'straw vote' and 'nem con', for committee meetings.

Environmental setting and pieces

Most situations involve special environmental settings and

props. Cricket needs bat, ball, stumps, and so on; a seminar requires a blackboard, slide projector and lecture notes.

How do persons fit into situations, conceived in this way? To begin with, there are certain pervasive aspects of persons, corresponding to the 20 per cent or so of person variance found in P x S (personality and situation) studies. This consists of scores on general dimensions like intelligence, extraversion, neuroticism and so on. In addition, persons have dispositions to behave in certain ways in classes of situations; this corresponds to the 50 per cent or so of the P x S variance in relation to dimensions of situations like formal-informal, and friendly-hostile. Third, there are more specific reactions to particular situations; for example, behaviour in social psychology seminars depends partly on knowledge of social psychology, and attitudes to different schools of thought in it. Taken together these three factors may predict performance in, and also avoidance of, certain situations - because of lack of skill, anxiety, etc. - and this will be the main expectation in such cases.

Friendship

This is one of the most important social relationships: failure in it is a source of great distress, and so it is one of the main areas of social skills training. The conditions under which people come to like one another have been the object of extensive research, and are now well understood.

There are several stages of friendship: (i) coming into contact with the other, through proximity at work or elsewhere; (ii) increasing attachment as a result of reinforcement and discovery of similarity; (iii) increasing self-disclosure and commitment; and, sometimes, (iv) dissolution of the relationship. Friendship is the dominant relationship for adolescents and the unmarried; friends engage in characteristic activities, such as talking, eating, drinking, joint leisure, but not, usually, working.

Frequency of interaction

The more two people meet, the more polarized their attitudes to one another become, but usually they like one another more. Frequent interaction can come about from living in adjacent rooms or houses, working in the same office, belonging to the same club, and so on. So interaction leads to liking, and liking leads to more interaction. Only certain kinds of interaction lead to liking. In particular, people should be of similar status. Belonging to a co-operative group, especially under crisis conditions, is particularly effective, as Sherif's robbers' cave experiment (Sherif, Harvey, White, Hood and Sherif, 1961) and research on inter-racial attitudes have shown.

Reinforcement

The next general principle governing liking is the extent to which one person satisfies the needs of another. This was

shown in a study by Jennings of 400 girls in a reformatory
(1950). She found that the popular girls helped and pro-
tected others, encouraged, cheered them up, made them
feel accepted and wanted, controlled their own moods so as
not to inflict anxiety or depression on others, were able
to establish rapport quickly, won the confidence of a wide
variety of other personalities, and were concerned with the
feelings and needs of others. The unpopular girls on the
other hand were dominating, aggressive, boastful, demanded
attention, and tried to get others to do things for them.
This pattern has been generally interpreted in terms of the
popular girls providing rewards and minimizing costs, while
the unpopular girls tried to get rewards for themselves, and
incurred costs for others. It is not necessary for the other
person to be the actual source of rewards: Lott and Lott
(1960) found that children who were given model cars by the
experimenter liked the other children in the experiment
more, and several studies have shown that people are liked
more in a pleasant environmental setting.

Being liked is a powerful reward, so if A likes B, B
will usually like A. This is particularly important for
those who have a great need to be liked, such as individuals
with low self-esteem. It is signalled, as discussed above,
primarily by non-verbal signals.

Similarity
People like others who are similar to themselves, in certain
respects. They like those with similar attitudes, beliefs
and values, who have a similar regional and social class
background, who have similar jobs or leisure interests, but
they need not have similar personalities. Again there is a
cyclical process, since similarity leads to liking and liking leads to similarity, but effects of similarity on liking
have been shown experimentally.

Physical attractiveness
Physical attractiveness (p.a.) is an important source of
both same-sex and opposite sex liking, especially in the
early stages. Walster, Aronson, Abrahams and Rottmann (1966)
arranged a 'computer dance' at which couples were paired at
random: the best prediction of how much each person liked
their partner was the latter's p.a. as rated by the experimenter. Part of the explanation lies in the 'p.a. stereotype'. Dion, Berscheid and Walster (1972) found that attractive people were believed to have desirable characteristics
of many other kinds. However, people do not seek out the
most attractive friends and mates, but compromise by seeking
those similar to themselves in attractiveness.

Self-disclosure
This is a signal for intimacy, like bodily contact, because
it indicates trust in the other. Self-disclosure can be
measured on a scale (1-5) with items like:

What are your favourite forms of erotic play and sexual lovemaking? (scale value 2.56)

What are the circumstances under which you become depressed and when your feelings are hurt? (3.51)

What are your hobbies, how do you best like to spend your spare time? (4.98) (Jourard, 1971).

As people get to know each other better, self-disclosure slowly increases, and is reciprocated, up to a limit.

Commitment

This is a state of mind, an intention to stay in a relationship, and abandon others. This involves a degree of dependence on the other person and trusting them not to leave the relationship. The less committed has the more power.

Social skills training

The most common complaint of those who seek SST is difficulty in making friends. Some of them say they have never had a friend in their lives. What advice can we offer, on the basis of research on friendship?

* As we showed earlier, social relations are negotiated mainly by non-verbal signals. Clients for SST who cannot make friends are usually found to be very inexpressive, in face and voice.
* Rewardingness is most important. The same clients usually appear to be very unrewarding, and are not really interested in other people.
* Frequent interaction with those of similar interests and attitudes can be found in clubs for professional or leisure activities, in political and religious groups, and so on.
* Physical attractiveness is easier to change than is social behaviour.
* Certain social skills may need to be acquired, such as inviting others to suitable social events, and engaging in self-disclosure at the right speed.

The meaning and assessment of social competence

By social competence we mean the ability, the possession of the necessary skills, to produce the desired effects on other people in social situations. These desired effects may be to persuade the others to buy, to learn, to recover from neurosis, to like or admire the actor, and so on. These results are not necessarily in the public interest: skills may be used for social or antisocial purposes. And there is no evidence that social competence is a general factor: a person may be better at one task than another, for example, parties or committees. SST for students and other more or less normal populations has been directed to the skills of dating, making friends and being assertive. SST for mental patients has been aimed at correcting failures of social competence, and also at relieving subjective distress, such as social anxiety.

To find out who needs training, and in what areas, a detailed descriptive assessment is needed. We want to know, for example, which situations individual trainees find difficult (formal situations, conflicts, meeting strangers, etc.), and which situations they are inadequate in, even though they do not report them as difficult. And we want to find out what individuals are doing wrong: failure to produce the right non-verbal signals, low rewardingness, lack of certain social skills, and so on.

Social competence is easier to define and agree upon in the case of professional social skills: an effective therapist cures more patients, an effective teacher teaches better, an effective salesperson sells more. When we look more closely, it is not quite so simple: examination marks may be one index of a teacher's effectiveness, but usually more is meant than just this. Salespersons should not simply sell a lot of goods, they should make the customers feel they would like to go to that shop again. So a combination of different skills is required and an overall assessment of effectiveness may involve the combination of a number of different measures or ratings. The range of competence is quite large: the best salesmen and saleswomen regularly sell four times as much as some others behind the same counter; some supervisors of working groups produce twice as much output as others, or have 20-25 per cent of the labour turnover and absenteeism rates (Argyle, 1972).

For everyday social skills it is more difficult to give the criteria of success; lack of competence is easier to spot: failure to make friends, or opposite sex friends, quarrelling and failing to sustain co-operative relationships, finding a number of situations difficult or a source of anxiety, and so on.

Methods of SST training

Role-playing with coaching

This is now the most widely-used method of SST. There are four stages:

* instruction;
* role-playing with other trainees or other role partners for five to eight minutes;
* feedback and coaching, in the form of oral comments from the trainer;
* repeated role-playing.

A typical laboratory set-up is shown in figure 3. This also shows the use of an ear-microphone for instruction while role-playing is taking place. In the case of patients, mere practice does no good: there must be coaching as well.

For an individual or group of patients or other trainees a series of topics, skills or situations is chosen, and introduced by means of short scenarios. Role partners who can be briefed to present carefully graded degrees of difficulty are used.

It is usual for trainers to be generally encouraging, and also rewarding for specific aspects of behaviour, though there is little experimental evidence for the value of such reinforcement. It is common to combine role-playing with modelling and video-playback, both of which are discussed below. Follow-up studies have found that role-playing combined with coaching is successful with many kinds of mental patients, and that it is one of the most successful forms of SST for these groups.

Role-playing usually starts with 'modelling', in which a film is shown or a demonstration given of how to perform the skill being taught. The feedback session usually includes videotape-playback and most studies have found that this is advantageous (Bailey and Sowder, 1970). While it often makes trainees self-conscious at first, this wears off after the second session. Skills acquired in the laboratory or class must be transferred to the outside world. This is usually achieved by 'homework': trainees are encouraged to try out the new skills several times before the next session. Most

Figure 3

A social skills training laboratory

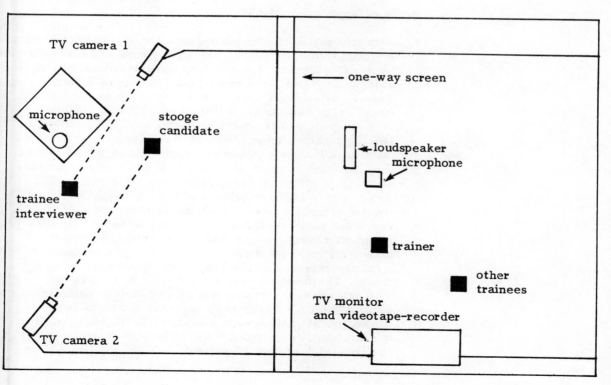

trainers take people in groups which provides a source of role partners, but patients may need individual sessions as well for individual problems.

Other methods of training

*   Training on the job: this is a widely used traditional method. Some people improve through experience but others do not, and some learn the wrong things. The situation can be improved if there is a trainer who regularly sees the trainee in action, and is able to hold feedback sessions at which errors are pointed out and better skills suggested. In practice this method does not appear to work very well, for example with trainee teachers (see Argyle, 1969).
*   Group methods: these, especially T-groups (T standing for training), are intended to enhance sensitivity and social skills. Follow-up studies have consistently found that 30-40 per cent of trainees are improved by group methods, but up to 10 per cent are worse, sometimes needing psychological assistance (e.g. Lieberman, Yalom and Miles, 1973). It has been argued that group methods are useful for those who are resistant to being trained.
*   Educational methods: these, such as lectures and films, can increase knowledge, but to master social skills it is necessary to try them out, as is the case with motor skills. Educational methods can be a useful supplement to role-playing methods.

Areas of application of SST

*   Neurotic patients: role-playing and the more specialized methods described above have been found to be slightly more effective than psychotherapy, desensitization, or other alternative treatments, but not much (Trower, Bryant and Argyle, 1978). Only one study so far has found really substantial differences: Maxwell (1976), in a study of adults reporting social difficulties and seeking treatment for them, in New Zealand, insisted on homework between training sessions. However, SST does produce more improvement in social skills and reduction of social anxiety. A few patients can be cured by SST alone, but most have other problems as well, and may require other forms of treatment in addition.
*   Psychotic patients: these have been treated in the USA by assertiveness training and other forms of role-playing. Follow-up studies have shown greater improvement in social behaviour than from alternative treatments. The most striking results have been obtained with intensive clinical studies of one to four patients, using a 'multiple baseline' design: one symptom is worked on at a time over a total of 20-30 sessions. It is not clear from these follow-up studies to what extent the general condition of patients has been improved, or

how well they have been able to function outside the hospital (Hersen and Bellack, 1976). It has been argued by one practitioner that SST is more suitable than psychotherapy for working-class patients in view of their poor verbal skills (Goldstein, 1973).

Other therapeutic uses of SST

*   Alcoholics: alcoholics have been given SST to improve their assertiveness, for example in refusing drinks, and to enable them to deal better with situations which they find stressful and make them drink. Similar treatment has been given to drug addicts. In both cases treatment has been fairly successful, though the effects have not always been long-lasting; SST is often included in more comprehensive packages.
*   Delinquents and prisoners: these have often been given SST with some success, especially in the case of aggressive and sex offenders. SST can also increase their degree of internal control.
*   Teachers, managers, doctors, etc.: SST is increasingly being included in the training of those whose work involves dealing with people. The most extensive application so far has been in the training of teachers by 'micro-teaching'. They are instructed in one of the component skills of teaching, such as the use of different kinds of question, explanation or the use of examples; they then teach five or six children for 10-15 minutes, followed by a feedback session and 're-teaching'. Follow-up studies show that this is far more effective than a similar amount of teaching practice, and it is much more effective in eradicating bad habits (Brown, 1975). In addition to role-playing, more elaborate forms of simulation are used, for example to train people for administrative positions. Training on the job is a valuable addition or alternative, provided that trainers really do their job.
*   Normal adults: students have received a certain amount of SST, especially in North American universities, and follow-up studies have shown that they can be successfully trained in assertiveness (Rich and Schroeder, 1976), dating behaviour (Curran, 1977), and to reduce anxiety at performing in public (Paul, 1966). Although many normal adults apart from students have social behaviour difficulties, very little training is available unless they seek psychiatric help. It would be very desirable for SST to be more widely available, for example in community centres.
*   Schoolchildren: a number of attempts have been made to introduce SST into schools, though there are no follow-up studies on its effectiveness. However, there have been a number of successful follow-up studies of training schemes for children who are withdrawn and unpopular or aggressive, using the usual role-playing methods (Rinn and Markle, 1979).

Conclusion

In this chapter we have given an account of those aspects of social psychology which are most relevant to the work of teachers, social workers and others, both in understanding the behaviour of their clients and also in helping them with their own performance. We have used various models of social behaviour, such as the social skills model and the model of social behaviour as a game. Some of the phenomena described cannot be fully accounted for in terms of these models: for example, the design of sequences of interaction. A number of practical implications have been described; in particular, discussion of the skills which have been demonstrated to be the most effective in a number of situations, and the methods of SST which have been found to have most impact. I should be emphasized that much of this research is quite new and it is expected that a great deal more will be found out on these topics in the years to come.

References

Argyle, M. (1969)
Social Interaction. London: Methuen.

Argyle, M. (1972)
The Social Psychology of Work. London: Allen Lane and Penguin Books.

Argyle, M. (1975)
Bodily Communication. London: Methuen.

Argyle, M. and Cook, M. (1976)
Gaze and Mutual Gaze. London: Cambridge University Press.

Argyle, M., Furnham, A. and Graham, J.A. (1981)
Social situations. London: Cambridge University Press.

Argyle, M. and Kendon, A. (1967)
The experimental analysis of social performance. In L. Berkowitz (ed.), Advances in Experimental Social Psychology, Volume 3. New York: Academic Press.

Argyle, M., Salter V., Nicholson, H., Williams, M. and Burgess, P. (1970)
The communication of inferior and superior attitudes by verbal and non-verbal signals. British Journal of Social and Clinical Psychology, 9, 221-231.

Bailey, K.G. and Sowder, W.T. (1970)
Audiotape and videotape self-confrontation in psychotherapy. Psychological Bulletin, 74, 127-137.

Bales, R.F. (1950)
Interaction Process Analysis. Cambridge, Mass.: Addison-Wesley.

Brown, G.A. (1975)
Microteaching. London: Methuen.

Curran, J.P. (1977)
Skills training as an approach to the treatment of heterosexual-social anxiety. Psychological Bulletin, 84, 140-157.

Davitz, J.R. (1964)
The Communication of Emotional Meaning. New York: McGraw-Hill.

Dion, K., Berscheid, E. and Walster, E. (1972)
What is beautiful is good. Journal of Personality and
Social Psychology, 24, 285-290.

Flavell, J.H. (1968)
The Development of Role-taking and Communication Skills
in Children. New York: Wiley.

Goldstein, A.J. (1973)
Structured Learning Therapy: Toward a psychotherapy for
the poor. New York: Academic Press.

Harré, R. and Secord, P. (1972)
The Explanation of Social Behaviour. Oxford: Blackwell.

Hersen, M. and Bellack, A.S. (1976)
Social skills training for chronic psychiatric patients:
rationale, research findings, and future directions.
Comprehensive Psychiatry, 17, 559-580.

Jennings, H.H. (1950)
Leadership and Isolation. New York: Longmans Green.

Jones, E.E. and Nisbett, R.E. (1972)
The actor and the observer: divergent perceptions of the
causes of behavior. In E.E. Jones, D. Kanouse, H.
Kelley, R.E. Nisbett, S. Valins and B. Weiner (eds),
Attribution: Perceiving the causes of behavior.
Morristown, NJ: General Learning Press.

Jourard, S.M. (1971)
Self Disclosure. New York: Wiley Interscience.

Lieberman, M.A., Yalom, I.D. and Miles, M.R. (1973)
Encounter Groups: First facts. New York: Basic Books.

Lott, A.J. and Lott, B.E. (1960)
The formation of positive attitudes towards group
members. Journal of Abnormal and Social Psychology, 61,
297-300.

Maxwell, G.M. (1976)
An evolution of social skills training. (Unpublished,
University of Otago, Dunedin, New Zealand.)

Mehrabian, A. (1972)
Nonverbal Communication. New York: Aldine-Atherton.

Meldman, M.J. (1967)
Verbal behaviour analysis of self-hyperattentionism.
Diseases of the Nervous System, 28, 469-473.

Paul, G.L. (1966)
Insight v. Desensitization in Psychotherapy. Stanford,
Ca: Stanford University Press.

Rich, A.R. and Schroeder, H.E. (1976)
Research issues in assertiveness training. Psychological
Bulletin, 83, 1081-1096.

Rinn, R.C. and Markle, A. (1979)
Modification of social skill deficits in children. In
A.S. Bellack and M. Hersen (eds), Research and Practice
in Social Skills Training. New York: Plenum.

**Sherif, M., Harvey, O.J., White, B.J., Hood, W.R. and
Sherif, C.** (1961)
Intergroup Conflict and Cooperation: The Robbers' Cave
experiment. Norman, Oklahoma: The University of Oklahoma
Book Exchange.

Trower, P., Bryant, B. and Argyle, M. (1978)
Social Skills and Mental Health. London: Methuen.
Walster, E., Aronson, E., Abrahams, D. and Rottmann, L.
(1966)
Importance of physical attractiveness in dating
behavior. Journal of Personality and Social Psychology,
5, 508-516.

Questions

1. Is it useful to look at social behaviour as a kind of skill?
2. What do bad conversationalists do wrong?
3. What information is conveyed by non-verbal communication, and in what ways do non-verbal signals supplement verbal ones?
4. How is the perception of other people different from the perception of other physical objects?
5. What information about a social situation would a newcomer to it need to know?
6. Do we like other people primarily because they are rewarding?
7. Why do some people have difficulty in making friends?
8. What criticisms have been made of experiments in social psychology? What other methods are available?
9. Does social behaviour take the same form in other cultures?
10. Are there fundamental differences between social behaviour in families, work-groups and groups of friends?

Annotated reading

Argyle, M. (1978) The Psychology of Interpersonal Behaviour
(3rd edn). Harmondsworth: Penguin.
Covers the field of the chapter, and related topics at
Penguin level.

Argyle, M. and Trower, P. (1979). Person to Person. London
Harper & Row.
A more popular account of the area covered by the
chapter, with numerous coloured illustrations.

Argyle, M. (1975). Bodily Communication. London: Methuen.
Covers the field of non-verbal communication in more
detail, with some illustrations.

Berscheid, E. and Walster, E.H. (1978). Interpersonal
Attraction (2nd edn). Reading, Mass.: Addison-Wesley.
A very readable account of research in this area.

Bower, S.A. and Bower, G.H. (1976). Asserting Yourself.
Reading, Mass.: Addison-Wesley.
An interesting and practical book about assertiveness,
with examples and exercises.

Cook, M. (1979). Perceiving Others. London: Methuen.
A clear account of basic processes in person perception.

Goffman, E. (1956). The Presentation of Self in Everyday Life. Edinburgh: Edinburgh University Press.
A famous and highly entertaining account of self-presentation.

Trower, P., Bryant, B. and Argyle, M. (1978). Social Skills and Mental Health. London: Methuen.
An account of social skills training with neurotics, with full details of procedures.

Chapter 10

Interviewing: the social psychology of the inter-view

Robert Farr

Interviewing is an everyday social phenomenon as well as being a widely used technique for gathering data both in professional practice and in social research. It is essentially a technique or method for establishing or discovering that there are perspectives or viewpoints on events other than those of the person initiating the interview. Those who work professionally in the media are accustomed to conducting interviews in the course of a day's work. Many thousands more listen to, view, or read about these self-same interviews. The interview is thus a common event, though many participate only vicariously in such encounters.

An interview is a social encounter between two or more individuals with words as the main medium of exchange. It is, in short, a peculiar form of conversation in which the ritual of turn-taking is more formalized than in the commoner and more informal encounters of everyday life. A conversation or interview is a co-operative venture. Despite the common assumptions that make conversations or talks possible, the interface between the individuals involved is always potentially present. When talks break down or conversation proves difficult this highlights the interface which is always potentially present within the inter-view. Conversations are embryonic interviews even though the participants might not so conceive of them. This general approach is compatible with the viewpoint adopted by Gorden (1975): 'I consider as an interviewer any person who uses conversation as a means of obtaining information from another person.'

The distinctive approach of this chapter

This chapter is intended to be an introduction to the social psychology of the inter-view. As such, it is a modest contribution to the development of a theory appropriate to the practice and conduct of interviews. There is, at present, no adequate theory in psychology of direct relevance to the practice of interviewing. This may surprise the reader. There is much advice offered and many guides are to be found in the literature as to how best to conduct interviews. There is also much research relevant to certain aspects of the interview, such as research in cognitive psychology on how we perceive persons (inspired by Heider's seminal work) and purely behavioural research on various aspects of non-verbal communication, etc. There is, however, no overall framework within which these theoretically opposed areas of research could be integrated with one another and made relevant to the practice of interviewing. We need theory in order to understand what goes on in the interview situation.

Any purely psychological theory is likely to be inadequate as the interview is so obviously a social encounter. Any adequate social psychology of the interview must enable us to account for the actions and experience both of the person being interviewed and of the person conducting the interview. Any theory of the interview which was not also at one and the same time a theory of the human self would be inadequate to the task in hand. Any theory which failed to account for states of awareness or consciousness in the parties to the interaction would similarly be inappropriate. We have sought to keep salient the inherently social nature of the interview by the simple expedient of using a hyphen: that is, by talking about inter-views rather than interviews, and similarly, inter-face and inter-action.

In devising an appropriate theory for the understanding of the interview we have drawn on Heider's psychology of interpersonal relations; on Goffman's work in sociology on the presentation of self in everyday life; on the work of Freud, in psychiatry, in devising a psychology based on listening rather than one based exclusively on visual observation; and on the philosophy of George Herbert Mead. While the influences derive from a number of disciplines the theory is an explicitly social psychological one. We have also found it convenient to adopt and adapt the divergence in perspective between actors and observers first noted by Jones and Nisbett in 1971. We have been impressed by the advantages which Becker and Geer (1957) claim for participant observation as a methodology over an exclusive reliance upon the interview alone. We have sought to include in this approach to the inter-view some of the advantages which Becker and Geer claim for participant observation. In our approach to the inter-view we are, therefore, influenced by the experience of social anthropologists and of sociologists.

The psychology of inter-personal relations

There is much that psychologists can learn from a study of the social psychology of everyday life. This is the viewpoint taken by the psychologist Fritz Heider (1958). He was particularly interested in how we perceive other persons and the evidence we use when we make inferences as to what is going on in the minds of those with whom we inter-act. He referred to the perceiver as P and the person whom he observes as O (i.e. the 'other'). The man-in-the-street does not hesitate to infer the attitudes, hopes, fears, motives, opinions, intentions, etc., of those with whom he inter-acts. Indeed, he is only intermittently aware that most of what he 'knows' about others is highly conjectural. The professional psychologist, however, is more acutely aware of the extent to which our knowledge of the minds of others involves our going beyond the information available; that is, it is based on inference rather than strictly on observation. We cannot directly 'observe' another's motives, intentions, aspirations, attitudes, and so on.

Heider's psychology of inter-personal relations is highly relevant to the inter-view situation. While Man is seldom aware that most of his knowledge of others is based on conjecture, he is sometimes acutely aware that what others know about him is highly conjectural. This is particularly true in the inter-view situation. The persons being interviewed (i.e. the interviewees) are only too well aware that the other (i.e. the interviewer) is likely to be making inferences concerning their motives, intentions, etc., on the basis of what they say and do in the interview.

Heider was primarily concerned with how P perceives O. In common with many other psychologists Heider's primary interest was in what we can learn about others by observing them from the outside. O, however, need not remain silent in the presence of P. O can talk about, or 'reveal', opinions, attitudes, aspirations, motives, hopes, fears and so on. The interview is the technique par excellence for eliciting such self-reports. When O speaks, a perspective other than that of P is revealed. P and O engage in conversation while the unique perspective of each is retained. This difference in perspective between them helps to produce an inter-view in the literal sense of that term.

An interview is also a form of social encounter between persons. Heider set out to devise a psychology of inter-personal relations. It is worth reflecting briefly on what we understand by the word 'person'. The philosopher Strawson considered it to be a characteristic of persons that they can monitor their own actions and give an 'account' of them (see Harré and Secord, 1972). We are accustomed in everyday life to accounting for our actions. Persons have names. When we know people's names we can address them as individuals rather than needing to hail them as strangers. They are 'accountable' and normally 'respond' when others address them. In the technical literature relating to the interview as a research tool in social science, the person being interviewed is normally referred to as the 'respondent'. Persons readily respond to being inter viewed because it is a constituent part of their everyday social experience. It is not an alien or obtrusive mode of investigation.

The divergence in perspective between actors and observers

Heider introduced us to the perspective of P, the observer or perceiver. An actor is any person whose behaviour is currently the focus of attention. In the language of drama which suffuses the writing of Goffman, the actor is the person who is currently 'on stage'. Jones and Nisbett (1971) note an important divergence in perspective between actors and observers: 'There is a pervasive tendency for actors to attribute their actions to situational requirements, whereas observers tend to attribute the same actions to stable personal dispositions' (Jones and Nisbett, 1971). Actors are more likely to consider their actions to be situationally appropriate whilst observers are more likely to make inferences about the sort of person an actor is on the basis of observable actions.

The awareness of actors that they are objects in the social worlds of others leads them to become 'apprehensive' as to how those others might evaluate them. The actors are here clearly aware of the divergence in perspective between themselves and the observing others. Too acute an awareness of this may cause an inter-viewee to perform poorly. For the chronically shy this is likely to be a particular problem. A certain measure of self-confidence is necessary if a person is to create a favourable impression in the inter-view situation. In his description of the art of impression management, Goffman (1959) makes telling use of the metaphor of the theatre. In his everyday presentation of himself, Man as an actor is putting on a 'performance' for a particular audience. The audience may be the 'other' with whom he is inter-acting. This obviously is the case in the typical inter-view. Goffman describes action in terms of its relation to the observing and listening other: that is, his conception of the audience is critical to his portrayal of action. This is why he is so much more genuinely sociopsychological in his approach than any mere psychologist could be. This is an important contribution to an understanding of the dynamics of the inter-view.

Goffman notes that the mirror is one of the most useful devices to be found backstage in any theatre. The mirror enables an actor to become an object to himself before he goes 'on stage' and becomes an object to others. In preparing for inter-views candidates often find mirrors to be similarly useful. The work of Goffman beautifully illustrates why a theory of the human self is necessary in order to understand what occurs in the inter-view. We also believe that an adequate analysis of the nature of human consciousness is an essential ingredient in any theory which purports to shed significant light on what occurs in the course of an inter-view. Mead's theory of action provides us with the necessary theory both of human consciousness and of the human self.

We have drawn on the work of Goffman for an account of human action and for his portrayal of Man as agent or actor; and on the work of Heider for his delineation of the perspective of Man as an observer of others. We are indebted to Jones and Nisbett for suggesting that these two perspectives might be different. It is worth considering how we might apply their distinction to accounting for differing views of the same actions. In a series of experimental studies, Milgram (1974) obtained high levels of obedience to an experimental request to administer what the subject believed to be high levels of electric shock to a fellow subject. Those who complied with the experimental request regarded their actions as being entirely appropriate in the particular experimental setting in which they occurred. This is the perspective of Jones and Nisbett's 'actor'.

The majority of subjects in Milgram's experiment would reject the inference which any who observed their acts of obedience might have made about them as persons on the basis of their actions. That this is so is revealed in an interesting variation on his main theme which Milgram later introduced. He described his experiment to a number of subjects whom he then invited to respond by saying how they would act in this situation. This is more akin to the hypothetical questions which persons being inter-viewed are often invited to consider. Indeed, this particular study was an inter-view rather than being an experiment in any strict sense of the term. The actual task in the original experiment involved increasing the level of shock administered, by way of punishment, to a subject in a learning task each time he made a mistake. Few subjects in this hypothetical situation saw themselves as advancing much beyond the earlier low levels of shock on the generator. It was almost as if there were different 'selves' for each button on the shock generator. In considering how they would act, subjects were able to reject the selves corresponding to the buttons at the 'high shock' end of the generator. They were thus able to consider what they would think of themselves if they were to press each of these buttons. This 'pause for reflection' enabled subjects to adopt the perspective of being an observer of their own hypothetical actions. They were thus able to inter-act with themselves. This is a process which the philosopher, G. H. Mead, called thinking.

In the analysis of Jones and Nisbett, actor and observer are two different persons. The actual face-to-face encounter of the inter-view, however, produces social states of awareness which are infinitely more complex and subtle than those envisaged by Jones and Nisbett. These more complex states of awareness arise because each of the interactants in an inter-view is both an actor and an observer and each is capable of alternating between these two perspectives.

The demise of the interview as a way of assessing persons and the rise of the psychological test: a brief historical note

Humans are liable to 'react' to the knowledge that their actions are being observed. If the very act of investigating behaviour alters what is there to be observed, then the techniques of investigation used can be described as 'reactive' (Webb, Campbell, Schwartz and Sechrest, 1966). The interview is clearly a highly 'reactive' way of appraising people. The inter-view, as proposed in this chapter, is even more explicitly 'reactive' than the commoner and more conventional varieties of the same species. Psychologists, early in the history of their discipline, rejected the interview as a valid way of assessing either the intelligence of children or the suitability of adults for jobs. At the time this rejection was hailed as an important scientific advance. It is worth briefly considering why this was so.

The amount of information potentially present in the face-to-face encounter of an interview is liable to over-whelm even the most experienced of interviewers. Different interviewers sample from the available evidence differently. They use and combine the information they do select in highly impressionistic or subjective ways. Psychologists were quick to prove their worth by reducing the amount of 'noise' (i.e. irrelevant information) present in the appraisal setting. Rather than ranging over the whole gamut of information potentially available they instead preferred to 'tune in' to information transmitted on much narrower wavebands. This information could be collected under quite rigorously controlled conditions. The psychological test yielded much more precise information and this information could be combined objectively in ways which research had demonstrated to be valid. This is how the psychological test – or rather a battery of such tests – came to supersede the interview as the preferred way of assessing persons.

It is worth briefly noting certain aspects of this early critique of the interview. The origins of the doubts which still linger on in the minds of psychologists concerning the validity of the interview can be found in the very success of this early critique. This is one reason why psychologists so far have done so little to improve the interview as a method of investigation. Eysenck (1953) presents a convenient account:

> One of the earliest investigations of the interview is reported by Binet, the creator of modern intelligence tests. Three teachers interviewed the same children and estimated the intelligence of each. These estimates were based on the results of an interview conducted by each teacher as he saw fit. Binet reports two outcomes of this experiment which have since been verified over and over again. Each interviewer was confident that his judgement was right. Each interviewer disagreed almost completely with the judgement of the other interviewers.

This was the kind of evidence which highlighted, at an early stage, the unreliability of the interview as an appraisal device. The failure amongst interviewers to agree in their judgements led to the development of standardized tests. Here psychologists were quite consciously adopting a scientific perspective: that of being the detached observer of others. In commenting on the significance of Binet's first conclusion concerning the confidence with which each interviewer held his judgement, Eysenck notes that this 'explains why, in spite of all the factual information regarding its inadequacy, the interview has remained the firm favourite of most people who have to select personnel for industrial and other purposes' (Eysenck, 1953). Here interviewers are behaving like Jones and Nisbett's 'actors':

that is, they see their actions as being situationally appropriate. Eysenck neatly captures the difference in perspective noted above between the 'actor' (i.e. the interviewer as agent) and the 'observer' (i.e. the scientist who 'validates' the predictive accuracy of the interviewer's judgements).

Interviewers, naturally, feel that their actions are justifiable and so seek to maintain their autonomy even in the face of scientific evidence:

> Time and time again does one encounter the individual who admits all the evidence about the inadequacy of the interview but stoutly maintains that he or she is the one outstanding exception to this general rule, and that his or her opinions are almost invariably correct. (Needless to say, experimental studies of such individuals fail to disclose any greater ability to forecast success and failure among them than is found among other people) (Eysenck, 1953).

This very human tendency to consider oneself to be an exception may derive from the unique perspective of the 'actor'. Kay (1971) has noted a similar tendency with respect to the occurrence of accidents. Individuals find it difficult to conceive of themselves as having an accident. However, scientists, as observers of others, can afford from the greater distance of their own quite different perspectives to be more sceptical. From this perspective, accidents do not just 'happen': they are caused.

The early pioneers of psychological tests who so readily dismissed the interview as a valid way of assessing people were bewitched by the magic of measurement. Their perspective was that of being a scientific observer of others. Their basic strategy was to standardize the conditions under which they made their observations and then to attribute all of the variance in observed performance to the existence of individual differences. In so doing, they unwittingly adopted the perspective of Jones and Nisbett's 'observer': that is, on the basis of test scores they inferred the existence of 'traits', 'abilities', 'attitudes', etc., as relatively permanent dispositions in those whom they observed or tested.

The social antecedents of mind and self: the philosophy of G. H. Mead

Our sense of our own 'selfhood' has its origin in the experience of interacting with others within the framework of a shared culture and of a common language. This was the viewpoint of the American philosopher, G. H. Mead, who developed a form of social behaviourism at Chicago in the opening decades of the present century (Mead, 1934). Mead understood the symbolic nature of language and its key role in the development and creation of 'mind' in Man.

The model of Man which emerges from the writings of Mead is one of Man as being both speaker and listener. The social behaviourism of Mead is thus more directly relevant to an understanding of the dynamics of inter-viewing than are any of the forms of behaviourism which developed within psychology. Our own approach in this chapter to the dynamics of inter-viewing is much influenced by the work of Mead. Man, according to Mead, is self-reflexive; that is, he is self-aware as distinct from being merely conscious..Consciousness is something which Man shares with other species. Self-consciousness is a distinctly human state of mind. Man is unique as a species in that he can act towards himself as an object. He can do so because he is an object in the social world of those others with whom he interacts. By 'assuming the role of the other' (Mead) with respect to himself, he becomes an 'other' to himself. Man can thus engage himself in inter-action. When he does so we refer to this activity as thinking. Thinking, for Mead, was a kind of internalized dialogue between 'I' and various 'me's. We have already noted above how some of the subjects in Milgram's experiment engaged in such internalized dialogues.

A theory of the human self is needed if we are to understand the dynamics of the inter-view. The meaning of an act for Mead was to be found in the response which it elicits from observing others. Man not only acts but also re-acts to his own actions. He reacts to his own behaviour on the basis of the actual or anticipated reactions of others.

These processes of action and of reaction are highly characteristic of what happens in the course of an interview. Individuals will often anticipate in imagination a formal interview, in the outcome of which they have a personal stake. They may rehearse what they intend to say and do and they may anticipate likely questions which might be asked. After the event they are also likely to 're-enact' what actually occurred in the course of the interview. Sometimes these re-enactments are purely 'private' ones which they carry out solely for their own benefit. Sometimes they are more explicitly social in that they are 'accounts' which the individual provides for others as to what occurred in the course of the interview. Without an adequate theory of the human self the psychologist could not possibly give a coherent account of these important mental events which both precede and follow the interview proper. These fairly familiar experiences can be accounted for, given a theory of the inherently social nature of the mind of Man. Mead provides just such a theory.

Mead developed a purely behavioural account of the origins of mind in Man: a theory of the human self. He also shed important new light on the social nature of 'perspectives'. As children develop, according to Mead, they learn to 'assume the role of the other' with respect to themselves. These social skills are first acquired in role-playing and are then further developed in the playing of games. Commercial transactions, such as those which were of interest to Adam Smith, depend for their success on the reciprocal ability of buyer and seller to assume each other's role. Those who excel in interviewing, either as interviewers or as interviewees, are adept at assuming each other's role in the interview situation.

In his later writings, Mead was much influenced by Einstein. He preferred to talk of 'assuming the perspective' of the other instead of his earlier preference for 'assuming the role' of the other. For Mead these 'perspectives' were objectively real: that is, they represented points in space/ time from which one could view events. It was, therefore, entirely possible to change one's perspective by the simple expedient of changing one's position in space/time. It is thus possible both literally and metaphorically to 'turn the tables' and for interviewers and interviewees to 'exchange places'. Successful interviewees already do this mentally in preparing themselves for an interview. Poor interviewers may experience much difficulty in imagining such an exchange of roles or places. Role-playing exercises and the techniques of self-confrontation (e.g. where interviewers watch a videotape of themselves actually conducting an interview) are now increasingly used in the training of interviewers. If the theoretical approach developed in the present chapter is a sound one then such training devices are well-founded.

Observing, questioning and listening: interpreting what we see and hear

Goffman belonged to that important tradition of social psychological thought at Chicago which drew at least some of its inspiration from the work of Mead. In referring to the social interactions of everyday life, Goffman had this to say: 'Many crucial facts lie beyond the time and place of interaction, or lie concealed within it' (1959). This is particularly true of the interview. One fails to grasp the significance of what is happening in an interview if one's attention is confined, in the interest of science, only to what can be directly observed from the outside.

Psychologists, when they accepted behaviourism, came to value what they could see and measure over what they could hear. It was only too easy to overlook the signifi- cance of something as invisible to the human eye as speech. In their attempts to make psychology a branch of natural science, the early pioneers stressed the physical rather than the symbolic nature of stimuli. Speech was thought of in terms of sound waves: as changes in the patterns of energy impinging on the human ear. The outcome of collabor- ation between psychologists and telecommunications engineers was the development within psychology of information theory as a specialism. To reduce language to 'information' as the human engineer uses that term is to destroy something distinctly human. In order properly to appreciate the significance of speech in human development it would first have been necessary to understand the symbolic nature of language. Only a philosopher like Mead would be likely to ask such a preliminary question.

If, instead of observing the actions of others one listens to them talking, one arrives at a totally different type of psychology. Freud established a whole new psychology based entirely upon listening. It is called psychoanalysis. As a theory about human behaviour, psychoanalysis was born and developed within the context of the clinical interview. Rather than visually exploring the natural world as a research physiologist, which was Freud's early training, he became instead, reluctantly, a practising clinician. He spent hours listening to his clients talking about themselves and their problems.

The difference in perspective between speaker and listener in Freud's consulting room gave birth to a psychology of the unconsciousness. There were aspects of the analysand's 'account' of his own actions which were more apparent to the listener than to the speaker. Listener and speaker were here two separate persons. Speakers are less likely to be aware of the non-verbal aspects of their own accounts than listeners. 'Actors' generally are unaware of their own non-verbal behaviour. Non-verbal cues are more salient to the observers/listeners than they are to the actors themselves. The study of non-verbal behaviour is a significant contribution to an understanding of the interview which flows from the perspective of the behaviourist as an observer of others. Behaviourists tend to note or record this behaviour rather than to 'interpret' it. It is worth quoting Freud (1905) on this issue:

> When I set myself the task of bringing to light what human beings keep hidden within them, not by the compelling power of hypnosis, but by observing what they say and what they show I thought the task was a harder one than it really is. He that has eyes to see and ears to hear may convince himself that no mortal can keep a secret. If the lips are silent, he chatters with his finger tips; betrayal oozes out of him at every pore. And thus the task of making conscious the most hidden recesses of the mind is one which it is quite possible to accomplish.

The difference in perspective between analyst and analysand (i.e. the person undergoing analysis) may have important therapeutic implications. It corresponds to the difference in perspective between actors and observers previously noted. In seeking therapy the analysand might consider himself to be the victim of circumstances; for instance, as being, like King Lear, 'more sinned against than sinning'. The therapist, however, may not accept this 'account'. Therapists usually make the opposite attributional assumption: that is, they see the analysand as being the cause of their own problems. It is possible to consider psychoanalysis as a protracted negotiation of the analysand's original account by two persons who initially make opposite attributional assumptions.

Psychoanalysis, however, is not held in high esteem within scientific circles. As a science based on listening rather than one founded on observation, it is highly marginal within the context of natural science. It is, at one and the same time, both an odd kind of psychology and an odd kind of medicine. Its oddity in both respects may reflect, in part, a strong preference for vision over hearing as the preferred modality of research in both psychology and medicine.

Within psychology, behaviourists sought to make their discipline a branch of natural science by concentrating on what they could observe rather than by striving to understand what they could hear. Watson and Skinner typify this general strategy while Freud remains a striking, but solitary, example of someone who chose the latter alternative. There could scarcely be a more marked contrast than the one between behaviourism and psychoanalysis. This contrast is further mirrored in the differences between behaviour therapy and psychotherapy. In the former one 'treats' people, whilst in the latter one interviews them. In the former one removes 'symptoms', whilst in the latter one 'interprets' them.

The question of interpretation is an important one for the professional interviewer. Freud, in his early clinical interviews, listened to his clients relating how, as young girls, they had been seduced by their own fathers. He was inclined, at first, to believe in the truth of these accounts. When the number of such incidents, of which he had heard tell, came to greatly exceed his own prior expectations concerning the likelihood of such events occurring in Viennese society, he dramatically changed his interpretation of these 'accounts'. His decision to interpret these accounts as fantasy rather than as reflecting reality had dramatic consequences for the subsequent development of psychoanalysis. He was forced to distinguish between fantasy and reality and to oppose the pleasure to the reality principle. This was how he resolved his obligations as an interviewer to indicate the level of reality to which his observations referred.

There are two opposing dangers which threaten to ensnare the unwary social scientist. The first is to believe that he does not need to ask questions in order to establish the veracity of what he can observe for himself. The asking of questions helps to establish the existence of perspectives other than that of the investigator who has initiated the study. This leads to the establishment of an inter-view. There are a number of professional groups whose work directly involves them in observing and recording behaviour, yet who only rarely conduct interviews in the conventional sense of the term, such as nurses and classroom teachers. The written reports of these professional groups, summarizing their observations of behaviour on the wards or in the classroom, are often included as background information on the basis of which others, elsewhere in the organization, conduct clinical or educational interviews. However, persons in the higher reaches of these professions (nursing and teaching) almost certainly spend a great deal of their time interviewing in the more conventional sense of the term. This is probably true of almost anyone in a position of managerial responsibility. When a nurse on the ward, or a teacher in the classroom, asks questions in order to clarify or to verify what they observe, they are engaging in the process of inter-viewing as that term is used in this chapter. This is also true of the manager or supervisor in industry. The process of inter-viewing as outlined·here is just such a process of checking on the veracity of one's observations. It is, therefore, a wider process of research than the interview as conventionally conceived. Failure to supplement and verify what one can observe by the asking of questions results in one type of error: that is, the limitations and biasses inherent in one's perspective as an observer are not subject to any process of cross-checking and hence one remains blind to them. A different sort of error arises if one accepts at face value the 'accounts' one elicits. In relation to the work of Herzlich on people's conceptions of health and illness (Herzlich, 1973) and of Herzberg on the nature of work motivation, Farr has identified some of the consequences that can flow from a too uncritical acceptance of what people say in the course of an unstructured or semi-structured research interview (Farr, 1977a,b).

Harré and Secord (1972) advocate the collection of 'accounts' as a brave new methodology for research in psychology. They base their case on Strawson's criterion of a person as being someone who can monitor his own behaviour and give an account of it. Collecting 'accounts' is thus equivalent to treating people as people. 'In order to be able to treat people as if they were human beings it must be possible to accept their commentaries upon their actions as authentic, though revisable, reports of phenomena, subject to empirical criticism' (Harre and Secord, 1972). If their plea were heeded then the interview would become the privileged mode of research in psychology, much as the experiment has been in the past and is still currently. The inter-view, as outlined here, might be more defensible from a scientific point of view, as it highlights the fact that the perspectives of researcher and informant are different and so sensitizes one to the possibility that important consequences might flow from this divergence in perspective.

Harré and Secord's proposal is not a particularly revolutionary one. Social psychologists traditionally have relied upon the collection of just such self-reports. This reflects the influence of Gestalt psychologists on the historical development of social psychology. Gestalt psychologists were interested in the study of perception. In order to explain a person's behaviour it was first necessary, in the opinion of Gestalt psychologists, to understand how that person perceived the world. The best way of finding out about a person's unique perspective, of course, is to invite him to tell you about it. You can best establish that his perspective is different from your own by means of an inter-view. Behaviourists, by directly relating aspects of the physical environment to observable responses, had completely by-passed perception as an important field of study.

In the study of attitudes the 'view of the world' approach which stems from Gestalt psychology came to prevail over the 'consistency of response' approach associated with behaviourism (see Campbell, 1963). To date, in the history of psychology, either the one or the other of these two perspectives has prevailed. How to inter-relate two such contrasting perspectives is perhaps the most interesting single problem which psychologists now face. By studying attitudes, social psychologists had hoped to avoid the laborious task of noting consistencies in a person's res-ponse to his social environment. The relationships between what people say and what they do turn out to be rather tenuous. These findings continue to pose problems for the social psychologist (see Deutscher, 1973). They also pose problems for the professional interviewer. Can one accept at face value what people say? Or does one have to 'interpret' what they tell you? Can one accept oral accounts obtained in interviews as a basis for predicting behaviour in con-texts other that that of the interview? Can a knowledge of a person's 'attitudes' help us to predict his behaviour?

Harré and Secord contend that one does not have to accept 'accounts' at face value. They can be 'negotiated'. Here the inter-face within the inter-view enables one to question the face validity of any particular account. The co-existence of more than one perspective helps to ensure that work gets done in the course of the inter-view. The perspec-tive of the interviewer is always different from that of the interviewee. This divergence in perspective is an adequate basis on which to negotiate. Work on inter-views needs to be integrated with work on inter-actions. We have noted above, more than once, how rarely an actor's view of his own actions corresponds to an observer's view of those same actions. Individuals may remain blissfully unaware of all that they communicate in the course of an interview. Goffma observed that impressions are 'given off' as well as 'man-aged'. One could view psychoanalytic theory as an elaborate set of rules for 'interpreting' the significance of a per-son's words and actions, especially those which occur in the course of therapy. Whilst most interviewers would agree with the truth of Goffman's observation, quoted earlier, that 'many crucial facts lie beyond the time and place of interaction, or lie concealed within it', few have need to draw on 'depth' psychologies such as psychoanalysis in order to interpret what they hear and observe. Good interviewers, however, listen not only to what persons choose to talk about but also to what they may not want to talk about or cannot say without help.

The recent explosion of research on non-verbal behaviour is of considerable relevance to the practice of interviewing (e.g. Weitz, 1974; Argyle, 1975; Ekman and Friesen, 1975).

It accurately reflects the perspective of the outside observer on the behaviour of others. Much of the classic literature on interviewing is highly 'cognitive' in tone and is
now rather dated (Cannell and Kahn, 1968). It tends to
reflect the perspective of the interviewer as 'actor': that
is, presenting the rationale for conducting interviews in
particular ways. Having to sample, in the writing of this
chapter, from two such separate, but unrelated, literatures
has not been an easy task. The fact that the two literatures
are unrelated testifies to the absence of a relevant theory
on the basis of which they might be integrated. Much recent
research of a purely behavioural nature (e.g. on non-verbal
aspects of social interaction), while highly relevant to
the practice of interviewing, has not yet been satisfac-
torily integrated into the literature on interviewing. We
would claim that this failure in integration reflects the
absence of an appropriate theory of the interview. It is
highly artificial, in practice, to distinguish between
inter-views and inter-actions. For the theory and practice
of inter-viewing it is necessary to understand both: hence
the priority we accord in this chapter to the development of
suitable theory. My approach to theory is a very Lewinian
one; there is nothing so practical as a good theory.

The model of the observer favoured in psychological
circles is that of the detached and objective scientist.
The role of psychologists in relation to selection is often
of this nature: they are usually to be found at several
removes from the face-to-face encounter between assessors
and candidates at the point of selection. There are, of
course, important exceptions such as Civil Service Selection
Boards, where psychologists are actively involved in conducting interviews. The model of the observer which pre-
vails more widely in social science is a more active one;
the researcher is often a participant observer. Becker and
Geer (1957), in what is now a classic paper, argue that
participant observation is a more complete method of research than the interview used alone: 'Participant observation can thus provide us with a yardstick against which to
measure the completeness of data gathered in other ways, a
model which can serve to let us know what orders of information escape us when we use other methods' (Becker and
Geer, 1957).

By participant observation Becker and Geer mean 'that
method in which the observer participates in the daily life
of the people under study, either openly in the role of
researcher or covertly in some disguised role, observing
things that happen, listening to what is said, and questioning people, over some length of time'. Inter-viewing as
outlined in this chapter is virtually synonymous with Becker
and Geer's characterization of participant observation.

This wider conception of the inter-view enables us to
encompass professional groups who rarely interview in the
conventional sense: for instance, classroom teachers,
nurses, supervisors in industry, etc. The skills involved in

participant observation are akin to those which a social anthropologist might employ. The seminal work of Goffman, which is highly relevant to an understanding of the dynamics of inter-viewing, is largely based on participant observation; for example, his studies of the under-life of mental institutions (Goffman, 1961) or his study of life in the Hebrides (Goffman, 1959). One can observe and ask questions about what one has observed. One can test out that one has correctly learnt the native language by trying it out in the presence of skilled users of that language. This is synonymous with the process of inter-viewing as outlined here.

We have previously noted the distinction which Jones and Nisbett make between the perspective of the actor and the perspective of the observer. Participant observation preserves both perspectives within the one methodology, as does inter-viewing. The observer is an actor in so far as he is also a participant in the scene he observes. In inter-viewing the participants alternate between the roles of actor and of observer, of speaker and of listener. Observers and inter-viewers, if they are to be effective, need to be conscious of their own actions and of the effects of these on those whom they are observing or interviewing. This awareness of being an 'object' in the social world of the 'other' is enhanced by the face-to-face nature of the inter-view situation. The mechanisms of gaze and mutual gaze help to maintain this duality of awareness in being both observer and observed (Argyle and Cook, 1976). This social psychology of the inter-view applies equally well both to inter-viewers and to inter-viewees.

It is easy to be aware of one's 'other-ness' when the person whom one is observing or inter-viewing comes from a different culture from one's own. This is the typical experience of the social anthropologist. Becker and Geer trenchantly note that persons within the one culture often inhabit different social worlds but that this is not always recognized. There is much merit, in their eyes, in approaching the social worlds of others in much the same way as a social anthropologist approaches a strange culture.

> In interviewing members of groups other than our own,
> then, we are in somewhat the same position as the
> anthropologist who must learn a primitive language, with
> the important difference that, as Ichheiser has put it,
> we often do not understand that we do not understand and
> are thus likely to make errors in interpreting what is
> said to us (Becker and Geer, 1957).

This inter-face is more explicitly recognized in the literature on participant observation than it is in the literature on interviewing. We have tried to introduce into the literature on interviewing some of the advantages of participant observation by choosing, on occasion, to distinguish between inter-viewing and interviewing.

Becker and Geer are critical of the interview 'when it is used as a source of information about events that have occurred elsewhere and are described to us by informants'. We noted above the problems Freud faced in regard to estimating the likely incidence of incest in Viennese society. Becker and Geer continue:

> In working with interviews, we must necessarily infer a great many things we could have observed had we only been in a position to do so. We add to the accuracy of our data when we substitute observable fact for inference. More important, we open the way for the discovery of new hypotheses for the fact we observe may not be the fact we expected to observe.

It may be that it is only through the process of interviewing that Man develops an awareness of the social world of others. It is only through Piaget's brilliant use of the inter-view that we are today as aware of just how different the world of the child is from the world of the adult (Farr, 1982). Adults often falsely assume, because they were children once themselves, that they therefore understand the world of a child. By the simple device of inter-viewing Piaget made quite explicit the many different ways in which the world of the child and the world of the adult failed to coincide. Thanks to Piaget, many teachers-in-training become sensitive to such differences before they encounter children face-to-face in the classroom.

Postscript on industrial psychology

A good deal is known in industrial psychology about the behaviour of candidates in selection contexts and the experience of assessors, for example, advice concerning how best to conduct interviews, etc. Here again, there is the same dichotomy between the perspective of the observer and the perspective of the 'actor'. The time is now ripe to redress this imbalance in our current knowledge by studying the behaviour of assessors and sampling the experience of candidates within selection contexts. Such additional information could significantly contribute to the emergence of a social psychology of selection which would be highly compatible with the dynamics of inter-viewing as outlined in this chapter. The recognition of the existence of more than one viewpoint or perspective is quite explicit in the notion of the inter-view. At present we know very little about the perspective of candidates within selection contexts.

The classic approach in selection is to collect standardized data about candidates by means of psychological tests, the results of which are then entered into a decision formula based on a regression analysis. The outcome is an 'institutional' decision. The candidate either is or is not offered a job. Such 'objective' test data could, however, be analysed in relation to the candidate's own response to the system either at the time of selection or subsequently on receiving a job offer. Are the inferences that candidates might make about their suitability for a particular job radically different from those which the organization might make concerning their suitability? This is a question which only research can resolve. We have presented evidence elsewhere on the possible use of self-appraisal within a selection context (Downs, Farr and Colebeck, 1978).

References

Argyle, M. (1975)
Bodily Communications. London: Methuen.

Argyle, M. and Cook, M. (1976)
Gaze and Mutual Gaze. Cambridge: Cambridge University Press.

Becker, H.S. and Geer, B. (1957)
Participant observation and interviewing: a comparison. Human Organization, 16, 28-32. Reprinted in G. McCall and J. Simmons (eds), Issues in Participant Observation: A text and readings. Reading, Mass.: Addison-Wesley.

Campbell, D.T. (1963)
Social attitudes and other acquired behavioral dispositions. In S. Koch (ed.), Psychology: A study of a science, Vol. 6. New York: McGraw-Hill.

Cannell, C.F. and Kahn, R.L. (1968)
Interviewing. In G. Lindzey and E. Aronson (eds), Handbook of Social Psychology, Vol. 2: Research methods (2nd edn). Reading, Mass: Addison-Wesley.

Deutscher, I. (1973)
What we say/What we do: Sentiments and acts. Glenview, Illinois: Scott, Foresman & Co.

Downs, S., Farr, R.M. and Colebeck, L. (1978)
Self-appraisal: A convergence of selection and guidance. Journal of Occupational Psychology, 51, 271-278.

Ekman, P. and Friesen, W.V. (1975)
Unmasking the Face: A guide to recognizing emotions from facial clues. Englewood Cliffs, NJ: Prentice-Hall.

Eysenck, H.J. (1953)
Uses and Abuses of Psychology. Harmondsworth: Penguin.

Farr, R.M. (1977a)
Heider, Harré and Herzlich on health and illness: some observations on the structure of 'representations collectives'. European Journal of Social Psychology, 7, 491-504.

Farr, R.M. (1977b)
On the nature of attributional artifacts in qualitative research: Herzberg's two-factor theory of work motivation. Journal of Occupational Psychology, 50, 3-14.

Farr, R.M. (1982)
Social worlds of childhood. In V. Greaney (ed.), The Rights of Children. New York: Irvington Publications.

Freud, S. (1905)
Fragments of an analysis of a case of hysteria. In The Standard Edition of the Complete Psychological Works of Sigmund Freud (1953), Volume 7. London: Hogarth Press.

Goffman, E. (1959)

The Presentation of Self in Everyday Life. New York: Doubleday.

Goffman. E. (1961)

Asylums: Essays on the social situations of mental patients and other inmates. New York: Anchor Books.

Gorden, R.L. (1975)

Interviewing: Strategy, techniques and tactics (revised edition). Homewood, Ill.: The Dorsey Press.

Harré, R. and Secord, P.F. (1972)

The Explanation of Social Behaviour. Oxford: Blackwell.

Heider, F. (1958)

The Psychology of Interpersonal Relations. New York: Wiley.

Herzlich, C. (1973)

Health and Illness: A social-psychological analysis. European Monographs in Social Psychology, No. 5. London: Academic Press.

Jones, E.E. and Nisbett, R.E. (1971)

The actor and the observer: divergent perspectives of the causes of behaviour. In E.E. Jones, D.E. Kanouse, H.H. Kelly, R.E. Nisbett, S. Valins and B. Weiner (eds), Attribution: Perceiving the causes of behaviour. Morristown, NJ: General Learning Press.

Kay, H. (1971)

Accidents: some facts and theories. In P.B. Warr (ed.), Psychology at Work. Harmondsworth: Penguin.

Mead, G.H. (1934)

Mind, Self and Society: From the standpoint of a social behaviorist. Edited and introduced by C.W. Morris. Chicago, Ill.: University of Chicago Press.

Milgram, S. (1974)

Obedience to Authority: An experimental view. London: Tavistock.

Weitz, S. (ed.) (1974)

Non-verbal Communication: Readings with commentary. New York: Oxford University Press.

Webb, E.J., Campbell, D.T.M, Schwartz, R.D. and Sechrest, L. (1966)

Unobtrusive Measures. Nonreactive research in the social sciences. Chicago: Rand McNally.

Questions

1. Why might a theory of the human self be a necessary prerequisite to understanding the social psychology of the interview?

2. What are the dangers of relying exclusively on the interview as a source of information in social research?

3. What were the inadequacies of the interview as a way of appraising a person's fitness for a particular job?

4. Discuss the similarities and differences between interviewing and participant observation as techniques of research in social science.

5. 'Many crucial facts lie beyond the time and place of interaction, or lie concealed within it' (Goffman). Discuss with reference to the interview.
6. Can one accept at face value what people say in an interview or does one have to 'interpret' what one hears? If you advocate the first strategy, are there any qualifications to your acceptance? If you advocate the latter strategy, suggest the guidelines you might use in making your interpretations.
7. What are the problems of inter-relating what one hears in an interview with what one observes?
8. Compare and contrast interviews with conversations.
9. 'It is crucial to an understanding of the interview situation to appreciate that more than one perspective is involved'. Discuss.
10. Discuss the strengths and weaknesses of behavioural approaches to the study of interviews.

Annotated reading

Argyle, M. (1975) Bodily Communication. London: Methuen.
A popular account of different aspects of non-verbal behaviour. Compare and contrast this approach with Goffman. Goffman is much more 'cognitive', whilst Argyle is more 'behavioural'. Is there scope for both approaches?

Goffman, E. (1959) The Presentation of Self in Everyday Life. Harmondsworth: Penguin.
Based on astute observations of everyday life. It is essentially a theory of action in relation to the observing and listening other (i.e. his conception of the audience is critical to his portrayal of action). Consider the relevance of this book to the problems faced by the interviewee as he prepares for an interview.

Kahn, R.L. and Cannell, C.F. (1957) The Dynamics of Interviewing: Theory, technique and cases. New York: Wiley.
Available in paperback. This has been the standard work for over 20 years. Presents a group dynamic approach to the interview. Concerned with the events of feedback as a way of improving interviewing skills, for example, such self-confrontation devices as tape-recorders. Needs to be up-dated to include video-feedback. Basically very sound.

Chapter 11

Interviewing: practical aspects
Russell P. Wicks

If there is one universally applied technique to be found
in behavioural research it is 'interviewing'. If there is
one technique basic to all professional practice it is the
interaction between people that is called 'interviewing'. It
is the nature of this interaction between people which is
the concern of this chapter. It is to be hoped that what
is said can be applied not simply to 'the interview' in
'an interview situation' but to all purposive contacts
between individuals; the critical feature, it is claimed,
being the purposive nature of the encounter. The participants bring hopes, fears, expectations, misconceptions and
many other cognitions to the situation, most times in the
hope that their wishes will be met, fears reduced and so on.
Customarily this view is found in the characterization of an
interview as a 'conversation with a purpose'. So it is, but
all those participating in an interview have their purposes
and not simply, for example, the interviewer. In the complex
transactions of getting and giving information we observe
effort aimed at achieving purposes. Thus the psychologist
testing a client by means of, say, the Wechsler Adult
Intelligence Scale is conducting an interview as defined.
The purpose from one point of view is to help the client in
some way, from the other to be helped. In the exchange of
information each has purposes and expectations that they
hope will be met. Each may be optimizing their strategies
towards fulfilling these purposes. Roles will be assumed
constraining and shaping behaviour. If participants in
interviews can become more skilful and aware of the processes involved there is some hope of raising levels of
satisfaction. It is, therefore, the aim of this chapter to
examine such interview processes with this goal in mind. For
this purpose a simple model of an interview is described
(see figure 1) and for illustrative purposes reference made
to three particular interview situations; occupational
counselling, job interviews and research interviewing.

Initiation

The view that it is the purposive nature of the interview that is crucial leads us to consider the motives of
the participants. An individual approaching a counselling
situation may be motivated by a complex of needs, and

Figure 1

Model of an interview

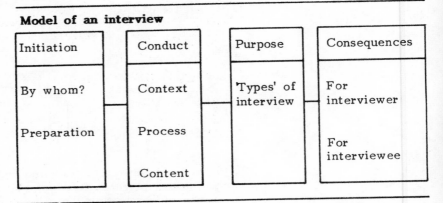

Initiation	Conduct	Purpose	Consequences
By whom?	Context	'Types' of interview	For interviewer
Preparation	Process		For interviewee
	Content		

voluntary or compulsory attendance may be crucial in structuring these needs. Whether these needs are shared and whether they can be fulfilled is another matter. It may well be the case that some frequently voiced criticisms of interviews arise, in part, from a failure to make explicit the needs and expectations of the parties involved. Nowhere is this more important than in those situations with a high level of emotional involvement. Two people may look back on an interview as a total failure because each had different expectations which unfortunately were not fulfilled. We all, interviewers and interviewees, bring hopes and fears to the task. Just as Orne (1962) draws our attention to the 'demand characteristics' of the experimental situation as a result of which subjects perform as they believe they are expected so to do, so participants in interviews will seek a role that they perceive as being appropriate. Not always, unfortunately, do they choose correctly.

In analysing an interview it follows, therefore, that attention to preliminaries and preparation is vital. Many writers on interviewing stress the physical preparations needed, literally setting the scene. Here, 'cognitive' scene setting is judged to be more important; for example, in employment interviewing paying attention to providing information about the organization, or providing an adequate job description. Considering the contribution of application forms and references, together with other 'scene setting' activities, will go a long way towards minimizing the cognitive gap that may occur. Furthermore, such preparations are in fact part of the information exchange that lies at the heart of an interview. In general, preparation from the interviewer's point of view means careful planning of all aspects of the situation. Briefing oneself, rehearsing the interview, anticipating needs; all contribute to an efficiently managed, worth-while encounter.

Recently, increasing attention has been given to preparation on the part of the interviewee, especially for those about to be interviewed for a job. For example, a great deal of work stemming from careers work with young people has resulted in programmes aimed at developing 'life skills'. There is clear evidence that all can profit from paying attention to the activities and skills involved in job seeking. The material included in such programmes varies widely but may cover:

* where to get job information;
* work experience;
* how to reply to advertisements;
* how to become more self-aware;
* how to be interviewed.

The techniques employed range from self-instructional material to the use of video-recording of role-play situations. In general, however, the emphasis is on providing guidelines, improving social skills, self-presentation and making people more aware of the processes of social interaction.

Conduct

Context

What effect on the behaviour of the participants in an interview might the following environments have: a police station; a doctor's surgery; a street corner; a psychology laboratory? Clearly the effect can be dramatic. We have the clearest evidence here for the importance of the frame of reference, role expectations and construal of the situation upon behaviour in an interview. Indeed, the subtlety of the rules of the 'games' played out in different contexts is such that we spend our lives refining and editing our private rule books. Within each context there may be a range of indicators signalling to us how to behave, how to address people, what to say and what not to say, an obvious example being dress, particularly a uniform which may be anything from a pin-stripe suit to a white coat. What is the experience of people who customarily wear a 'uniform' when they discard it? What might people say to a priest in mufti that they would not say if he donned his clerical garb? Thus our perception of the interview context is an essential part of the scene setting previously discussed. Most interviewers, being aware of this, go to some trouble to ensure that the physical setting signals what they wish it to: they dress in a particular style, arrange the seats appropriately, adjust the lighting, ensure that interruptions do or do not occur. They try to ensure that the interview is conducted in a 'good mannered' way.

A further aspect is that participants bring substantial resources to the task: their background knowledge, and skills expectations. Whilst these resources may bring benefits to an interview, they sometimes create problems. Such difficulties have been extensively investigated by Rosenthal and his co-workers (e.g. Rosenthal and Rosnow, 1969) in studies of the characteristics of 'volunteers' in research and studies of the expectations of subjects in experiments, as well as the experimenters. Avoiding bias and error arising from these factors is a major concern of investigators; thus one should be aware that volunteers for survey research tend to be better educated; if male, they score higher on IQ tests; and they are better adjusted than non-volunteers. Such factors should be taken into account in evaluating data. Similarly, the survey interviewer asked to find a sample of five people, even though certain characteristics of the sample are specified, may unwittingly choose those they feel it would be 'nice' to interview.

Process

A great deal of what we know about interpersonal communication has been learnt by systematic study of interviews, especially the face-to-face two-person encounter. What is offered here, however, is a general communication model which may be used to analyse an interview (see figure 2). The utility of this model as a tool for examining interpersonal behaviour rests upon the conceptualization of communication as a system; the model is dynamic because it has independent parts with provision for feedback.

Figure 2

A communication model

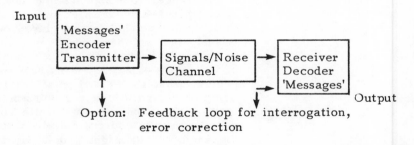

Such a model could stand for many communication systems: radio or television transmission; a nervous system; or, in this case, an interview. A useful procedure arising from the 'system' model is that we can examine its integrity. In other words, we can see what happens when one part of the system is distorted or eliminated.

In this model, 'message' is taken to stand for that which we wish to transmit. Embedded in this is the difficult problem of meaning, and an obvious use of the model is to compare inputs and outputs according to some criterion of meaningfulness. Such a comparison is the basis of an often hilarious game in which the distortion occurring when a 'message' is passed along a line of people by word of mouth is examined. Bartlett (1972) showed in his method of serial reproduction the simplifications and intrusions which occur in this process.

Within the interview, 'meaning' arises at a number of levels. First, it arises at the level of verbal content. What was the question and what is the answer? Much has been written about asking the right sort of question in an interview, whether to use direct or indirect questions, the appropriate form of words, and the dangers of certain questions such as leading or multiple forms. Skilful interviewers do not seem to be constrained by rigid rules but show flexibility, constantly probing and following up interesting leads. They tend to ask: 'Tell me', 'When was that?', 'How was that?', 'What did you do?' and perhaps the most difficult question of all, 'Why?'

Second, the question of meaning arises at the level of recording the interview material. What gets lost or distorted when an interviewer distils a reply into notes or makes a decision? Third, a consideration arising especially in the research interview is: what has happened to the original meaning when a response is coded, probably into a pre-determined category, and is lumped together with others when the study is reported?

However, the verbal content of the message is only a small part of the signal. Many researchers assert that the non-verbal component of a signal is of greater importance. Argyle (1973, 1975) in particular has drawn our attention to the role of non-verbal communication factors such as:

* bodily movements: body language: gestures;
* facial expression;
* eye movements and eye contact;
* personal space: proximity.

Socially skilled performers are simultaneously transmitting signals using all these components together with verbal material whilst reacting to similar signals constituting feedback from their partners.

Utilizing and decoding this complex of information involves us in consideration of interpersonal perception, a key area in the analysis of interviewing. How we form judgements about other people is at the heart of interview decisions: the substantial literature on this topic, for example Cook (1979), suggests that the information we use includes:

* a person's actions;
* the situation in which the person is observed;
* appearance (including facial expression, physique, speech characteristics and dress style);
* non-verbal cues mentioned previously.

The powerful influence of some cues is seen most clearly in the study of stereotypes. Picking up one piece of information and building often unwarranted assumptions upon it is the classic error in judging others. Reacting to a regional accent, to hair colour, to ethnic origin or any other isolated item is all too common. Such a reaction, especially to irrelevant information, is usually dubbed the 'halo effect'. Since the judge or interviewer is striving for cognitive consistency, information is often interpreted in such a way that it fits this single judgement. Thus favourable material or even attributions will be ascribed to a liked person. Contrariwise, undue weight may be given to negative indications in the case of dislike. Clearly, interviewers must be constantly on their guard against introducing bias of this kind. Awareness of their prejudices and the sorts of errors we make in judging others will help.

It is the process component of interviewing which has received most attention in the training of interviewers. Such training commonly takes the form of general social skills training together with exercises directed at the specialization of the interviewer; for example, obtaining clinically relevant material in the hospital setting. Just how effective training may be is not easy to assess. Largely this is so because published studies of interview training tend to use different criteria, thus making comparisons difficult. The benefits to the trainee probably come from receiving informed feedback in role-playing or group tasks about their performance together with enhanced self-awareness.

Content

The point has been made that the absence of a shared common aim or the lack of a clear plan in an interview leads to many difficulties. Specifically, criticisms in terms of interview decisions tend to the view that they may leave much to be desired. It is claimed, for example, that the research literature points overwhelmingly in this direction. Without wishing to dismiss the many studies leading to this conclusion, it must be pointed out that they cover a wide range of interview outcomes made by many interviewers at different levels of experience and training with their decisions based on imprecise criteria. The message of these studies seems to be that all concerned with interviews should be aware of the shortcomings and take steps to overcome them. Apart from errors arising from factors already mentioned in describing context and process aspects at an interview, the principal source is often the lack of a clear plan for an interview; in other words, content must be tailored to the particular aim in mind, each interview requiring careful planning with preparation related to a desired outcome. By way of illustration let us consider the content of interviews within the three professional contexts of counselling, job interviews and research interviewing.

COUNSELLING: OCCUPATIONAL GUIDANCE. What is the aim of an occupational guidance procedure? At one time the approach was modelled upon the notion of talent matching: specify the job, specify the person and attempt to match

the two. On the job side of the equation, techniques of task
analysis, job description and content specification were
developed whilst evidence of congruent relevant behaviour
was sought from the interviewee. It is no coincidence that
the heyday of this approach coincided with the early boom in
psychological test production. Aptitude tests, occupational
interest guides, and tests of specific skills were all produced to aid the matching. Today, with the application of
computer-based matching procedures, the approach is enjoying
a revival. The role of the interview in this model was
largely to establish the congruence of job and applicant
profiles by comparison through discussion. From this approach evolved the contemporary developmental model, with an
emphasis on career decision making as a process over time,
starting in the early years with educational counselling,
proceeding to occupational counselling and then to career
development counselling, with perhaps counselling for retirement in later years. Thus there may be many interviews
within this model each with a specific aim, the sum aimed at
the overall development of the individual. Among the sub-
goals of this process we can recognize the following:

*   self-appraisal: equipping the client to achieve
     realistic self-assessment;
*   self-perception: providing frames of reference,
     categories of occupationally significant behaviours;
*   job perception: acquiring the skills required to assess
     the world of work in terms of job content, values, roles
     and life style;
*   reality testing: matching aspirations and goals with
     opportunities within one's limitations;
*   setting goals and objectives: specifying attainable
     goals and precise objectives;
*   hypothesis generation: helping the client to generate
     occupational 'theories';
*   interaction of the person and the job environment:
     examining the complexities of the person/work situation
     interaction;
*   sharing information: providing the client with educa-
     tional and occupational information, and providing the
     counsellor with perceptions of the client;
*   task setting: translating immediate goals into discrete
     tasks, such as finding an address, seeking information,
     reading a pamphlet, etc.

The task of the interviewer/counsellor therefore becomes
that of achieving these goals at the appropriate time and in
a manner which meets the client's needs. Flexibility, wide
background knowledge and the ability to relate to the client
are clearly prerequisites on the part of the counsellor.
Similar goals are shared by modern staff appraisal schemes
and staff development procedures.

JOB INTERVIEWS. Being interviewed for a job, for promotion

or for annual assessment is probably the most commonly experienced form of interview. It has certainly attracted a substantial body of folk-lore, myth, jokes and hard-luck stories. That this is so is, in itself, of considerable psychological significance. The job interview comes in many varieties, not least the panel interview. Here especially the crucial importance of planning an interview is seen. The justifiable criticism of such encounters is frequently due first to poor interviewing skills on the part of the individual board members, and second to the lack of an agreed role for each.

Whilst not normally included under the heading of interviews, such behavioural observation techniques as role-playing by candidates, group discussions, problem-solving exercises and others raise the same problems previously mentioned of reliable and valid judgements about other people.

Two examples of interview plans used in job interviews will be presented here: one is a general approach commonly employed, namely, the biography; the second a well-known technique called the Seven-Point Plan.

1. The biography: the majority of job interviews employ this approach, often, however, in an undisciplined fashion, hunting and pecking at a person's history. However, a simple structure which can be readily shared consists of establishing landmarks within relevant areas; commonly times of change such as leaving school. Bearing in mind the selectivity of recall, in itself an important indicator within an interview, and that the recent past may be more accessible, one should not expect uniform coverage of a life history. This raises the problem of breadth and depth within the interview in relation to the relevance of the information. Too often an interviewer will spend time on an irrelevant area, missing the opportunity to explore a significant point in detail.

However, a plan such as that shown in figure 3 provides a secure frame of reference for interviewer and interviewee. Not least, the interviewee can be assembling information and anticipating questions; the task is not unlike talking through a curriculum vitae. A final benefit of this approach is that it enables the interviewer to check dates, spot gaps in the account and draw out the inter-relationships between

Figure 3

	Education	Interests	Home	Work
The past Landmarks The present	Dates			

events. This approach is underpinned by application forms
and curricula vitae, which are customarily set out in
biographical order.

2. The Seven-Point Plan: probably the best known of all
assessment and interview formats, the plan was originally
developed by Alec Rodger within the framework of the talent
matching approach to occupational guidance. It was intended
to apply to both candidates and jobs, to obtain relevant
information about people and, by asking the same questions
of a job, to facilitate matching.

The plan was rapidly adopted for job interviewing and
has undoubtedly been highly influential in so far as it
provides the unskilled interviewer with a robust, easily
understood framework within which to work. Over the years,
a number of modifications have been suggested to the original plan. Similarly based schemes have been published, but
what is essentially the original is presented here (Rodger,
1974).

1. Physical characteristics:
   Physical abilities of occupational importance.
   State of health. Vision, hearing. Appearance. Speech.
2. Attainments (and previous experience):
   Educational background, achievements. Occupational and
   professional training. Experience. How well has this
   person done? Personal achievements in any area: sports,
   pursuits, etc.
3. General ability:
   Especially general intelligence and cognitive skills -
   words, numbers, relationships.
4. Special aptitudes:
   Particularly occupationally applicable talents -
   scientific, mechanical, mathematical, practical,
   literary, artistic, social skills.
5. Interests:
   Often the core information: type of interests, how they
   are pursued, to what effect. Intellectual, practical,
   physical, social and artistic interests may be
   occupationally significant.
6. Personality:
   What is this person like? Especially in terms of self-
   perception. Social relationships, behaviour indicative
   of self-reliance, dependability.
7. Circumstances:
   The context of the person's life in so far as it affects
   his aspirations. Family circumstances, financial background, current problems.

The first six points apply particularly to the study of
jobs. What physical characteristics, what attainments and so
on are required for this job? It should be added that Rodger
emphasized the importance of paying attention to individual
likes and dislikes, to difficulties or distastes mentioned

by people, and to the individual's strengths and weaknesses when applying the plan; in particular, stressing the importance of negative information in making selection decisions and the noting of danger signs.

Finally, in considering job interviews it should be noted that advice and preparation for interviewees is widely available in relation to the job interview. Social skills training and self-presentation courses are examples.

RESEARCH INTERVIEWS. The place of the interview in social research is central. Its contribution ranges from preliminary information gathering to a place as the principal research tool. Clearly it takes many forms but the main dimension along which it varies is that of being unstructured/structured, from free to semi-structured to structured. Here, the highly structured form typically found in market research and surveys is considered, the characteristics of the unstructured form being similar to counselling interviews. For the structured approach a unique feature is the use of an interview schedule: in effect, a carefully prepared script meticulously adhered to by the interviewer. A great deal of thought is put into preparing the schedule in order that question form and content, question order, response mode, use of response aids and other factors can be taken into account.

Customarily these factors are checked by conducting pilot studies. Another feature of research interviewing is the attention paid to teaching interviewers how to present a particular schedule, together with supervision of their work in the field. Finally, since it is often the case that large numbers of respondents are involved, it is usual to design the schedules with data analysis in mind: for example, the coding of responses by interviewers for data entry.

As an example of research interviewing the approach of the Government Social Survey is now described. The Social Survey began work dealing with wartime problems of the 1940s. It is now a Division of the Office of Population Censuses and Surveys carrying out a wide range of studies of social and economic interest for public departments. A detailed description of the practices and procedures it employs is to be found in the handbook for interviewers (Atkinson, 1971).

Steps in producing such surveys include:

* identifying research question: decide on form and content of survey, consider costs;
* draft proposals: content of schedule, sampling of respondents;
* pilot stage: explore degree of structure appropriate, such as free to highly. Coding of replies. Analyse pilot material;
* brief and train interviewers: careful training including practice on schedule. How to contact the public. Identifying the person to be interviewed (e.g. by age,

sex, role). Putting over the purpose of the survey; problem of refusals or lack of co-operation. Conducting the interview: defining the roles of interviewer and informant;

* timetable: prepare addresses, number of interviewees, target dates;

* carry out field survey: interviewers adhere to research officers' instructions on each question. Comprehend the purpose of each question: (i) factual information; (ii) expression of opinion; (iii) attitude measures.

Deploy response modes without distortion: open questions with free response, closed/forward choice questions with pre-coded or scaled responses.

Interviewers practise use of response aids: prompt cards for scaled responses, self-completion scales, repertory grids, examples of products in market research.

Interviewers pay particular attention to prompting and probing.

Guard against distortion in recording data: both precoded and open response items are susceptible;

* coding: check schedules and categorize response;
* computing: produce tables, analyse data;
* conclusion: write report.

Purpose

At this stage in the discussion of our model of an interview it must be clear that so many varieties exist as to demand careful consideration of each in terms of purpose. The variety of purposes has been mentioned, and also that the approach may vary from structured to unstructured according to purpose. Thus a number of recognizable forms of interview have emerged to meet particular needs. Examples include:

* non-directive counselling, client-centred therapy;
* psychotherapeutic encounters of many kinds;
* depth interviews emphasizing motivational factors;
* group interviews involving a number of respondents in a discussion group type format;
* psychological testing, especially individual tests such as WAIS (Wechsler Adult Intelligence Scale);
* problem-solving interviews such as individual role-playing for a variety of purposes.

Consequences

Accepting the purposive nature of the interview implies that outcomes are important for all concerned and that their nature depends on the situation, and not least how the situation is perceived. For the interviewer, this will involve achieving the particular aims which have been identified together with maintenance of professional competence; for example, in the research interview maintaining the validity, reliability and precision of data with errors eliminated as far as possible.

For the interviewee or respondent one might ask: what do they get out of the experience? All too often what might be called the public relations aspect of interviewing is ignored. Symptoms of this include fears on the part of correspondents regarding the confidentiality of data, or that in some way they are being threatened. Such considerations appear to bring us full circle, for if attention is paid to the initiation stage of the proceedings by way of setting the scene such alarms can be reduced. Nevertheless, the sometimes necessary use of subterfuge in research needs to be handled with great care, a minimum requirement being the provision of an adequate explanation after the event or an account of the research.

References

Argyle, M. (1973)
  Social Interaction. London: Tavistock.

Argyle, M. (1975)
  Bodily Communication. London: Methuen.

Atkinson, J. (1971)
  A Handbook for Interviewers (2nd edn). London: HMSO.

Bartlett, F.C. (1932)
  Remembering. Cambridge: Cambridge University Press.

Cook, M. (1979)
  Perceiving Others. London: Methuen.

Orne, M.T. (1962)
  On the social psychology of the psychology experiment. American Psychologist, 17, 776-783.

Rodger, A. (1974)
  Seven Point Plan. London: NFER.

Rosenthal, R. and Rosnow, R.L. (1969)
  The volunteer subject. In R. Rosenthal and R.L. Rosnow (eds), Artifact in Behavioral Research. New York: Academic Press.

Questions

1. 'The interview is a wide-band procedure with low fidelity'. Discuss.
2. Assess the contribution of the study of social skills to the improvement of job selection interviewing.
3. 'Interviewing is the most commonly used selection tool'. Why do you think this is and what else are its strengths and weaknesses?
4. What future do you see for the interview?
5. Discuss the significance of role expectations for the conduct of an interview.
6. Write an account of the function of non-verbal communication in the interview.
7. Critically assess the form of an interview in a counselling situation with which you are familiar.
8. What are the advantages and disadvantages of using a scheme such as the Seven Point Plan for job interviewing?
9. Identify common sources of error in research interviewing. How might these be eliminated?

10. Choose a particular type of interview and design an appropriate interviewer training course.

Annotated reading

Anstey, E. (1976) An Introduction to Selection Interviewing. London: HMSO.
> Originally prepared for staff training in the Civil Service, this practical guide is useful for the advice it gives on general preparation for selection interviewing as well as the conduct of interviews.

Bingham, W.V. and Moore, B.V. (1959) How to Interview (4th edn). New York: Harper & Row.
> A classic work. An early attempt to offer general guidance for those engaged in selection, survey interviews and counselling. Rather general in its approach.

Cannell, C.F. and Kahn, R.L. (1968) Interviewing. In G. Lindzey and E. Aronson (eds), Handbook of Social Psychology, Volume 2: Research methods (2nd edn). London: Addison-Wesley.
> A systematic account of the research interview. Tends towards a theoretical presentation; for example in its discussion of problems of reliability and validity and measurement. Includes discussion of interview technique, question form and the training of interviewers.

Cross, C.P. (1974) Interviewing and Communication in Social Work. London: Routledge & Kegan Paul.
> A useful guide to the 'helping' interview. Represents the movement towards enhancing social skills of all involved in such encounters.

Sidney, E. and Brown, M. (1973) The skills of Interviewing. London: Tavistock.
> Aimed at managers, especially personnel staff. A generally acclaimed book, based on the extensive experience of the authors, it offers a very practical guide to the selection interview.

Sidney, E., Brown, M. and Argyle, M. (1973) Skills with People. London: Hutchinson.
> A guide for managers. Concerns itself with a wide range of topics: communication in general, social skills, interviews, meetings and committees, interpersonal skills and training in social skills.

Ungerson, B. (ed.) (1975) Recruitment Handbook (2nd edn). London: Gower Press.
> Very useful guide to the context of job interviewing, preparing job specifications, advertising, references; all the supporting activities of selection are covered.

Chapter 12

Bargaining and negotiation
Ian E. Morley

According to Adam Smith, 'Man is an animal that makes bargains - no dog exchanges bones with another.' More generally, people exchange ideas. They negotiate, or confer, in an attempt to define or redefine the terms of their relationships.

We believe that psychologists can contribute to our understanding of the ways negotiators prepare for bargaining and negotiate their case. In particular, we argue that:

* to understand the process of negotiation we need to combine 'models of negotiation' with 'models of man';
* planning and process may be regarded as the intra-group and inter-group aspects of a task which engage the 'core' processes of information interpretation, influence and decision-making;
* structure in the process of negotiation is determined by the working out of the core processes which are involved;
* attempts to influence the other depend upon the ways in which negotiators resolve 'dilemmas' built into the negotiation task;
* an understanding of the effects of uncertainty, complexity and stress is central to the psychology of bargaining and negotiation;
* negotiation is a skill. More precisely, 'the skilful negotiator is one who understands the risks and opportunities associated with his work; knows what resources he can bring to bear, and is able to protect or pursue the values and interests seen at stake' (Morley, 1981).

Recent work on the psychology of conflict, commitment and choice is considered in some detail. Following Janis and Mann (1977), we emphasize:

Man's vulnerability to gross errors in arriving at a decision through superficial search and biased information processing ... we see man not as a cold fish but as a warm-blooded mammal, not as a rational calculator always ready to work out the best solution but as a reluctant decision-maker - beset by conflicts, doubts, and worry, struggling with incongruous longings, antipathies and loyalties, and seeking relief by procrastinating, rationalizing or denying responsibility for his own choices (Janis and Mann, 1977).

We discuss psychology's view of 'rational man' and present evidence that 'skilled' negotiators bargain in ways which help others to manage the uncertainties and complexities of the negotiation task.

Persons, parties and models of negotiation

Model 1: Negotiation as a game of strategy

Negotiation is sometimes regarded as a game of strategy, analogous to games such as poker or chess. Furthermore, like chess, it is sometimes compared to an exercise in war in which moves are visible to each of the sides. It is, however, probably a mistake to think of negotiation in this latter way. Therefore, rather than study poker or chess, psychologists have utilized abstract games of a kind which are thought to reveal the logical structure of certain of the bargaining problems negotiators face. Research suggests that those who show dissimilar behaviour in one game may appear almost indistinguishably alike in another. What is important is the reward structure of the game, the way that structure is displayed, and the social meaning participants read into the game.

The process of negotiation is analysed in terms of a sequence of behavioural dilemmas inherent in the nature of the task: for example, shall I stand firm or risk signalling flexibility? Negotiators make choices guided by expectations about the others' response. Outcomes depend upon the accuracy of their diagnoses and the skill with which they construct appropriate moves.

Model 2: Negotiation as struggle

'Pressure bargaining' or 'dispute settlement' models preserve the flavour of strategic thinking by emphasizing 'concealment' and 'competitive' strategies (Winham, 1977a). They recognize the truth in the common-sense view that negotiators only modify their positions when they have fought to the limit. Negotiation is seen as a struggle in which negotiators move stepwise toward an agreement which will be acceptable to both. It is a struggle which in itself validates the final terms, demonstrating that participants have done the best they can.

Model 3: Negotiation as collaboration

Common sense would suggest that in some cases negotiators are more willing to work towards agreement than in others. Negotiation may, therefore, be viewed in terms of a 'collaborative model' in which parties make sacrifices, rather than concessions, in the pursuit of some overriding goal. For example, Strauss' description of the negotiations to achieve economic union between Belgium, the Netherlands, and Luxembourg shows the parties 'kept major focus on the shared benefits of economic union' (Strauss, 1978). Elements of threat and manipulation were still there but negotiators did not, in general, openly exploit asymmetries in the balance of power. In Winham's terms, strategy was more a matter of forestalling the consideration of certain unattractive solutions than a matter of extracting change of position from an adversary (Winham, 1977a).

Model 4: The 'two-track' or 'boundary role' model

Frequently, negotiators belong to, and work for, organizations. They negotiate rules or interpret the manner in which they are to be applied. The attitude they adopt is determined by internal negotiations which place various kinds of restriction on their autonomy at the negotiation table. In some cases the restriction applies to 'latitude of decision'. In others it comes from uncertainty about the policy the organization wishes to pursue. Negotiators therefore monitor their constituents (where should we be?) as well as their opponents (where are they?) (Druckman, 1977). The process of negotiation may be charted by mapping the extent to which they are responsive to the one or the other. Following Druckman, we call this the 'two-track' or 'boundary role' model of negotiation.

Model 5: Negotiation as interpersonal and interparty exchange

The work of Douglas (1962) may be used to elaborate the nature of the two tracks which follow from negotiators' boundary roles. Let us say, rather, that negotiators operate at two levels; that it is possible to distinguish interpersonal and interparty forces which act on the members of negotiation groups. Party forces operate insofar as negotiators are representatives of groups. Personal forces derive from relationships built up at the bargaining table. The former (party) relationship is the superordinate (or dominant) one; the main struggle. The latter (personal) relationship is the subordinate (or diplomatic) one, which 'tidies up the battle'. The relative emphasis upon the one or the other changes as negotiation proceeds.

Studies of bargaining relationships have recently come to the fore in industrial relations research. 'Strong' relationships have important cognitive, affective, and motivational elements. They allow negotiators to exchange information freely, indicating (say) the likely reaction of one organization to proposals from the other. They are affectively positive in terms of trust, respect, liking, and so on. They are 'co-operative', rather than 'individualistic' or 'competitive'.

A systems view of industrial negotiations

Each of the models we have outlined draws our attention to certain aspects of the process of negotiation. What is not yet clear is how descriptions of process are to be linked to descriptions of the environment of which the negotiation forms a part. A 'systems model', adapted from Allen, is shown in figure 1.

Conflict begins when some change in existing circumstances, sometimes inadvertent, sometimes deliberate, creates a situation in which one party feels it must confront another. That is, conflict starts with some input from the environment.

The 'working core' of the model is the transformation element, the process of negotiation. Input is coded, summarized and sorted and a decision made to act. The activity is activity of information search and influence. The 'core processes' of the model are the processes of information interpretation (including the search for information), influence, and decision making.

The control element contains policies, decision rules, and goals. In negotiation, policies and decision rules (themselves the product of social action) operate upon the process of intra-organizational bargaining to produce a more detailed specification of goals. Controls are also imposed by various background factors and negotiating conditions.

The memory element contains the data storage facilities of the management and union organizations.

The output element contains the product of the negotiation including effects on the attitudes of the negotiators, and members of the domestic groups (constituencies) which they represent.

Finally, the model contains a loop for feedback of effects, emphasizing once again the importance of continuity in the relationships between the sides. The loop also reminds us that negotiations are part of a more general process in which practitioners learn about the methods and expectations of the other side. Allen's model underlines the importance for practitioners of working out what their opponents are trying to do.

First, negotiation is described as a transformation element. That is, input requires interpretation (diagnosis) as well as action (treatment). It is all too easy to think of negotiation in terms of strategy, tactics, and struggle without considering why the struggle is perceived in this or that kind of way. The systems model reminds us that negotiators are operating in an uncertain, threatening environment in which they use their mental resources to make sense of what is going on.

Second, the language of control suggests that negotiators operate within a system of constraints. To understand an opponent's behaviour it may be necessary to identify the constraints, perceived from the point of view of that opponent. Strong bargaining relationships help negotiators do this kind of job.

Differences in issue emphasis

The control element

Bonham (1971) set up a laboratory simulation of some of the

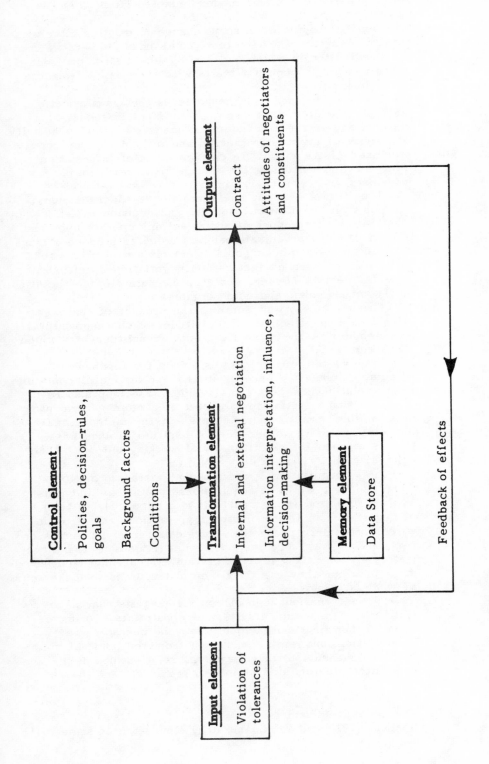

Figure 1

A 'systems model'
From Allen, 1971.

disarmament negotiations which took place between 1946 and 1961. Differences in issue emphasis (priority to arms reduction versus priority to problems of inspection) led to two rather different patterns of behaviour. Either participants exchanged fewer messages and tried to 'avoid the problem'; or they increased their activity, partly to make more attacks on the motives of the others. All in all, Bonham felt it legitimate to conclude that differences in the relative saliency of the issues produce misunderstanding, negative attitudes, hostile interaction, fewer concessions and a lower probability of eventual agreement (Bonham, 1971).

Problems of social judgement

Typically, negotiators balance gains on one issue against losses on another. 'Cognitive conflict' arises when negotiators trade off values in different ways. Balke, Hammond and Meyer (1973) asked practitioners to 're-enact' negotiations, rating the acceptability of different kinds of agreement. the results obtained from this study and others show that 'inconsistency' in judgement is a major source of conflict in negotiation between groups. To quote Brehmer and Hammond (1977):

> the inability to describe judgement policies accurately and completely is one of the major reasons why cognitive conflict between persons is so hard to resolve and successful negotiation is so elusive. For while the student of human judgement will realize that the descriptions of judgement policies produced by introspection are likely to be inaccurate and incomplete because of human INABILITY to be otherwise, the lay person will attribute inconsistencies, inaccuracies, and incompleteness to an INTENTION TO BE DEVIOUS; current folklore suggests that it is naive to do otherwise. Failure to acknowledge the limitations of human judgement results in the attribution of evil intent to the other person.

Background factors

Negotiators define their representative task in different ways, depending on control factors which, in a sense, 'link' them to their constituency groups. Broadly speaking, the greater the 'pressure' on representatives the greater their concern explicitly to demonstrate their commitment to group positions, and to 'confirm and validate' the final settlement by their behaviour at the negotiation table. Thus negotiation takes longer when representatives face post-negotiation evaluation by members of a cohesive group.

Psychologists also investigated the ways in which a constituency looks at its spokesman. For example, Klimoski and Breaugh (1977) have argued that, in some cases, 'performance doesn't count'. In their study the 'behaviour of outsiders was censured and their agreements rejected', despite a level of performance comparable to representatives who came from inside the group.

It is not just that negotiation takes longer in certain circumstances than others. Settlements may exhibit greater variability, reflecting unilateral domination by one of the sides, depending (say) upon perceptions of the 'win-lose' character of the conflict, or its links with more ideo-logical disputes.

Conditions of negotiation

To conclude our discussion of the control element, let us say a little about some of the conditions which may be important. We have two lines of research in mind.

The first is geared to Douglas' model of negotiation. It has investigated the proposition that formal systems of communication (which restrict the cues one person can transmit to another) affect the balance between inter-personal and interparty forces. Evidence has been obtained to show that negotiators given the stronger case drive harder bargains when formal rather than informal systems of communication are used (Morley and Stephenson, 1977).

The second line of research deals with some of the effects of 'situational complexity'. Put simply, negotia-tions become complex:

> when there are a lot of 'things' to be kept in mind, either issues being debated or positions taken by different parties, or implications that the negotiation might have for the environment. Complexity is created also under conditions of uncertainty, when information that is needed is difficult or costly to obtain or is simply unavailable (Winham, 1977b).

Following Winham we refer to the 'size' of the negotiation situation when there are lots of things to be kept in mind. We use the term uncertainty when information is difficult to obtain or is ambiguous once it is obtained. As the size the negotiation situation is increased, negotiators may not have time to study important documents and work out what is going on. More generally, increasing the size of negotiation may lead to uncertainty about value judgements of one's own. Parties are less likely to agree on the nature of conces-sions, or even that concessions have been made. The more complex the negotiation (particularly if it is multilateral rather than bilateral), the harder it will be to establish that a breakthrough has been made. Uncertainty will in-crease. It will be harder to estimate what opponents are likely to accept. Note that the negotiators questioned by Balke et al (1973) were confident they understood their counterpart's policies, a belief based on years of association and negotiation. Yet they were wrong.

The transformation element

In Allen's framework the transformation element contains the process of negotiation, both internal (within parties) and external (between parties). It also contains the processes of conciliation, mediation, or arbitration. We are not sure what Allen intended but, except for arbitration, psychologists have emphasized the similarities between what might seem like disparate elements in the process of transformation.

Here we want to emphasize that preparation and process are linked by virtue of the fact that they are intra-group and inter-group phases of a complex task. The output of one is input to the other which provides input in its turn: and so on. Both involve the core processes of information interpretation, influence, and decision making. We are not sure that the internal process can 'be explained in precisely the same terms as the external process' (Anthony, 1977) but we do think that the similarities are more important than the differences.

1. THE PROCESS OF INTERNAL ADJUSTMENT. By and large the process of internal adjustment has been taken for granted, rather than studied in detail. So far as laboratory research is concerned there have been studies of the effects of role reversal; preparation in strategy versus study groups; the effects of linking conflicts to more basic values (system maintenance versus system change); and the effects of preparation for negotiation in a group.

Much the most important research, however, has been conducted by Rackham and Carlisle (1978b), who compared the planning techniques used by 'effective' and 'average' negotiators. By 'effective', Rackham and Carlisle meant a negotiator (i) rated as such by both sides, union and management, supplier and purchaser; (ii) with a good 'track record' in terms of reaching agreements; and (iii) able to reach agreements which 'stick'. 'Average' negotiators were those who failed with respect to (i) or (ii) or (iii), or negotiators for whom no criterion data were available.

Briefly, the 'effective' negotiators considered a wider range of 'options for action' than 'average' negotiators, and were more likely to identify a range of possible outcomes than think in terms of fixed objectives. In short, they recognized that what can be achieved is partly a function of what is available. An 'effective' plan is a plan which survives contact with the opposition and does not require a 'mental change of gear' when they fail to react as they should. It is, for example, a mistake to rely on verbalizations such as, 'First I'll bring up A, then B, then C, then D'. Effective negotiators used plans which were independent of sequence: 'issue planning' rather than 'sequence planning', as Rackham and Carlisle say.

2. THE PROCESS OF EXTERNAL ADJUSTMENT: STAGES IN NEGOTIATION. Research by Douglas implies that, to be successful, negotiators must separate in time the interpersonal and inter-party demands of their task. Apparently,

negotiations which end in agreement go through stages, so that: 'changes in overt behavior come as spurts, often rather abrupt ones, following periods of prolonged circular activity which appear to accomplish remarkably little in a forward direction' (Douglas, 1962). Indeed, Douglas goes so far as to say that, during the first stage of negotiation, it is precisely 'to the extent that the contenders can intrench their seeming disparity' that they 'enhance their chances for a good and stable settlement in the end' (Douglas, 1957). That is, in some sense, not to disagree means not to solve the problem.

Initially (stage I) the negotiators observed by Douglas showed 'prodigious zeal' for discrediting their opponents. Speeches were exceptionally long and emphasized the representative role participants had to play. Apparently the activity functioned to provide 'a thorough and exhaustive determination of the range within which the parties will have to do business' (Douglas, 1957). Presumably this helped participants to avoid positions which were non-starters. It may also have forced negotiators to look beyond the easy, obvious solutions. Subsequently (stage II) negotiators subordinated their representative roles whilst engaging in unofficial behaviours designed to reconnoitre the bargaining range and give a more precise idea of the settlements which might be obtained. Finally (stage III) negotiators returned to an emphasis upon their representative roles, as they moved to commit their parties to an agreement and 'precipitate a decision-making crisis'.

Stages I and II allow negotiators to assess the 'strength of position' of the parties (Morley and Stephenson, 1977). Initially,

> the parties are either uncertain or mistaken about relative bargaining power, primarily because they cannot know the value of each other's interests at stake and how firm the other ultimately will be. Toward the end of the confrontation stage, the parties develop fairly clear, if not correct, pictures of mutual resolve and hence relative bargaining power, and then a process of resolution occurs - either compromise or one-sided capitulation depending on the revealed power relations. Process is therefore practically inseparable from power since it is through process that the true power relations become manifest in the parties' values and perceptions (Snyder and Diesing, 1977).

If the first stage of negotiation allows negotiators to 'get on the record a turgid edition of what they wish to say about themselves and their positions', the second allows the argument to get truly under way. It allows the bargaining relationship between the negotiators to come to the fore.

In this respect it is interesting to note that 'the systems of argument employed tend to differ between stewards who have a strong bargaining relationship and those who do not' (Batstone, Boraston and Frenkel, 1977). When stewards enjoyed a strong bargaining relationship with an opponent they were more likely (i) to emphasize their 'leader' role within the workforce; (ii) stress 'the men are on my back' rather than 'the men have instructed me'; (iii) demonstrate their understanding of management politics; and (iv) attempt to work out how particular goals could be achieved.

Accordingly, there is an important sense in which stage II can be regarded as a 'problem-solving' stage, but it is problem-solving with an irreducibly political component. The behaviour followed by the negotiators follows from and functions to develop or maintain the bargaining relationship between the negotiators 'at the table'.

3. THE PROCESS OF EXTERNAL ADJUSTMENT: BID AND COUNTERBID: social scientists have assumed (frequently) that negotiation involves little more than a process of bid and counterbid. Douglas' analysis does not necessarily diminish the importance of bid and counterbid but makes it clear that any concession-convergence process is likely to occur late in the day, once the participants have established an 'exchange rate' determining what sized concession from A is equivalent to what sized concession from B.

Magenau and Pruitt (1979) take the view that current levels of demand, are to be understood in terms of negotiators' levels of aspiration (LOA) and the minimum necessary share (MNS). Thus, if negotiator A is asking for an increase of 25 per cent as part of a strategy designed to secure 15 per cent, his LOA is defined by the value (to him) of achieving a settlement at 15 per cent. A's MNS, if he has one, is defined by 'the smallest level of value acceptable in the foreseeable future' or the 'level below which he would rather break off negotiation than reach agreement' (Magenau and Pruitt, 1979).

What is important is the suggestion that the nature of the concession-convergence process depends upon the presence or absence of a solution that is above the negotiators' minimum necessary shares (i.e. can be sold to domestic organizations), is perceptually prominent (to emphasize this really is the end), and is supported by one or more moral rules.

Given such a solution it seems that negotiators are inclined to match the other's offers. That is, 'the more he demands initially, the more they will demand ... The more rapidly he concedes, the faster are their concessions' (Magenau and Pruitt, 1979). Otherwise, a mismatch occurs. That is, 'If he makes a large initial demand, they make a small one ... If he makes a large concession they make small ones' (Magenau and Pruitt, 1979). Almost certainly, a detailed analysis has to be more complicated than this to take account of deadlines, time cost, and so on, but enough has been said to indicate some of the moves which might be made.

Walton and McKersie's behavioural theory

Walton and McKersie in 'A Behavioral Theory of Labor Negotiations' (1965) have provided the 'classic' statement of certain psychological aspects of the process of collective bargaining. Labour negotiations are treated as one example of the more general class of 'social negotiations' which occur whenever 'two or more complex social units ... are attempting to define or re-define the terms of their inter-dependence' (Walton and McKersie, 1965). More precisely, their theory contains five main elements.

The elements of the theory

First, Walton and McKersie identify four 'sub-processes' which serve different goals and operate according to different internal dynamics: distributive bargaining, in which negotiators settle the issues which divide them; integrative bargaining, in which they work through problem areas of joint concern; attitudinal structuring, by which they modify or maintain the bargaining relationships they have built up; and intra-organizational bargaining, the process of internal adjustment in which negotiators influence, and respond to, the demands of the domestic organizations they represent.

Second, there is a theory of individual choice behaviour in distributive bargaining, namely maximization of 'subjectively expected utility' or SEU. Third, there is a theory of individual choice behaviour in integrative bargaining, namely 'utility matching'. Fourth, there is a discussion of the tactical possibilities that negotiators can exploit, with tactics classified according to the 'internal logic' of the sub-processes they are designed to serve. Fifth, there is a discussion of the ways in which the 'sub-processes' place conflicting demands upon the participants. For example, Walton and McKersie argue that: 'the techniques for fostering the integrative process are generally the reverse of the techniques for implementing the distributive process' (Walton and McKersie, 1965).

Distributive and integrative bargaining

What is immediately apparent is the contrast between distributive and integrative bargaining which Walton and McKersie's theory contains. However, the nature of this distinction is not at all clear. Anthony (1977) has developed the point in the following way:

> Bargaining implies a difference in interests and objectives. Collective bargaining is concerned to reach accommodations, often of a temporary nature, between different interests and expectations. In this sense collective bargaining is almost always what Walton and McKersie define merely as a subprocess; it is always distributive bargaining in which the parties are negotiating over the distribution of scarce resources, money, status, or power.

From this point of view 'integrative bargaining' is simply

distributive bargaining in which participants adopt a collaborative rather than a competitive approach to the problems of distribution which are involved.

Research on integrative bargaining

Before moving on to the other aspects of Walton and McKersie's theory it is, perhaps, worth considering the kind of research psychologists have conducted under the heading of 'integrative' bargaining. To do so, we should note that some laboratory tasks, often those which simulate negotiation between buyer and seller, allow one negotiator to increase the profit obtained by the other at little or no personal cost. In other words, one negotiator (say A) may be able to maintain a given level of profit whilst maximizing the joint gain (A's profit plus B's profit). Some writers use the term 'integrative' to refer to distributive bargaining which is efficient in this kind of way.

One line of research shows that under some circumstances joint profit is maximized provided only that 'one individual behaves systematically and that the other one terminates the process by accepting the highest offer available to him' (Kelley and Schenitzki, 1972). A second shows that 'a period of conflict is often necessary before people look beyond the easy obvious options in search of those that provide more joint profit' (Pruitt and Lewis, 1975). The conflict which was productive was, however, conflict guided by a co-operative rather than a competitive 'mode of thought'.

The sub-processes of attitudinal structuring and intra-organizational bargaining

Attitudinal structuring and intra-organizational bargaining may be described as 'sub-processes' in ways distributive bargaining and integrative bargaining may not. Nevertheless, their status is not entirely clear. Anthony (1977) has argued that attitudinal structuring is best regarded as identifying tactics which may be selected as part of an overall co-operative or collaborative approach. He has added that 'There is a further confusion over the sub-process "intra-organizational" bargaining because this represents neither strategic nor tactical concerns but rather an environmental characteristic of the total field within which bargaining takes place' (Anthony, 1977).

Evaluation

Despite this, 'A Behavioral Theory of Labor Negotiations' remains a valuable work. First, the discussion of strategy and tactics is extremely thorough. Second, the discussion of attitudinal structuring reminds us that negotiation skill is not just a matter of learning which tactical opportunities are available. Rather, the bargaining process is 'constrained' by continuities in the relationships between the persons and parties involved: tactics must be seen to follow naturally from that process as it 'unfolds'. Third, Walton and McKersie have demonstrated the multiplicity of outputs from the process of collective bargaining: obtaining favourable agreements, avoiding disasters, maintaining good-will, improving bargaining relationships, educating constituents and the like. To the extent that negotiators seek different outputs, and establish different objectives, we may say that their choice of strategy is 'constrained' in various ways. Finally, Walton and McKersie have demonstrated the importance of a theory of individual decision-making, or choice, one of the 'core' processes which we now consider in rather more detail.

Information interpretation, influence and decision making

Walton and McKersie predicated their account of distributive bargaining upon a prescriptive theory which says that the rational thing for negotiators to do is to choose that outcome which maximizes subjectively expected utility (SEU). What is important here is that SEU theory is one example of a more general class of theories which define rational behaviour in 'analytic' terms (Steinbruner, 1974). 'Analytic' decision makers recognize that different policies lead to different benefits and carry different costs. As information comes in, they are able to spell out the implications of different choices in more and more detail. The 'optimal' choice is identified by comparing, however roughly, the costs and benefits attached to each option, explicitly identifying the trade-off relationships which are involved. The decision-makers confront the uncertainties in their environment and do their best to work out the most sensible policy, all things considered.

There are good reasons, however, to suppose that, in many cases, people have neither the time, the energy, nor the ability to carry out the mental operations required by analytic theories of choice. As negotiations become more complex settlements may be accumulated 'from the bottom up' rather than conceptualized in advance. Thus, negotiators SATISFICE rather than maximize; they control uncertainty by looking for a settlement which is 'good enough' in terms of a few key variables such as domestic support, precedent, and so on. The risk is, of course, that they will fail to appreciate important implications of the agreements which are reached.

A negotiator is likely to use different strategies, at different times and in different circumstances (Janis and Mann, 1977). Broadly speaking, the more complex the negotiation the lower the probability that negotiators will proceed according to the analytic paradigm which has been outlined. However, the more general point is that to understand the process of negotiation it is important to ask whether, and if so how, negotiators cope with the information processing demands of their task.

Essentially, given input ('violation of tolerances'), negotiators must first define the nature of the 'challenge' and work out what is going on. Second, they must decide what they will try to do; consider means to achieve those ends; take note of likely reactions from the other side; and decide on a strategy for 'sorting things out'. Third, they must revise their policies in the light of information obtained once bargaining is under way.

Information interpretation and rationality in negotiation

Negotiation is one example of decision making under uncertainty, not least because values, interests, and power relations have to be worked out as arguments are presented and moves are made. Negotiators cannot escape questions about the validity of information presented by the other side. Negotiation as a process includes negotiators' attempts to impose order and certainty, and work out what is going on. However, there is a sense in which negotiators may exercise too much ingenuity in sorting what is essential from what is not.

The interpretation of input, 'violations of tolerances', requires an assessment of the intentions of the other side. People look for some kind of 'master script' which defines in ordinary language the threats and opportunities which they are likely to face (Morley, 1981).

Initially, it is inevitable that messages will be interpreted in the light of scripts formulated at a very high level of generality, in terms of 'images' of the other. However, following Snyder and Diesing (1977) we may then distinguish two kinds of development. 'Rational' bargainers are those who learn from the process of negotiation so that their images of the others are corrected or updated by what happens 'at the table'. More precisely, 'rational' bargainers sharpen their images of the others, differentiating general knowledge of the opponents' aims from what is implied by their behaviour at the time.

In contrast, 'irrational' bargainers are those whose perceptions, from first to last, are dominated by the general characteristics of their images of the others. In some cases of 'endemic conflict' the image of the other appears more like the image of an 'enemy' and it is, perhaps, appropriate to say 'the bargainer "knows" what is going on and is not going to be fooled by any new information' (Snyder and Diesing, 1977).

'Irrational' bargainers are 'irrational' in two kinds of way. They hold a rigid system of beliefs, retain and defend images and policies even when, to outsiders, they are clearly 'out of date'. Furthermore, their beliefs are organized so that all considerations point to the same strategic choice. This policy is seen as superior to others in all important respects. Jervis (1976) argues that this is a kind of 'overkill' in which the belief system minimizes the conflict between different kinds of constraint. It is 'irrational' because we can be fairly sure that the world is not so benign; negotiation is complex because it requires one kind of constraint to be balanced, or traded-off, against another.

It is in recognition of this that Drucker (1970) describes 'The Effective Executive' as one who understands 'the need for organized disagreement'.

> Decisions of the kind the executive has to make are made
> well only if based on the clash of conflicting views,
> the dialogue between different points of view, the
> choice between different judgments. The first rule in
> decision-making is that one does not make a decision
> unless there is disagreement (Drucker, 1970).

The 'rational' bargainer described by Snyder and Diesing is
rather like the 'effective executive' described by Drucker.
Each begins with tentative judgements and initiates an
active search for new information. The search is designed to
root out ideas which are plausible, but false or incomplete.
It is designed to test hypotheses so that conclusions follow
from, rather than precede, the 'facts' which are obtained.
Each attempts to understand the problem from the perspective
of the other side, and makes moves designed to reduce
ambiguity, clarify communications, and slow negotiation down
(Rackham and Carlisle, 1978a; Morley, 1981).

Three aspects of this treatment deserve further comment.
First, the search for information involves elements such as
diagnosing the basic cause of a given demand; looking for
alternative means to achieve the same ends; determining
which aspects of the other's position are flexible, and by
how much; and so on. If negotiators are to do these jobs
they must attempt a realistic assessment of the bargaining
power they have relative to their opponents. That is to say,
they must make estimates of the kind: how do the costs to
the others of rejecting my proposals compare with their
costs if they accept my proposal?

Second, rational bargainers concentrate their efforts in
attempts to work out the strategies of the others, since to
ask, 'Is my strategy working?', is to invite wishful thinking of one kind or another (Snyder and Diesing, 1977).
Furthermore, although Snyder and Diesing do not make this
explicit, we are tempted to extend the analogy with the
effective executive and argue that rational bargainers ask,
'What does this fellow have to see if his position were,
after all, tenable, rational, intelligent?' (Drucker, 1970).

Third, rational bargainers appreciate that signals clear
to them may be interpreted differently by others. Accordingly, a rational bargainer

> builds redundancy into his ... messages ... He does not
> assume that the opponent 'must know' what he is doing,
> but rather assumes the situation is pretty confused.
> Consequently he tries to send a message several dif-
> ferent ways, always through a different channel, and
> keeps repeating the same theme. The purpose is to break
> through the resistance set up by the opponent's mistaken
> expectations and also to give him time to test, retest,
> and adjust his expectations (Snyder and Diesing, 1977).

The reader should note that this is not just a theoretical
analysis. Snyder and Diesing's account is derived from the

empirical study of documents describing crisis bargaining between nations. It is consistent with other work.

For example, the 'effective' negotiators studied by Rackham and Carlisle (1978a) tended to label messages as questions, suggestions, warnings (rather than threats) and so on; they were less likely to respond immediately to proposals with counter-proposals of their own, possibly because they recognized the proposal might not be perceived as a proposal at all (but as 'blocking' or 'disagreement'); they made frequent attempts to summarize positions and test the other's understanding of what was going on; they organized disagreement so that ambiguities were cleared up and each gained an understanding of how the other would proceed; and they showed a proper respect for difficulties likely to arise when agreements were put into effect.

Power and influence

Psychologists have taken the view that power is to be analysed in terms of potential for influence: that there is a kind of 'negotiation power' deriving from the personal resources of the negotiators, from 'facility and shrewdness in the execution of negotiation tactics' (Stevens, 1963).

From one point of view the power derives from negotiators' ability to choose an appropriate strategy, meaning a set of tactics ordered in a certain kind of way. Here we argue that the selection and sequencing depends on the way negotiators view certain 'behavioural dilemmas' inherent in their task. Some of the dilemmas are linked to questions of information interpretation which have already been raised. For example, should an issue be treated on its merits or as a symptom of a more basic conflict which happens to have been expressed in this particular way? Does this clause have to be spelled out in detail? Or will the other keep the spirit of the agreement in areas not explicitly put into words?

Other dilemmas follow from a negotiator's concern to protect his reputation for resolve. Consider the question, 'Shall I make a concession or not?' According to Pruitt (1971), negotiators face costs whichever decision they make. To stand firm may be to nail my colours to a position I cannot possibly maintain, or make it look as if I am not trying to reach an agreement at all. But to move too early may give my opponents the expectation that more will follow if they persist. Some ways of dealing with the dilemma are outlined in Morley (1981).

Strategies are, of course, designed to influence others' behaviour. Consequently, it is important to realize that negotiation is not the same as other forms of debate. 'Effective' negotiators tend 'to advance single reasons insistently' rather than provide mutually supporting reasons to back up proposals they have made. Apparently, a negotiating position is only as credible as the weakest argument in the chain, but to influence others it is necessary to know what counts as a strong argument from their point of view.

Negotiation as decision making

In one sense negotiators continually face a threefold choice: to accept the offer on the table, to continue in the hope of negotiating better terms, or to break off negotiation, for the time being at any rate. However, it is perhaps more useful, analytically, to identify major choice points in terms of the decision whether to negotiate or not; the decision to pursue these objectives rather than those; the choice of this strategy rather than that; the decision to stay with this strategy rather than that; and, finally, the decision whether or not to accept the 'final' offer which has been made.

Decisional conflicts as sources of stress

The negotiators studied by Douglas were not only experienced but had a good deal of third-party help. Douglas described one mediator as 'a perceptualizer of each to the other',

> and in the course of fashioning ready-made perceptions about each for the other, he appended his own embellishments in such a manner as, not to deceive, but to highlight, intensify, or otherwise single out certain elements for special attention ... Such tactics would unquestionably influence a party's estimate of the status of the conflict (Douglas, 1962).

Without such help it is not too difficult to believe that the concession dilemma identified by Pruitt may have deepened to the point where negotiators felt whatever they did was likely to be wrong. Under such circumstances, particularly when issues are complex, or there is a feeling that the environment cannot be controlled at all, negotiators may 'short circuit' the activities of information interpretation and information search, ignoring authentic warnings that things are going wrong.

Essentially, we propose to treat the concession dilemma as one example of a 'decisional conflict' in which there are 'simultaneous opposing tendencies within the individual to accept and reject a given course of action' (Janis and Mann, 1977). According to Janis and Mann, decisional conflicts produce intense stress when individuals face a 'crisis situation' in which each course of action carries serious risks and they see little hope of obtaining new information to reduce some of the uncertainty.

They argue, further, that the individual seeks forms of 'defensive avoidance' which enable him 'to escape from worrying about the decision by not exposing himself to cues that evoke awareness of anticipated losses' (Janis and Mann, 1977). If the decision can be postponed or delayed the individual will procrastinate; if the deadline is tight the individual will try to shift the responsibility to someone else, or 'bolster' the decision in various ways, warding off stress 'by selective attention and distorted information processing' (Janis and Mann, 1977).

Finally, Janis and Mann argue that their analysis applies not only to individuals but also to groups, to teams. In their view, being in a group amplifies the tendency of individuals to avoid raising controversial issues or confront difficulties head on. Apparently, group members are motivated (i) to shift responsibility, by seeking out the policy alternative favoured by the leader, or the most esteemed person, and (ii) to pool their resources collectively to bolster (rationalize) the choice the individual would like to make.

Janis and Mann refer to this collective tendency as 'groupthink' and argue that it is fostered when members belong to a cohesive group, 'insulated' from others in the organization; when leaders direct attention to the policy they would prefer; and when the group lacks systematic procedures for information appraisal and search. They argue, also, that the way to reduce tendencies towards groupthink is not to change the composition of the group. Rather, it is to ensure that the group devotes its energies to the right kinds of task.

Essentially, Janis and Mann have extended work on emergency decision making to cover all cases of decision making in which participants are concerned or anxious about the possibility that they may not attain the objectives which they seek. Details of the analysis are still being worked out, but one thing is clear; not to disagree, not to express 'organized dissent', means not to solve the problem. Dissent, properly conducted, is essential to clarify one's own position, and the position of the other side.

References

Allen, A.D. Jr (1971)
A systems view of labor negotiations. Personnel Journal, 50, 103-114.

Anthony, P.D. (1977)
The Conduct of Industrial Relations. London: Institute of Personnel Management.

Balke, W.M., Hammond, K.R. and Meyer, G.D. (1973)
An alternative approach to labor-management relations. Administrative Science Quarterly, 18, 311-327.

Batstone, E., Boraston, I. and Frenkel, S. (1977)
Shop Stewards in Action: The organization of workplace conflict and accommodation. Oxford: Blackwell.

Bonham, M.G. (1971)
Simulating international disarmament negotiations. Journal of Conflict Resolution, 15, 299-315.

Brehmer, B. and Hammond, K.R. (1977)
Cognitive factors in interpersonal conflict. In D. Druckman (ed.), Negotiations: Social psychological perspectives. Beverly Hills: Sage.

Douglas, A. (1957)
The peaceful settlement of industrial and inter-group disputes. Journal of Conflict Resolution, 1, 69-81.

Douglas, A. (1962)
Industrial Peacemaking. New York: Columbia University Press.

Drucker, P.F. (1970)
The Effective Executive. London: Pan Business Management.

Druckman, D. (1977)
Boundary role conflict: negotiation as dual responsiveness. In I.W. Zartman (ed.), The Negotiation Process: Theories and applications. Beverly Hills: Sage.

Janis, I.L. and Mann, L. (1977)
Decision Making: A psychological analysis of conflict, choice and commitment. London: Collier Macmillan.

Jervis, R. (1976)
Perception and Misperception in International Politics. Princeton, NJ: Princeton University Press.

Kelley, H.H. and Schenitzki, D.P. (1972)
Bargaining. In C.G. McClintock (ed.), Experimental Social Psychology. New York: Holt, Rinehart & Winston.

Klimoski, R.J. and Breaugh, J.A. (1977)
When performance doesn't count: a constituency looks at its spokesman. Organizational Behavior and Human Performance, 20, 301-311.

Magenau, J.A. and Pruitt, D.G. (1979)
The social psychology of bargaining: a theoretical synthesis 1. In G.M. Stephenson and C.J. Brotherton (eds), Industrial Relations: A social psychological approach. Chichester: Wiley.

Morley, I.E. (1981)
Negotiation and bargaining. In M. Argyle (ed.), Handbook of Social Skills, Volume 2. London: Methuen.

Morley, I.E. and Stephenson, G.M. (1977)
The Social Psychology of Bargaining. London: George Allen & Unwin.

Pruitt, D.G. (1971)
Indirect communication and the search for agreement in negotiation. Journal of Applied Social Psychology, 1, 205-239.

Pruitt, D.G. and Lewis, S.A. (1975)
Development of integrative solutions in bi-lateral negotiation. Journal of Personality and Social Psychology, 31, 621-633.

Rackham, N. and Carlisle, J. (1978a)
The effective negotiator - Part 1: the behaviour of successful negotiators. Journal of European Industrial Training, 2, 6-11.

Rackham, N. and Carlisle, J. (1978b)
The effective negotiator - Part 2: planning for negotiations. Journal of European Industrial Training, 2, 2-5.

Snyder, G.H. and Diesing, P. (1977)
Conflict Among Nations: Bargaining decision making and system structure in international crises. Princeton, NJ: Princeton University Press.

Steinbruner, J.D. (1974)
   The Cybernetic Theory of Decision. Princeton, NJ:
   Princeton University Press.
Stevens, C.M. (1963)
   Strategy and Collective Bargaining Negotiation. New
   York: McGraw-Hill.
Strauss, G. (1978)
   Negotiations: Varieties, contexts, processes, and social
   order. London: Jossey-Bass.
Walton, R.E. and McKersie, R.B. (1965)
   A Behavioral Theory of Labor Negotiations: An analysis
   of a social interaction system. New York: McGraw-Hill.
Winham, G.R. (1977a)
   Negotiation as a management process. World Politics, 30,
   97-114.
Winham, G.R. (1977b)
   Complexity in international negotiation. In D. Druckman
   (ed.), Negotiations: Social psychological perspectives.
   Beverly Hills: Sage.

Questions

1. Write an essay on negotiation, considered as a skill.
2. Outline the Janis and Mann model of decisional conflict
   and evaluate its significance for the study of
   negotiation.
3. Outline and discuss Douglas' model of successful
   negotation.
4. Why are negotiations sometimes more difficult than they
   need to be?
5. 'The basic operation of interests which exists within
   negotiation is mediated by personal relationships which
   facilitate the constructive resolution of problems'.
   Discuss.
6. What do effective negotiators do?
7. Discuss the link between bargaining power and bargaining
   process.
8. Evaluate the Walton and McKersie 'behavioural theory'.
9. Outline and discuss the distinction between rational and
   irrational kinds of bargaining.
10. Outline and discuss some of the 'behavioural dilemmas'
    inherent in the negotiation task.

Annotated reading

Atkinson, G.M. (1975) The Effective Negotiator. London:
Quest.
   One of the best of the 'how to do it' books, including
   a number of extremely interesting suggestions designed
   to help negotiators set objectives based firmly on the
   realities of the power position between the sides.

Druckman, D. (ed.) (1977) Negotiations: Social psychological
perspectives. Beverly Hills: Sage.
   Contains 13 chapters illustrating the kinds of problems
   psychologists take to be important in the study of
   negotiation. Some of the chapters are technical and

require a background in psychology. Others may be read
without detailed preparation.

Lockhart, C. (1979) Bargaining in International Conflicts.
New York: Columbia University Press.
    A clear and well-written statement of the processes of
information interpretation, influence and decision-
making as they occur in negotiation groups.

Miron, M.S. and Goldstein, A.P. (1979) Hostage. Oxford:
Pergamon Press.
    An extremely interesting account of the skills involved
in 'hostage negotiations'. In many respects the book is
a manual to be used in training the police.

Morley, I.E. (1980) Negotiation and Bargaining. In M. Argyle
(ed.), Handbook of Social Skills, Volume 2. London:
Methuen.
    Provides an account of negotiation skill. Discusses some
of the psychological factors which promote success in
negotiation. Readers may be interested in some of the
other social skills outlined in Argyle's book.

Morley, I.E. and Stephenson, G.M. (1977) The Social
Psychology of Bargaining. London: George Allen & Unwin.
    Provides a detailed review of laboratory research and a
report of a programme of research designed to investi-
gate Douglas' ideas. Includes transcripts of actual
cases.

Stephenson, G.M. (1978) Negotiation and collective
bargaining. In P.B. Warr (ed.), Psychology at Work (2nd
edn). Harmondsworth: Penguin.
    A concise account which places negotiation for agree-
ment in the context of a more general treatment of
relations between groups.

Stephenson, G.M. and Brotherton, C.J. (eds) (1979)
Industrial Relations: A social psychological approach.
Chichester: Wiley.
    A collection of 16 chapters reviewing the contribution
of psychology to various aspects of industrial
relations.

Part four

Some special problems

Chapter 13

Introduction to Part 4
Cary L. Cooper and Peter Makin

In this final section we look at some of the problems that face managers. Space prevents us from looking at more than a few such problems but we have chosen one from an area that affects managers as individuals, one that concerns their dealings with other people, and one that concerns new technology, especially in the office.

One of the major areas of concern in recent years has been the effect of working under pressure on the health, both physical and mental, of managers. Research carried out by Cooper and Melhuish (1980) has found that managers drink excessive amounts of alcohol, smoke a higher than average number of cigarettes, do not exercise as much as they should and are at risk of coronary heart disease (particularly male managers). The main sources of stress on managers are job insecurity, industrial relations difficulties, role conflict and ambiguity, relationships with senior management, lack of autonomy and participation at work, and a variety of other organizational stressors which are discussed in chapter 14. Methods of coping with these stressors range from changes in corporate personnel policy, to training, to better selection.

Although we have considered the sources of stress for managers, it should not be thought that it is solely a managerial phenomenon, or that it results only from pressure at work. Long-term pressures, such as those considered by Cooper or acute trauma, which were discussed in the chapter on transition in Part One, often lead to a situation where an individual may need help to overcome personal problems. Obviously, in some situations there will be a need for professional help but, in his chapter on counselling and helping, Hopson shows how counselling can be 'demystified'.

One of the many responsibilities of a manager is the development of staff. Few managers would consider themselves as 'counsellors' but the skills required to help develop individuals are as appropriate to the shopfloor as they are to the psychiatrist's couch. Counselling is, according to Hopson, 'a process through which a person attains a higher state of personal competence' - this surely is an important part of a manager's job. The situation in management is perhaps slightly different in as much as the goals cannot be totally determined by the individual; they have also to be goals that are desired and/or accepted by the employer. To quote Hopson again 'counselling is helping people to help themselves'. To this we might add 'and in doing so help the organization'. The process of career development and advancement, for example, is a mixture of counselling and helping plus some bargaining and negotiation, hopefully in an atmosphere of mutual trust and understanding.

Finally we turn to office automation, an area which has been receiving considerable attention in recent years. New 'micro-chip' technology has meant that electronic storage, retrieval and communication systems are within the range of even the smallest businesses. Often overlooked, however, are the human aspects of such systems. At both the input and output ends of such technology are people, and people as we have seen, differ considerably. If they do not satisfy these individual demands the full potential of such systems will not be fulfilled, or possibly over-fulfilled with resultant waste of money. The potential of this new technology should not be underestimated, but neither should the human element. The authors are aware of one small firm whose owner has installed a 'fictitious' computer. Despairing of large firms who do not pay invoices for months, he can now deal with those to whom he owes money in a similar fashion to the multi-nationals. When creditors phone up he replies 'well, I'm surprised you haven't received it - it's gone in the computer'!

References

Cooper, C.L. and Melhuish, A. (1980) Occupational stress in managers. Journal of Occupational Medicine, 22, 588-592.

Chapter 14

Stress
Cary L. Cooper

Sources of stress on managers at work

The complexity of industrial organizational life is increasingly a source of stress for managers. Brummet, Pyle and Flamholtz (1968) suggest that managers are suffering extreme physiological symptoms from stress at work, such as disabling ulcers or coronary heart disease (CHD), which force them to retire prematurely from active work before they have had an opportunity to complete their potential organizational life. These and other stress-related effects (e.g. tension, poor adjustment, etc.) also feed into the family, becoming potential sources of disturbance and thus pervading the whole quality of managerial life. The mental and physical health effects of job stress are not only disruptive influences on individual managers, but also a 'real' cost to the organization, on whom many individuals depend: a cost which is rarely, if ever, seriously considered either in human or financial terms by organizations, but one which they incur in their day-to-day operations. In order to do something positive about sources of stress on managers at work, it is important to be able to identify them. The success of any effort to minimize stress and maximize job satisfaction will depend on accurate diagnosis, for different stresses will require different action. Any approach to the management of stress in an organization which relied on one particular technique (e.g. OD or job enrichment or TM), without taking into account the differences within work groups or divisions, would be doomed to failure. A recognition of the possible sources of management stress, therefore, may help us to arrive at suggestions of ways to minimize its negative consequences.

A survey of the management literature reveals a formidable list of over 40 interacting factors which might be sources of managerial stress and satisfaction: those to be dealt with here were drawn mainly from a wider body of theory and research in a variety of fields; medicine, psychology, management sciences, etc. Additional material has been drawn from exploratory studies carried out by Cooper and Marshall (1978). Seven major categories of

Figure 1

Seven major categories of stress

SOURCES OF MANAGERIAL
STRESS (AND SATISFACTION)

MANIFESTATIONS OF
MANAGERIAL STRESS

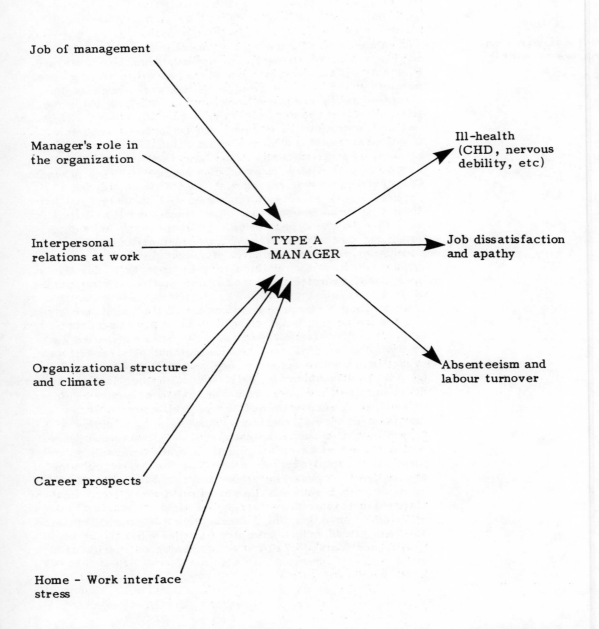

stress can be identified. Figure 1 is an attempt to represent these diagramatically: they are dealt with in a natural progression from those related to the job, organization and individual.

The job of management

Factors intrinsic to the 'job of management' were a first and vital focus of study for early researchers in the field, and 'shop-floor' (as opposed to management) studies are still the main preoccupation. Stress can be caused by too much or too little work, time pressures and deadlines, having too many decisions to make, working conditions, excessive travel, long hours, having to cope with changes at work and the expenses (monetary and career) of making mistakes. It can be seen that every job description includes factors which for some individuals at some time will be a source of pressure.

One of the most important sources of stress for managers is their tendency to work long hours and to take on too much work. Research into work overload has been given substantial empirical attention. French and Caplan (1973) have differentiated overload in terms of quantitative and qualitative overload. Quantitative refers to having 'too much to do', while qualitative means work that is 'too difficult'. Miller (1960) has theorized that 'overload' in most systems leads to breakdown, whether we are dealing with single biological cells or managers in organizations. In an early study, French and Caplan (1970) found that objective quantitative overload was strongly linked to cigarette smoking (an important risk factor or symptom of CHD). Persons with more phone calls, office visits, and meetings per given unit of work time were found to smoke significantly more cigarettes than persons with fewer such engagements. In a study of 100 young coronary patients, Russek and Zohman (1958) found that 25 per cent had been working at two jobs and an additional 45 per cent had worked at jobs which required (due to work overload) 60 or more hours per week. They add that, although prolonged emotional strain preceded the attack in 91 per cent of the cases, similar stress was only observed in 20 per cent of the controls. Breslow and Buell (1960) have also reported findings which support a relationship between hours of work and death from coronary disease. In an investigation of mortality rates of men in California, they observed that workers in light industry under the age of 45, who are on the job more than 48 hours a week, have twice the risk of death from CHD compared with similar workers working 40 or under hours a week. Another substantial investigation on quantitative work load was carried out by Margolis et al (1974) on a representative national US sample of 1,496 employed persons of 16 years of age or older. They found that overload was significantly related to a number of symptoms or indicators of stress: escapist drinking, absenteeism from work, low motivation to work, lowered self-esteem, and an absence of suggestions to employers. The results from these and other studies (Cooper and Marshall, 1978) are relatively consistent and indicate that this factor is indeed a potential source of managerial stress that adversely affects both health and job satisfaction.

There is also some evidence that 'qualitative' overload is a source of stress for managers. French et al (1965) looked at qualitative work overload in a large university. They used questionnaires, interviews and medical examinations to obtain data on risk factors associated with CHD for 122 university administrators and professors. The greater the 'quality' of work expected of the professor, the lower the self-esteem. Several other studies have reported an association of qualitative work overload with cholesterol level, including one concerning a tax deadline for accountants, on medical students performing a medical examination under observation, etc. French and Caplan (1973) summarize this research by suggesting that both qualitative and quantitative overload produce at least nine different symptoms of psychological and physical strain: job dissatisfaction, job tension, lower self-esteem, threat, embarrassment, high cholesterol levels, increased heart rate, skin conductance, and more smoking. In analysing these data, however, one cannot ignore the vital interactive relationship of the job and manager: objective work overload, for example, should not be viewed in isolation but relative to the manager's capacities and personality.

Such caution is sanctioned by much of the American and some UK literature which shows that overload is not always externally imposed. Many managers (perhaps certain personality types more than others) react to overload by working longer hours. For example, in reports on an American study (Uris, 1972), it was found that 45 per cent of the executives investigated worked all day, in the evenings, and at weekends, and that a further 37 per cent kept weekends free but worked extra hours in the evenings. In many companies this type of behaviour has become a norm to which everyone feels they must adhere.

Manager's role in the organization

Another major source of managerial stress is associated with a person's role at work. A great deal of research in this area has concentrated on role ambiguity and role conflict, following the seminal investigations of the Survey Research Centre of the University of Michigan (Kahn et al, 1964).

Role ambiguity exists when a manager has inadequate information about his work role: that is, where there is lack of clarity about the work objectives associated with the role, about work colleagues' expectations of the work role and about the scope and responsibility of the job. Kahn et al (1964) found in their study that men who suffered from role ambiguity experienced lower job satisfaction, higher job-related tension, greater futility, and lower self-confidence. French and Caplan (1970) found, in a sample of 205 volunteer engineers, scientists, and administrators at one of NASA's bases, that role ambiguity was significantly related to low job satisfaction and to feelings of job-related threat to one's mental and physical well-being. This also related to indicators and physiological strain such as increased blood pressure and pulse rates. Margolis et al (1974) also found a number of significant relationships between symptoms or indicators of physical and mental ill health with role ambiguity in their representative national sample (n = 1,496). The stress indicators related to role ambiguity were depressed mood, lowered self-esteem, life dissatisfaction, low motivation to work, and intention to leave job.

Role conflict exists when an individual in a particular work role is torn by conflicting job demands or doing things he really does not want to do or does not think are part of the job specification. The most frequent manifestation of this is when a manager is caught between two groups of people who demand different kinds of behaviour or expect that the job should entail different functions. Kahn et al (1964) found that men who suffered more role conflict had lower job satisfaction and higher job-related tension. It is interesting to note that they also found that the greater the power or authority of the people 'sending' the conflicting role messages, the more role conflict produced job dissatisfaction. This was related to physiological strain as well, as the NASA study (French and Caplan, 1970) illustrates. They telemetered and recorded the heart rate of 22 men for a two-hour period while they were at work in their offices. They found that the mean heart rate for an individual was strongly related to his report of role conflict. A larger and medically more sophisticated study by Shirom et al (1973) found similar results. Their research is of particular interest as it tries to look simultaneously at a wide variety of potential work stresses. They collected data on 762 male kibbutz members aged 30 and above, drawn from 13 kibbutzim throughout Israel. They examined the relationships between CHD, abnormal electro-cardiograph readings, CHD risk factors (systolic blood pressure, pulse rate, serum cholesterol levels, etc.), and potential sources of job stress (work overload, role ambiguity, role conflict, and lack of physical activity). Their data were broken down by occupational groups: agricultural workers, factory groups, craftsmen, and managers. It was found that there was a significant relationship between role conflict and CHD (specifically, abnormal electro-cardiographic readings), but for the managers only. In fact, as we move down the ladder from occupations requiring great physical exertions (e.g. agriculture) to those requiring least (e.g. managerial), the greater was the relationship between role ambiguity/conflict and abnormal electro-cardiographic findings. It was also found that as we go from occupations involving excessive physical activities to those with less such activity, CHD increased significantly. Drawing together these data, it might be hypothesized that managerial and professional occupations are more likely to suffer occupational stress from role-related stress and other interpersonal dynamics and less from the physical conditions of work.

Another aspect of role conflict was examined by Mettlin and Woelfel (1974). They measured three aspects of interpersonal influence - discrepancy between influences, level of influence, and number of influences - in a study of the educational and occupational aspirations of high school students. Using the Langer Stress Symptom questionnaire as their index of stress, they found that the more extensive and diverse an individual's interpersonal communications network, the more stress symptoms he showed. A manager's role which is at a boundary - that is, between departments or between the company and the outside world - is, by definition, one of extensive communication nets and of high role conflict. Kahn et al (1964) suggest that such a position is potentially highly stressful. Margolis and Kroes (1974) found, for instance, that foremen (high role conflict-prone job) are seven times as likely to develop ulcers as shopfloor workers.

Another important potential source of stress associated with a manager's role is 'responsibility for people'. One can differentiate here between 'responsibility for people' and 'responsibility for things' (equipment, budgets, etc.). Wardwell et al (1964) found that responsibility for people was significantly more likely to lead to CHD than responsibility for things. Increased responsibility for people frequently means that one has to spend more time interacting with others, attending meetings, working alone and, in consequence, as in the NASA study (French and Caplan, 1970) more time in trying to meet deadline pressures and schedules. Pincherle (1972) also found this in the UK study of 2,000 executives attending a medical centre for a check-up. Of the 1,200 managers sent by their companies for their annual examination, there was evidence of physical stress being linked to age and level of responsibility; the older and more responsible the executive, the greater the probability of the presence of CHD risk factors or symptoms. French and Caplan support this: in their NASA study of managerial and professional workers, they found that responsibility for people was significantly related to heavy smoking, raised diastolic blood pressure, and increased serum cholesterol levels; the more the individual had responsibility for 'things' as opposed to 'people', the lower were each of these CHD risk factors.

Having too little responsibility, lack of participation in decision making, lack of managerial support, having to keep up with increasing standards of performance and coping with rapid technological change, are other potential role stressors mentioned repeatedly in the literature but with little supportive research evidence. Variations between organizational structures determine the differential distribution of these factors across differing occupational groups. Kay (1974) does suggest, however, that (independent of employing organizations) some pressures are to be found more at middle than at other management levels. He depicts today's middle manager as being particularly hard pressed:

* by pay compression, as the salaries of new recruits increase;
* by job insecurity: they are particularly vulnerable to redundancy or involuntary early retirement;
* by having little real authority at their high levels of responsibility;
* by feeling 'boxed' in.

Interpersonal relations

A third major potential source of managerial stress has to do with the nature of relationships with one's boss, subordinates, and colleagues. Behavioural scientists have long suggested that good relationships between members of a work group are a central factor in individual and organizational health (Cooper, 1980). Nevertheless, very little research work has been done in this area either to support or negate this hypothesis. French and Caplan (1973) define poor relations as 'those which include low trust, low supportiveness, and low interest in listening to and trying to deal with problems that confront the organizational member'. The most notable studies in this area are by Kahn et al (1964), French and Caplan (1970) and Buck (1972). Both the Kahn et al (1964) and the French and Caplan studies came to roughly the same conclusions, namely that mistrust of persons one works with is positively related to high role ambiguity, which leads to inadequate communications between people and to 'psychological strain in the form of low job satisfaction and to feelings of job-related threat to one's well-being'.

Relationships with boss

Buck (1972) focussed on the attitude and relationship of workers and managers to their immediate boss using Fleishman's leadership questionnaire on consideration and initiating structure. The consideration factor was associated with behaviour indicative of friendship, mutual trust, respect and a certain warmth between boss and subordinate. He found that those managers who felt that their boss was low on 'consideration' reported feeling more job pressure. Managers who were under pressure reported that their boss did not give them criticism in a helpful way, played favourites with subordinates, 'pulled rank' and took advantage of them whenever they got a chance. Buck concludes that the 'considerate behaviour of superiors appears to have contributed significantly inversely to feelings of job pressure'.

Relationships with subordinates

Officially, one of the most critical functions of a manager is his supervision of other people's work. It has long been accepted that an 'inability to delegate' might be a problem, but now a new potential source of stress is being introduced in the manager's interpersonal skills: he must learn to 'manage by participation'. Donaldson and Gowler (1975) point to the factors which may make today's zealous emphasis on participation a cause of resentment, anxiety and stress for the manager concerned:

* mismatch of formal and actual power;
* the manager may well resent the erosion of his formal role and authority (and the loss of status and rewards);
* he may be subject to irreconcilable pressures: for example, to be both participative and to achieve high production;
* his subordinates may refuse to participate.

Particularly for those with technological and scientific backgrounds (a 'things orientation'), relationships with subordinates can be a low priority (seen as 'trivial', 'petty', time consuming and an impediment to doing a job well) and one would expect their interactions to be more a source of stress than those of 'people-orientated' managers.

Relationships with colleagues

Besides the obvious factors of office politics and colleagues' rivalry we find another element here: stress can be caused not only by the pressure of poor relationships but also by its opposite: a lack of adequate social support in difficult situations (Lazarus, 1966). At highly competitive managerial levels, it is likely that problem sharing is inhibited for fear of appearing weak; and much of the (American) literature particularly mentions the isolated life of the top executive as an added source of strain (see Cooper and Marshall, 1978, for an extensive bibliography on this).

Morris (1975) encompasses this whole area of relationships in one model: what he calls the 'cross of relationships'. While he acknowledges the differences between relationships on two continua - one axis extends from colleagues to users and the other intersecting axis from senior to junior managers - he feels that the focal manager must bring all four into 'dynamic balance' in order to be able to deal with the stress of his position. Morris' suggestion seems 'only sensible' when we see how much of his work time the manager spends with other people. In a research programme to find out exactly what managers do, Mintzberg (1973) showed just how much of their time is spent in interaction. In an intensive study of a small sample of chief executives he found that in a large organization a mere 22 per cent of time was spent in desk work sessions, the rest being taken up by telephone calls (6 per cent), scheduled meetings (59 per cent), unscheduled meetings (10 per cent) and other activities (3 per cent). In small organizations basic desk work played a larger part (52 per cent), but nearly 40 per cent was still devoted to face-to-face contacts of one kind or another.

Career prospects

Two major clusters of potential managerial stressors can be identified in this area:

* lack of job security: fear of redundancy, obsolescence or early retirement, etc;
* status incongruity: under- or over-promotion, frustration at having reached one's career ceiling, etc.

For many managers their career progression is of overriding importance: by promotion they earn not only money but also status and the new job challenge for which they strive. Typically, in the early years at work, this striving and the aptitude to come to terms quickly with a rapidly changing environment is fostered and suitably rewarded by the company. Career progression is, perhaps, a problem by its very nature. For example, Sofer (1970) found that many of his sample believed that 'luck' and 'being in the right place at the right time' play a major role.

At middle age, and usually middle management levels, one's career becomes more problematic and most executives find their progress slowed, if not actually stopped. Job opportunities become fewer, those jobs that are available take longer to master, past (mistaken?) decisions cannot be revoked, old knowledge and methods become obsolete, energies may be flagging or demanded by the family, and there is the 'press' of fresh young recruits to face in competition. Constandse (1972) refers to this phase as the 'male menopause' and depicts the manager as suffering these fears and disappointments in 'silent isolation' from his family and work colleagues.

The fear of demotion or obsolescence can be strong for those who know they have reached their 'career ceiling': and most will inevitably suffer some erosion of status before they finally retire. Goffman (1952), extrapolating from a technique employed in the con-game, 'cooling the mark out', suggests that the company should bear some of the responsibility for taking the sting out of this (felt) failure experience.

From the company perspective, on the other hand, McMurray (1973) puts the case for not promoting a manager to a higher position if there is doubt that he can fill it. In a syndrome he labels 'the executive neurosis', he describes the over-promoted manager as grossly overworking to keep down a top job and at the same time hiding his insecurity: he points to the consequences of this for his work performance and the company. Age is no longer revered as it was; it is becoming a 'young man's world'. The rapidity with which society is developing (technologically, economically, and socially) is likely to mean that individuals will now need to change career during their working life (as companies and products are having to do). Such trends breed uncertainty and research suggests that older workers look for stability. Unless managers adapt their expectations to suit new circumstances 'career development' stress, especially in later life, is likely to become an increasingly common experience.

Organizational structure and climate

A fifth potential source of managerial stress is simply 'being in the organization' and the threat to an individual's freedom, autonomy, and identity this poses. Problem areas, such as little or no participation in the decision-making process, no sense of belonging, lack of effective consultation, poor communications, restrictions on behaviour, and office politics, are some of those with the most impact here. An increasing number of research investigations are being conducted in this area, particularly into the effect of employee participation in the work place. This research development is contemporaneous with a growing movement in North America and in the EEC countries of worke participation programmes, involving autonomous work groups, worker directors, and a greater sharing of the decision-making process throughout the organization. The early work on participation was in terms of its effect on production and attitudes of workers. For example, Coch and French (1948) examined the degrees of participation in a sewing factory. They found that the greater the participation, the higher was the productivity, the greater the job satisfaction, the lower the turnover and the better the relationship between boss and subordinate. These findings were later supported by a field experiment in a footwear factory in Southern Norway where greater participation led to significantly more favourable attitudes by workers towards management and more involvement in their jobs (French et al, 1960).

The research relevant to our interests here, however, is the more recent work on lack of participation and stress-related disease. In the NASA study (French and Caplan, 1970), for example, they found that managers and other professional workers who reported greater opportunities for participation in decision making reported significantly greater job satisfaction, low job-related feelings of threat, and higher feelings of self-esteem. Buck (1972) found that both managers and workers who felt 'under pressure' most, reported that their bosses 'always ruled with an iron hand and rarely tried out new ideas or allowed participation in decision making'. Managers who were under stress also reported that their bosses never let the persons under them do their work in the way they thought best. Margolis et al (1974) found that non-participation at work, amongst a national representative sample of over 1,400 workers, was the most consistent and significant predictor or indicator of strain and job-related stress. They found that non-participation was significantly related to the following health risk factors: overall poor physical health, escapist drinking, depressed mood, low self-esteem, low life satisfaction, low job satisfaction, low motivation to work, intention to leave job, and absenteeism from work. Kasl (1973) also found that low job satisfaction was related to non-participation in decision making, inability to provide feedback to supervisors, and lack of recognition for good performance; and that poor mental health was linked to close supervision and no autonomy at work. Neff (1968) has highlighted the importance of lack of participation and involvement by suggesting that 'mental health at work is to a large extent a function of the degree to which output is under the control of the individual worker'. To summarize, research seems to indicate that greater participation leads to lower staff turnover and higher productivity; and that when participation is absent lower job satisfaction and higher levels of physical and mental health risks may result.

Home-work interface stresses

The sixth 'source' of managerial stress is more of a 'catch-all' for all those interfaces between life outside and life inside the organization that might put pressure on the manager: family problems, life crises, financial difficulties, conflict of personal beliefs with those of the company, and the conflict of company with family demands (Cooper, 1981).

The area which has received most research interest here is that of the manager's relationship with his wife and family. (It is widely agreed that managers have little time for 'outside activities' apart from their families. Writers who have examined their effects on the local community have pointed to the disruptive effects of the executive's lack of involvement). The manager has two main problems vis-a-vis his family:

* the first is that of 'time management' and 'commitment-management'. Not only does his busy life leave him few resources with which to cope with other people's needs, but in order to do his job well the manager usually also needs support from others to cope with the 'background' details of house management, etc., to relieve stress when possible, and to maintain contact with the outside world;
* the second, often a result of the first, is the spill-over of crises or stresses in one system which affect the other.

As these two are inseparable we now go on to discuss them together.

Marriage patterns

The 'arrangement' the manager comes to with his wife is of
vital importance to both problem areas. Pahl and Pahl (1971)
found that the majority of wives in their middle-class sample
saw their role in relation to their husband's job as a
supportive, domestic one; all said that they derived their
sense of security from their husbands. Gowler and Legge
(1975) have dubbed this bond 'the hidden contract', in which
the wife agrees to act as a 'support team' so that her
husband can fill the demanding job to which he aspires. Handy
(1978) supports the idea that this is 'typical' and that it
is the path to career success for the manager concerned.
Based on individual psychometric data, he describes a number
of possible marriage-role combinations. In his sample of top
British executives (in mid-career) and their wives, he found
that the most frequent pattern (about half the 22 couples
interviewed) was the 'thrusting male-caring female'. This he
depicts as highly role segregated with the emphasis on
'separation', 'silence', and complementary activities.
Historically, both the company and the manager have reaped
benefits from maintaining the segregation of work and home
implicit in this pattern. The company thus legitimates its
demand for a constant work performance from its employee, no
matter what his home situation, and the manager is free to
pursue his career but keeps a 'safe haven' to which he can
return to relax and recuperate. The second and most frequent
combination was 'involved-involved': a dual career pattern,
with the emphasis on complete sharing. This, while
potentially extremely fulfilling for both parties, requires
energy inputs which might well prove so excessive that none
of the roles involved is fulfilled successfully.

It is unlikely that the patterns described above are
negotiated explicitly or that in the long term they are
'in balance'. Major factors in their continuing evolution
are the work and family demands of particular life stages.
One report (Beattie et al, 1974), for example, highlights the
difficult situation of the young executive who, in order to
build up his career, must devote a great deal of time and
energy to his job just when his young housebound wife, with
small children, is also making pressing demands. The report
suggests that the executive fights to maintain the distance
between his wife and the organization, so that she is not in
a position to evaluate the choices he has to make;
paradoxically, he does so at a time when he is most in need
of sympathy and understanding. Guest and Williams (1973)
examined the complete career cycle in similar terms, pointing
out how the demands of the different systems change over
time. The addition of role-disposition and personality-
disposition variations to their 'equations' would, however,
make them even more valuable.

Mobility

Home conflicts become particularly critical in relation to
managerial relocation and mobility. Much of the literature

on this topic comes from the United States where mobility is much more a part of the national character than in the UK but there is reason to believe that here, too, it is an increasingly common phenomenon.

At an individual level the effects of mobility on the manager's wife and family have been studied (Cooper and Marshall, 1978). Researchers agree that whether she is willing to move or not, the wife bears the brunt of relocations, and they conclude that most husbands do not appreciate what this involves. American writers point to signs that wives are suffering and becoming less co-operative. Immundo (1974) hypothesizes that increasing divorce rates are seen as the upwardly aspiring manager races ahead of his socially unskilled 'stay-at-home' wife. Seidenberg (1973) comments on the rise in the ratio of female to male alcoholics in the United States from 1:5 in 1962 to 1:2 in 1973 and asks the question, 'Do corporate wives have souls?' Descriptive accounts of the frustrations and loneliness of being a 'corporate wife' in the US and UK proliferate. Increasing teenage delinquency and violence is also laid at the door of the mobile manager and the society which he has created.

Constant moving can have profound effects on the life style of the people concerned: particularly on their relationships with others. Staying only two years or so in one place, mobile families do not have time to develop close ties with the local community. Immundo (1974) talks of the 'mobility syndrome', a way of behaving geared to developing only temporary relationships. Packard (1975) describes ways in which individuals react to the type of fragmenting society this creates: for example, treating everything as if it were temporary, being indifferent to local community amenities and organizations, living for the 'present' and becoming adept at 'instant gregariousness'. He goes on to point out the likely consequences for local communities, the nation, and the rootless people involved.

Pahl and Pahl (1971) suggest that the British reaction is, characteristically, more reserved and that many mobiles retreat into their nuclear family. Managers, particularly, do not become involved in local affairs due both to lack of time and to an appreciation that they are only 'short-stay' inhabitants. Their wives find participation easier (especially in a mobile rather than a static area) and a recent survey (Middle Class Housing Estate Study, 1975) suggested that, for some, involvement is a necessity to compensate for their husband's ambitions and career involvement which keep him away from home. From the company's point of view, the way in which a wife does adjust to her new environment can affect her husband's work performance. Guest and Williams (1973) illustrate this by an example of a major international company who, on surveying 1,800 of their executives in 70 countries, concluded that the two most important influences on overall satisfaction with the overseas assignment were the job itself and, more importantly, the executive's wife's adjustment to the foreign environment.

The Type A manager

Sources of pressure at work evoke different reactions from different managers. Some are better able to cope with these stressors than others; they adapt their behaviour in a way that meets the environmental challenge. On the other hand, some managers are psychologically predisposed to stress: that is, they are unable to cope or adapt to the stress-provoking situations. Many factors may contribute to these differences: personality, motivation, being able or ill-equipped to deal with problems in a particular area of expertise, fluctuations in abilities (particularly with age), insight into one's own motivations and weaknesses, etc. It would be useful to examine, therefore, those characteristics of the individual that research evidence indicates are predisposers to stress. Most of the research in this area has focussed on personality and behavioural differences between high- and low-stressed individuals.

The major research approach to individual stress differences began with the work of Friedman and Rosenman (Rosenman et al, 1966; Friedman, 1969) in the early 1960s and developed later showing a relationship between behavioural patterns and the prevalence of CHD. They found that individuals manifesting certain behavioural traits were significantly more at risk to CHD. These individuals were later referred to as the 'coronary-prone behaviour pattern Type A' as distinct from Type B (low risk of CHD). Type A w found to be the overt behavioural syndrome of style of living characterized by 'extreme of competitiveness, striving for achievement, aggressiveness, haste, impatience, restlessness, hyperalertness, explosiveness of speech, tenseness of facial musculature and feelings of being under pressure of time and under the challenge of responsibility'. It was suggested that 'people having this particular behavioural pattern were often so deeply involved and committed to their work that other aspects of their lives were relatively neglected' (Jenkins, 1971). In the early studies, persons were designated as Type A or Type B on the basis of clinical judgements of doctors and psychologists or peer ratings. These studies found higher incidence of CHD among Type A than Type B. Many of the inherent methodological weaknesses of this approach were overcome by the classic Western Collaborative Group Study (Rosenman et al, 1966). It was a prospective (as opposed to the earlier retrospective studies) national sample of over 3,400 men free of CHD. All these men were rated Type A or by psychiatrists after intensive interviews, without knowledge of any biological data about them and without the individuals being seen by a heart specialist. Diagnosis was made by an electro-cardiographer and an independent medical practitioner, who were not informed about the subjects' behavioural patterns. They found the following result: after $2\frac{1}{2}$ years from the start of the study, Type A men between the ages of 39 and 49, and 50 and 59, had 6.5 and 1.9 times respectively the incidence of CHD than Type B men. They also had a large number of stress risk factors (e.g. high serum cholesterol levels, elevated beta-lipoproteins, etc.). After 4½ years of the follow-up observation in the study, the same relationship of behavioural pattern and incidence of CHD was found. In terms of the clinical manifestations of CHD, individuals exhibiting Type A behavioural patterns had significantly more incidence of acute myocardial infarction and angina pectoris. Rosenman et al (1967) also found that the risk of recurrent and fatal myocardial infarction was significantly related to Type A characteristics. Quinlan and his colleagues (Quinlan et al, 1969) found the same results among Trappist and Benedictine monks. Monks judged to be Type A coronary-prone cases (by a double-blind procedure) had 2.3 times the prevalence of angina and 4.3 times the prevalence of infarction as compared to monks judged Type B.

An increasingly large number of studies have been carried out which support the relationship between Type A behaviour and ill-health From a management perspective the most significant work was carried out by Howard et al (1976). Two hundred and thirty-six managers from 12 different companies were examined for Type A behaviour and for a number of the known risk factors in CHD (blood pressure, cholesterol, triglycerides, uric acid, smoking and fitness). Those managers exhibiting extreme Type A behaviour showed significantly higher blood pressure (systolic and diastolic) and higher cholesterol and triglyceride levels. A higher percentage of these managers were cigarette smokers and in each age group studied, Type A managers were less interested in exercise (although differences in cardio-respiratory fitness were found only in the oldest age group). The authors conclude that Type A managers were found to be higher on a number of risk factors known to be associated with CHD than Type B managers.

The management of stress

Cooper and Marshall (1978) have argued that understanding the sources of managerial pressure, as we have tried to do here, is only the first step in stress reduction. Next, we must begin to explore 'when' and 'how' to intervene. There are a number of changes that can be introduced in organizational life to begin to manage stress at work. For example:

* to re-create the social, psychological, and organizational environment in the work place to encourage greater autonomy and participation by managers in their jobs;
* to begin to build the bridges between the work place and the home; providing opportunities for the manager's wife to understand better her husband's job, to express her views about the consequences of his work on family life,

253

and to be involved in the decision-making process of work that affects all members of the family unit;
* to utilize the well-developed catalogue of social and interactive skill training programmes in order to help clarify role and interpersonal relationship difficulties within organizations;
* and, more fundamentally, to create an organizational climate to encourage rather than discourage communication, openness and trust, so that individual managers are able to express their inability to cope, their work-related fears, and are able to ask for help if needed.

There are many other methods and approaches of coping and managing stress, depending on the sources activated and the interface between these sources and the individual make-up of the manager concerned, but the important point that we are trying to raise here is that the cure (intervention or training technique) depends on the diagnosis. It is important to try and encourage organizations to be sensitive to the needs of their managers and begin to audit managerial (di)stress. As Wright (1975) so aptly suggests, 'the responsibility for maintaining health should be a reflection of the basic relationship between the individual and the organization for which he works; it is in the best interests of both parties that reasonable steps are taken to live and work sensibly and not too demandingly'.

References

Beattie, R.T., Darlington, T.G. and Cripps, O.M. (1974) The management threshold. British Institute of Management Paper OPN 11.

Breslow, L. and Buell, P. (1960) Mortality from coronary heart disease and physical activity of work in California. Journal of Chronic Diseases, 11, 615-626.

Brummet, R.L., Pyle, W.C. and Flamholtz, E.G. (1968) Accounting for human resources. Michigan Business Review, 20, 20-25.

Buck, V. (1972) Working Under Pressure. London: Staples Press.

Coch, L. and French, J.R.P. (1948) Overcoming resistance to change. Human Relations, 11, 512-532.

Constandse, W.J. (1972) A neglected personnel problem. Personnel Journal, 51, 129-133.

Cooper, C.L. (1980) The Stress Check. London: Prentice Hall.

Cooper, C.L. (1981) Stressing Executive Families. London: Prentice Hall.

Cooper, C.L. and Marshall, J. (1978) Understanding Executive Stress. London: Macmillan.

Donaldson, J. and Gowler, D. (1975)
Prerogatives, participation and managerial stress. In Gowler, D. and Legge, K. (eds), Managerial Stress. Epping: Gower Press.

French, J.R.P. and Caplan, R.D. (1970)
Psychosocial factors in coronary heart disease. Industrial Medicine, 39, 383-397.

French, J.R.P. and Caplan, R.D. (1973)
Organizational stress and individual strain. In A.J. Marrow, (ed.), The Failure of Success. New York: AMACOM.

French, J.R.P., Israel, J. and As,D. (1960)
An experiment in participation in a Norwegian factory. Human Relations, 13, 3-20.

French, J.R.P., Tupper, C.J. and Mueller, E.I. (1965)
Workload of university professors. Unpublished research report. Ann Arbor, Mich.: University of Michigan.

Friedman, M. (1969)
Pathogenesis of Coronary Artery Disease. New York: McGraw-Hill.

Goffman, E. (1952)
On cooling the mark out. Psychiatry, 15, 451-463.

Gowler, D. and Legge, K. (1975)
Stress and external relationships - the 'Hidden Contract'. In D. Gowler and K. Legge (eds), Managerial Stress. Epping: Gower Press.

Guest, D. and Williams, R. (1973)
How home affects work. New Society, 23, 114-117.

Handy, C. (1978)
The family: help or hindrance. In C.L. Cooper and R. Payne (eds), Stress at Work. Chichester: Wiley.

Howard, J.H., Cunningham, D.A. and Rechnitzer, P.A. (1976)
Health patterns associated with Type A behaviour: a managerial population. Journal of Human Stress, 2, 24-31.

Immundo, L.V. (1974)
Problems associated with managerial mobility. Personnel Journal, 53, 910.

Jenkins, C.D. (1971)
Psychological and social precursors of coronary disease. New England Journal of Medicine, 284, 307-317.

Kahn, R.L., Wolfe, D.M., Quinn, R.P., Snoek, J.D. and Rosenthal, R.A. (1964)
Organizational Stress. New York: Wiley.

Kasl, S.V. (1973)
Mental health and the work environment. Journal of Occupational Medicine, 15, 509-518.

Kay, E. (1974)
Middle management. In J. O'Toole (ed.), Work and the Quality of Life. Cambridge, Mass.: MIT Press.

Lazarus, R.S. (1966)
Psychological Stress and the Coping Process. New York: McGraw-Hill.

McMurray, R.N. (1973)
   The executive neurosis. In R.L. Noland (ed.), Industrial Mental Health and Employee Counselling. New York: Behavioral Publications.

Margolis, B.L. and Kroes, W.H. (1974)
   Work and the health of man. In J. O'Toole (ed.), Work and the Quality of Life. Cambridge, Mass.: MIT Press.

Margolis, B.L., Kroes, W.H. and Quinn, R.P. (1974)
   Job stress: an unlisted occupational hazard. Journal of Occupational Medicine, 16, 654-661.

Marshall, J. and Cooper, C.L. (1978)
   Executives Under Pressure. London: Macmillan.

Mettlin, C. and Woelfel, J. (1974)
   Interpersonal influence and symptoms of stress. Journal of Health and Social Behavior, 15, 311-319.

Middle Class Housing Estate Study (1975)
   Unpublished paper. Civil Service College, UK.

Miller, J.G. (1960)
   Information input overload and psychopathology. American Journal of Psychiatry, 116, 695-704.

Mintzberg, H. (1973)
   The Nature of Managerial Work. New York: Harper & Row

Morris, J. (1975)
   Managerial stress and 'The Cross of Relationships'. In D. Gowler and K. Legge (eds), Managerial Stress. Epping: Gower Press.

Neff, W.S. (1968)
   Work and Human Behavior. New York: Atherton Press.

Packard, V. (1975)
   A Nation of Strangers. New York: McKay.

Pahl, J.M. and Pahl, R.E. (1971)
   Managers and Their Wives. London: Allen Lane.

Pincherle, G. (1972)
   Fitness for work. Proceedings of the Royal Society of Medicine, 65, 321-324.

Quinlan, C.B., Burrow, J.G. and Hayes, C.G. (1969)
   The association of risk factors and CHD in Trappist and Benedictine monks. Presented to the American Heart Association, Louisiana, New Orleans.

Rosenman, R.H., Friedman, M. and Jenkins, C.D. (1967)
   Clinically unrecognised myocardial infarction in the Western collaborative group study. American Journal of Cardiology, 19, 776-782.

Rosenman, R.H., Friedman, M. and Strauss, R. (1966)
   CHD in Western collaborative group study. Journal of American Medical Association, 195, 86-92.

Russek, H.I. and Zohman, B.L. (1958)
   Relative significance of heredity, diet and occupational stress in CHD of young adults. American Journal of Medical Science, 235, 266-275.

Seidenberg, R. (1973)
   Corporate Wives - Corporate Casualties. New York: American Management Association.

Shirom, A., Eden, D., Silberwasser, S. and Kellerman, J.J. (1973)
Job stress and risk factors in coronary heart disease among occupational categories in kibbutzim. Social Science and Medicine, 7, 875-892.

Sofer, C. (1970)
Men in Mid-career. Cambridge: Cambridge University Press.

Uris, A. (1972)
How managers ease job pressures. International Management, June, 45-46.

Wardwell, W.I., Hyman, M. and Bahnson, C.B. (1964)
Stress and coronary disease in three field studies. Journal of Chronic Diseases, 17, 73-84.

Wright, H.B. (1975)
Executive Ease and Dis-ease. Epping: Gower Press.

N.B. Some of the research literature reviewed here was drawn from Cary L. Cooper's book, written with Judi Marshall, 'Understanding Executive Stress', London: Macmillan, 1978.

Questions

1. What are the sources of occupational stress that are common to most jobs?
2. What is Type A behaviour and why is it important to be aware of it?
3. Studs Terkel in his book 'Working' suggests 'work is, by its very nature, about violence ... to the spirit as well as to the body. It is about ulcers as well as accidents, about shouting matches as well as fist fights, about nervous breakdowns as well as kicking the dog around. It is, above all, about daily humiliation'. Discuss.
4. Is there any evidence that 'worker participation' can work?
5. William Faulkner once said, 'You can't eat for eight hours a day nor drink for eight hours a day nor make love for eight hours a day ... all you can do for eight hours a day is work. Which is the reason why man makes himself and everybody else so miserable and unhappy'. Discuss.
6. Differentiate between 'qualitative' and 'quantitative' overload and between 'role ambiguity' and 'role conflict'.
7. Is stress a result of the mismatch between the person and the work environment?

Annotated reading

Buck, V.E. (1972) Working Under Pressure. London: Staples. This is an early book in the stress field, which highlights a seminal study in the area. It explores the nature of boss-subordinate relationships, but is limited by the method of data analysis and the theoretical framework it adopts.

Caplan, R.D., Cobb, S., French, J.R.P., Van Harrison, R. and Pinneau, S.R. (1975) Job Demands and Worker Health. Washington, DC: US Department of Health, Education and Welfare.
> This is a much more comprehensive study of a variety of occupations in terms of job stressors and their manifestations. It examines both blue and white collar occupations.

Cooper, C.L. and Marshall, J. (1978) Understanding Executive Stress. London: Macmillan.
> This book reviews the field of managerial stress, highlighting the potential stressors at work and in the home. It draws on work published in medical, social science and management journals and books.

Marshall, J. and Cooper, C.L. (1979) Executives Under Pressure. London: Macmillan.
> This book examines the quality of managerial life. It focusses on the problems of managerial redundancy, early retirement, job mobility, training and the home-work interface.

Cooper, C.L. and Payne, R. (1980) Current Concerns in Occupational Stress. Chichester: Wiley.
> This is an edited volume of distinguished contributors who explore a range of issues that affect people at work. It looks at the impact of job transfers, dual career marriages, shift work, hazardous occupations, boundary roles (e.g. shop stewards) and also explores the potential methods of coping with the exigencies of industrial life.

Chapter 15

Counselling and helping
Barrie Hopson

From a situation in the mid-1960s when 'counselling' was
seen by many in education as a transatlantic transplant
which hopefully would never 'take', we have today reached
the position of being on board a band-wagon; 'counsellors'
are everywhere: beauty counsellors, tax counsellors,
investment counsellors, even carpet counsellors. There are
'counsellors' in schools, industry, hospitals, the social
services. There is marriage counselling, divorce counselling, parent counselling, bereavement counselling, abortion
counselling, retirement counselling, redundancy counselling,
career counselling, psychosexual counselling, pastoral counselling, student counselling and even disciplinary counselling! Whatever the original purpose for coining the word
'counselling', the coinage has by now certainly been de-
based. One of the unfortunate consequences of the debasing
has been that the word has become mysterious; we cannot
always be sure just what 'counselling' involves. One of the
results of the mystification of language is that we rely on
others to tell us what it is: that is, we assume that we,
the uninitiated, cannot know and understand what it is
really about. That can be a first step to denying ourselves
skills and knowledge we already possess or that we may have
the potential to acquire.

It is vital that we 'de-mystify' counselling, and to do
that we must look at the concept within the broader context
of ways in which people help other people, and we must
analyse it in relation to objectives. 'Counselling' is often
subscribed to as being 'a good thing', but we must ask the
question, 'good for what?'

'Counselling' is only one form of helping. It is decidedly
not the answer to all human difficulties, though it can be
extremely productive and significant for some people, sometimes. Counselling is one way of working to help people
overcome problems, clarify or achieve personal goals. We can
distinguish between six types of helping strategies (Scally
and Hopson, 1979).

* Giving advice: offering somebody your opinion of what
  would be the best course of action based on your view
  of their situation.

* Giving information: giving a person the information he needs in a particular situation (e.g. about legal rights, the whereabouts of particular agencies, etc.). Lacking information can make one powerless; providing it can be enormously helpful.

* Direct action: doing something on behalf of somebody else or acting to provide for another's immediate needs; for example, providing a meal, lending money, stopping a fight, intervening in a crisis.

* Teaching: helping someone to acquire knowledge and skills; passing on facts and skills which improve somebody's situation.

* Systems change: working to influence and improve systems which are causing difficulty for people; that is, working on organizational development rather than with individuals.

* Counselling: helping someone to explore a problem, clarify conflicting issues and discover alternative ways of dealing with it, so that they can decide what to do about it; that is, helping people to help themselves.

There is no ranking intended in this list. What we do say is that these strategies make up a helper's 'tool-bag'. Each one is a 'piece of equipment' which may be useful in particular helping contexts. What a helper is doing is to choose from available resources whichever approach best fits the situation at the time.

There are some interesting similarities and differences between the strategies. Giving advice, information, direct action, teaching and possibly systems change recognize that the best answers, outcomes, or solutions rely on the expertise of the helper. The 'expert' offers what is felt to be most useful to the one seeking help. Counselling, on the other hand, emphasizes that the person with the difficulty is the one with the resources needed to deal with it. The counsellor provides the relationship which enables the clients to search for their own answers. The 'expert' does not hand out solutions. This does not deny the special skills of the helper, but does imply that having 'expertise' does not make a person an 'expert'. We all have expertise. In counselling, the counsellor is using personal expertise to help to get the clients in touch with their own expertise. Counselling is the only helping strategy which makes no assumption that the person's needs are known.

Teaching, systems change, and counselling are only likely to be effective if the 'helper' has relationship-making skills. Giving advice, information and direct action are likely to be more effective if he has them. Systems change is different in that it emphasizes work with groups, structures, rules and organizations.

The counsellor possibly uses most of the other strategies at some time or other, when they seem more appropriate than counselling. The other strategies would have an element of counselling in them if the 'helper' had the necessary skills. For example, a new student having difficulties making friends at school could lead to a counsellor, in addition to using counselling skills, teaching some relationship-building skills to the student, getting the staff to look at induction provision, making some suggestions to the student, or even taking the student to a lunchtime discotheque in the school club.

Who are the helpers?

Strictly speaking we are all potential helpers and people to be helped, but in this context it may be useful to distinguish between three groups.

Professional helpers
These are people whose full-time occupation is geared towards helping others in a variety of ways. They have usually, but not always, received specialist training. Social workers, doctors, teachers, school counsellors, nurses, careers officers and health visitors are a few examples. They define their own function in terms of one or more of the helping strategies.

Paraprofessional helpers
These people have a clearly defined helping role but it does not constitute the major part of their job specification or represent the dominant part of their lives, such as marriage guidance counsellors, priests, part-time youth workers, personnel officers and some managers. Probably they have received some short in-service training, often on-the-job.

Helpers in general
People who may not have any specially defined helping role but who, because of their occupational or social position or because of their own commitment, find themselves in situations where they can offer help to others, such as shop stewards, school caretakers, undertakers, social security clerks or solicitors. This group is unlikely to have received special training in helping skills. In addition to these groupings there are a variety of unstructured settings within which helping occurs: the family, friendships, and in the community (Brammer, 1973).

What makes people good helpers?

In some ways it is easier to begin with the qualities that quite clearly do not make for good helping. Loughary and Ripley (1979) people their helpers' rogue's gallery with four types of would-be helpers:

* the 'You think you've got a problem! Let me tell you about mine!' type;
* the 'Let me tell you what to do' type;
* the 'I understand because I once had the same problem myself' person;
* the 'I'll take charge and deal with it' type.

The first three approaches have been clearly identified as

being counter-productive (Carkhuff and Berenson, 1976) while the fourth one certainly deals with people's problems but prevents them ever learning skills or concepts to enable them to work through the problem on their own the next time it occurs. The only possible appropriate place for this person is in a crisis intervention. However, even this intervention would need to be followed up with additional counselling help if the needy person were to avoid such crises.

Rogers (1958) came out with clearly testable hypotheses of what constitutes effective helping. He said that helpers must be open and that they should be able to demonstrate the following qualities:

* unconditioned positive regard: acceptance of clients as worth while regardless of who they are or what they say or do;
* congruence: helpers should use their feelings, their verbal and non-verbal behaviour should be open to clients and be consistent;
* genuineness: they should be honest, sincere and without facades;
* empathic: they should be able to let clients know that they understand their frame of reference and can see the world as the client sees it, whilst remaining separate from it.

These qualities must be not only possessed but conveyed: that is, the client must experience them.

Truax and Carkhuff (1967) put these hypotheses to the test and found considerable empirical support for what they identified as the 'core facilitative conditions' of effective helping relationships - empathy, respect and positive regard, genuineness, and concreteness - the ability to be specific and immediate to client statements. They differed from Rogers in that whereas he claimed that the facilitative conditions were necessary and sufficient, they only claimed that they were necessary. Carkhuff has gone on to try to demonstrate (Carkhuff and Berenson, 1976) that they are clearly not sufficient, and that the helper needs to be skilled in teaching a variety of life and coping skills to clients. The other important finding from Truax and Carkhuff was that helpers who do not possess those qualities are not merely ineffective, for they can contribute to people becoming worse than they were prior to helping.

The evidence tends to suggest that the quality of the interpersonal relationship between helper and client is more important than any specific philosophy of helping adhered to by the helper. This has been demonstrated to be the case in counselling, psychotherapy and also teaching (Aspy and Roebuck, 1977). A recent review of the many research studies on this topic would suggest, as one might expect, that things are not quite that simple (Parloff, Waskow, and Wolfe, 1978), but after a reappraisal of the early work of Truax and Carkhuff and a large number of more recent studies, the authors conclude that a relationship between empathy, respect and genuineness with helper effectiveness has been established. They also shed light on a number of other factors which have been discussed periodically as being essential for effective therapists (their focus was therapy, not helping):

* personal psychotherapy has not been demonstrated to be a prerequisite for an effective therapist;
* sex and race are not related to effectiveness;
* the value of therapist experience is highly questionable; that is, someone is not necessarily a better therapist because of greater experience;
* therapists with emotional problems of their own are likely to be less effective;
* there is some support for the suggestion that helpers are more effective when working with clients who hold values similar to their own.

What they do point out is the importance of the match between helper and client. No one is an effective helper with everyone, although we as yet know little as to how to match helpers with clients to gain the greatest benefits.

Helping and human relationships

Carl Rogers states very clearly that psychotherapy is not a 'special kind of relationship, different in kind from all others which occur in everyday life' (1957). A similar approach has been taken by those theorists looking at the broader concept of helping. Brammer (1973) states that 'helping relationships have much in common with friendships, family interactions, and pastoral contacts. They are all aimed at fulfilling basic human needs, and when reduced to their basic components, look much alike'. This is the approach of Egan (1975) in his training programmes for effective interpersonal relating, of Carkhuff and Berenson (1976) who talk of counselling as 'a way of life', of Illich, Zola, McKnight, Kaplan and Sharken (1977) who are concerned with the de-skilling of the population by increasing armies of specialists, and of Scally and Hopson (1979) who emphasize that counselling 'is merely a set of beliefs, values and behaviours to be found in the community at large'. Considerable stress is placed later in this chapter on the trend towards demystifying helping and counselling.

Models of helping
Any person attempting to help another must have some model in mind, however ill-formed, of the process which is about to be undertaken. There will be goals, however hazy, ranging from helping the person to feel better through to helping the person to work through an issue independently. It is essential for helpers to become more aware of the value-roots of their behaviours and the ideological underpinning of their proffered support.

PFM–R

The helper builds his theory through three overlapping stages. First he reflects on his own experience. He becomes aware of his values, needs, communication style, and their impact on others. He reads widely on the experience of other practitioners who have tried to make sense out of their observations by writing down their ideas into a systematic theory ... Finally the helper forges the first two items together into a unique theory of his own (Brammer, 1973).

Fortunately, in recent years a number of theorists and researchers have begun to define models of helping. This can only assist all helpers to define their own internal models which will then enable them in turn to evaluate their personal, philosophical and empirical bases.

CARKHUFF AND ASSOCIATES: Carkhuff took Rogers' ideas on psychotherapy and expanded on them to helping in general. He has a three-stage model through which the client is helped to (i) explore, (ii) understand and (iii) act. He defines the skills needed by the helper at each stage of the process (Carkhuff, 1974), and has also developed a system for selecting and training prospective helpers to do this. Since the skills he outlines are basically the same skills which anyone needs to live effectively, he suggests that the best way of helping people is to teach them directly and systematically in life, work, learning and relationship-building skills. He states clearly that 'the essential task of helping is to bridge the gap between the helpee's skills level and the helper's skills level' (Carkhuff and Berenson, 1976). For Carkhuff, helping equals teaching, but teaching people the skills to ensure that they can take more control over their own lives.

BRAMMER (1973) has produced an integrated, eclectic developmental model similar to Carkhuff's. He has expanded Carkhuff's three stages into the eight stages of entry, classification, structure, relationship, exploration, consolidation, planning and termination. He has also identified seven clusters of skills to promote 'understanding of self and others'. His list of 46 specific skills is somewhat daunting to a beginner but a rich source of stimulation for the more experienced helper.

IVEY (1971) AND ASSOCIATES have developed a highly systematic model for training helpers under the label 'microcounselling'. Each skill is broken up into its constituent parts and taught via closed-circuit television, modelling and practice.

HACKNEY AND NYE (1973) have described a helping model which they call a 'discrimination' model. It is goal-centred and action-centred and it stresses skills training.

KAGAN, KRATHWOHL (1967) AND ASSOCIATES have also developed a microskills approach to counsellor training which is widely used in the USA. It is called Interpersonal Process Recall which involves an enquiry session in which helper and client explore the experience they have had together in the presence of a mediator.

EGAN (1975) has developed perhaps the next most influential model of helping in the USA after Carkhuff's and, indeed, has been highly influenced by Carkhuff's work. The model begins with a pre-helping phase involving attending skills, to be followed by Stage I: responding and self-exploration; Stage II: integrative understanding and dynamic self-understanding; and Stage III: facilitating action and acting. The first goal labelled at each stage is the helper's goal and the second goal is that of the client.

LOUGHARY AND RIPLEY (1979) approach helping from a different viewpoint, which, unlike the previous theorists, is not simply on the continuum beginning with Rogers and Carkhuff. They have used a demystifying approach aimed at the general population with no training other than what can be gleaned from their book. Their model is shown in figure 1.

Figure 1

Model of helping
From Loughary and Ripley (1979)

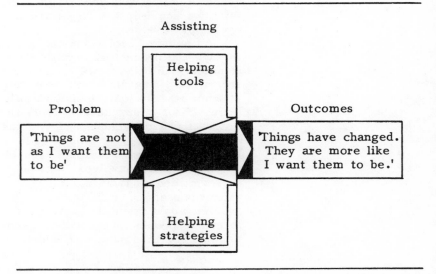

The helping tools include information, ideas, and skills (such as listening and reflecting dealings). The strategies are the plans for using the tools and the first step is always translating the problem into desired outcomes. Their four positive outcomes of helping are: changes in feeling states, increased understanding, decisions, and implementing decisions. Their approach does move away from the counselling-dominated approach of the other models.

HOPSON AND SCALLY: we reproduce our own model in some detail here, partly because it is the model we know best and it has worked very effectively for us and for the 3,000 teachers and youth workers who have been through our counselling skills training courses (Scally and Hopson, 1979), but also because it attempts to look at all the aspects of helping defined at the beginning of this chapter.

Figure 2 outlines three goal areas for helpers, central to their own personal development. It also defines specific helping outcomes. Helpers can only help people to the levels of their own skills and awareness (Aspy and Roebuck, 1977). They need to clarify their own social, economic and cultural values and need to be able to recognize and separate their own needs and problems from those of their clients. Helpers see in others reflections of themselves. To know oneself is to ensure a clarity of distinction between images: to know where one stops and the other begins. We become less helpful as the images blur. To ensure that does not happen, we need constantly to monitor our own development. Self-awareness is not a stage to be reached and then it is over. It is a process which can never stop because we are always changing. By monitoring these changes we simultaneously retain some control of their direction.

From a greater awareness of who we are, our strengths, hindrances, values, needs and prejudices, we can be clearer about skills we wish to develop. The broader the range of skills we acquire, the larger the population group that we can help.

As helpers involved in the act of helping we learn through the process of praxis. We reflect and we act. As we interact with others, we in turn are affected by them and are in some way different from before the interaction. As we attempt to help individuals and influence systems we will learn, change, and develop from the process of interaction, just as those individuals and systems will be affected by us.

Having access to support should be a central concern for anyone regularly involved in helping. Helpers so often are not as skilled as they might be at saying 'no' and looking after themselves.

We would maintain that the ultimate goals of helping are to enable people to become self-empowered and to make systems healthier places in which to live, work and play.

Self-empowerment

There are five dimensions of self-empowerment (Hopson and Scally, 1980a).

* Awareness: without an awareness of ourselves and others we are subject to the slings and arrows of our upbringing, daily events, social changes and crises. Without awareness we can only react, like the pinball in the machine that bounces from one thing to another without having ever provided the energy for its own passage.
* Goals: given awareness we have the potential for taking charge of ourselves and our lives. We take charge by exploring our values, developing commitments, and by

Figure 2

Goals of helping

GOALS OF HELPING

SELF-EMPOWERED INDIVIDUALS	PERSONAL DEVELOPMENT OF THE HELPER	HEALTHY SYSTEMS (MICRO, MACRO)	SPECIFIC OUTCOMES
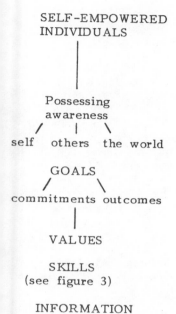	Increasing self-awareness and level and range of skills	Exist to serve the development of individuals	Increase understanding
	Monitoring own welfare and development	Value and promote behaviours which convey respect, genuineness and empathy	Changes in feeling states (discharge or exploration)
	Using skills to assist development of others	Encourage members to work co-operatively towards shared identifiable goals	Able to make a decision
	Giving and getting support	Are open to internal and external influences for change	Able to implement a decision
	Interacting with, learning from, changing and being changed by individuals and systems	Re-evaluate periodically goals, methods and effectiveness	Confirms a decision
		Are dynamic not static	Gets support
		Feature the giving and receiving of support by members	Adjusts to a situation which is not going to change
		Focus on individual's strengths	Examines alternative
			Receives direct action/ practical help
			Increases skills, develops new ones
			Receives information
		(continued)	(continued)

HEALTHY SYSTEMS (MICRO, MACRO) (continued)	SPECIAL OUTCOMES (continued)
And builds on them	Reflects on acts
Use problem solving strategies rather than scapegoating, blaming or focussing on faults	
Use methods which are consistent with goals	
Encourage power-sharing and enable individuals to pursue their own direction as a contribution to shared goals	
Monitor their own performance in a continuing cycle of reflection/action	
Allow people access to those whose decisions have a bearing on their lives	
Have effective and sensitive lines of communication	
Explore differences openly and use compromise, negotiation and contracting to achieve a maximum of win/win outcomes for all	
Are always open to alternatives	

specifying goals with outcomes. We learn to live by the question: 'what do I want now?' We reflect and then act.

* Values: we subscribe to the definition of values put forward by Raths, Harmin and Simon (1964): a value is a belief which has been chosen freely from alternatives after weighing the consequences of each alternative; it is prized and cherished, shared publicly and acted upon repeatedly and consistently. The self-empowered person, by our definition, has values which include recognizing the worth of self and others, of being proactive, working for healthy systems, at home, in employment, in the community and at leisure; helping other people to become more self-empowered.

* Life skills: values are good as far as they go, but it is only by developing skills that we can translate them into action. We may believe that we are responsible for our own destiny, but we require the skills to achieve what we wish for ourselves. In a school setting, for example, we require the skills of goal setting and action-planning, time management, reading, writing and numeracy, study skills, problem-solving skills and how to work in groups. Figure 3 reproduces the list of life skills that we have identified at the Counselling and Career Development Unit (Hopson and Scally, 1980b) as being crucial to personal survival and growth.

* Information: information is the raw material for awareness of self and the surrounding world. It is the fuel for shaping our goals. Information equals power. Without it we are helpless, which is of course why so many people and systems attempt to keep information to themselves. We must realize that information is essential (a concept), that we need to know how to get appropriate information, and from where (a skill).

Healthy systems

Too often counsellors and other helpers have pretended to be value free. Most people now recognize that fiction. Not only is it impossible but it can be dangerous. If we honestly believe that we are capable of being value free, we halt the search for the ways in which our value systems are influencing our behaviour with our clients. If we are encouraging our clients to develop goals, how can we pretend that we do not have them too? Expressing these goals can be the beginning of a contract to work with a client for, like it or not, we each have a concept, however shadowy, for the fully functioning healthy person to which our actions and helping are directed.

As with clients, so too with systems. If we are working towards helping people to become 'better', in whatever way we choose to define that, let us be clear about what changes we are working towards in the systems we try to influence. Figure 2 lists our characteristics of healthy systems. Each of us has our own criteria so let us discover them and bring them into the open. Owning up to our values is one way of demonstrating our genuineness.

Figure 3

Lifeskills: taking charge of yourself and your life

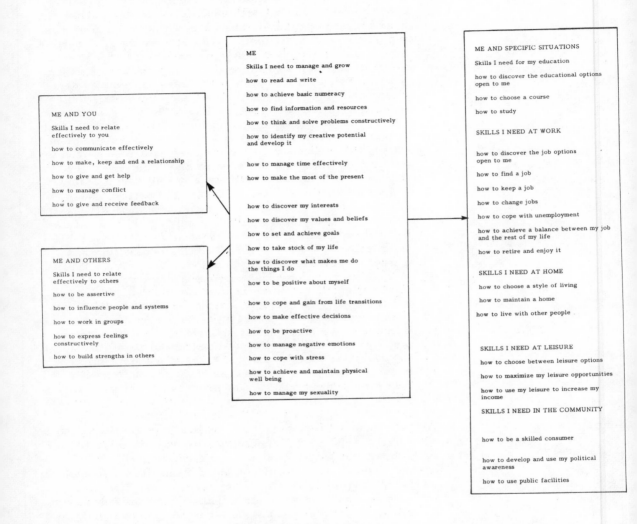

ME AND YOU

Skills I need to relate
effectively to you

how to communicate effectively

how to make, keep and end a relationship

how to give and get help

how to manage conflict

how to give and receive feedback

ME AND OTHERS

Skills I need to relate
effectively to others

how to be assertive

how to influence people and systems

how to work in groups

how to express feelings
constructively

how to build strengths in others

ME

Skills I need to manage and grow

how to read and write

how to achieve basic numeracy

how to find information and resources

how to think and solve problems constructively

how to identify my creative potential
and develop it

how to manage time effectively

how to make the most of the present

how to discover my interests

how to discover my values and beliefs

how to set and achieve goals

how to take stock of my life

how to discover what makes me do
the things I do

how to be positive about myself

how to cope and gain from life transitions

how to make effective decisions

how to be proactive

how to manage negative emotions

how to cope with stress

how to achieve and maintain physical
well being

how to manage my sexuality

ME AND SPECIFIC SITUATIONS

Skills I need for my education

how to discover the educational options
open to me

how to choose a course

how to study

SKILLS I NEED AT WORK

how to discover the job options
open to me

how to find a job

how to keep a job

how to change jobs

how to cope with unemployment

how to achieve a balance between my job
and the rest of my life

how to retire and enjoy it

SKILLS I NEED AT HOME

how to choose a style of living

how to maintain a home

how to live with other people

SKILLS I NEED AT LEISURE

how to choose between leisure options

how to maximize my leisure opportunities

how to use my leisure to increase my
income

SKILLS I NEED IN THE COMMUNITY

how to be a skilled consumer

how to develop and use my political
awareness

how to use public facilities

What is counselling?

Having identified six common ways of helping people, counselling will now be focussed on more intensively, which immediately gets us into the quagmire of definition.

Anyone reviewing the literature to define counselling will quickly suffer from data-overload. Books, articles, even manifestoes, have been written on the question.

In training courses run from the Counselling and Career Development Unit we tend to opt for the parsimonious definition of 'helping people explore problems so that they can decide what to do about them'.

The demystification of counselling

There is nothing inherently mysterious about counselling. It is merely a set of beliefs, values and behaviours to be found in the community at large. The beliefs include one that says individuals benefit and grow from a particular form of relationship and contact. The values recognize the worth and the significance of each individual and regard personal autonomy and self-direction as desirable. The behaviours cover a combination of listening, conveying warmth, asking open questions, encouraging specificity, concreteness and focussing, balancing support and confrontation, and offering strategies which help to clarify objectives and identify action plans. This terminology is more complex than the process needs to be. The words describe what is essentially a 'non-mystical' way in which some people are able to help other people to help themselves (see figure 4).

Training courses can sometimes encourage the mystification. They talk of 'counselling skills' and may, by implication, suggest that such skills are somehow separate from other human activities, are to be conferred upon those who attend courses, and are probably innovatory. In fact, what 'counselling' has done is to crystallize what we know about how warm, trusting relationships develop between people. It recognizes that:

* relationships develop if one has and conveys respect for another, if one is genuine oneself, if one attempts to see things from the other's point of view (empathizes), and if one endeavours not to pass judgement. Those who operate in this way we describe as having 'relationship-building skills';
* if the relationship is established, an individual will be prepared to talk through and explore thoughts and feelings. What one can do and say which helps that to happen we classify as exploring and clarifying skills (see figure 4);
* through this process individuals become clear about difficulties or uncertainties, and can explore options and alternatives, in terms of what they might do to change what they are not happy about;
* given support, individuals are likely to be prepared to, and are capable of, dealing with difficulties or problems they may face more effectively. They can be helped by somebody who can offer objective setting and action planning skills.

Counselling skills are what people use to help people to help themselves. They are not skills that are exclusive to one group or one activity. It is clear that the behaviours, which we bundle together and identify as skills, are liberally scattered about us in the community. Counselling ideology identifies which behaviours are consistent with its values and its goals, and teaches these as one category of helping skills.

Figure 4

The counselling process

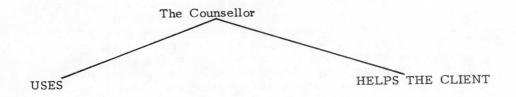

The Counsellor

USES   HELPS THE CLIENT

RELATIONSHIP   respect   to feel valued, understood
BUILDING   genuineness   and prepared to trust the
SKILLS   empathy   counsellor

                contracting   to talk and explore
                open questions   to understand more about
EXPLORING   summarizing   how he feels and why
AND   focussing   to consider options and
CLARIFYING   reflecting   examine alternatives
SKILLS   immediacy   to choose an alternative
                clarifying
                concreteness
                confronting

                objective setting   to develop clear objectives
                action planning   to form specific action plans
                problem-solving   to do (with support) what needs to
                strategies   be done

COUNSELLING IS HELPING PEOPLE TO HELP THEMSELVES

What may happen, unfortunately, is that the promotion of counselling as a separate training responsibility can increase the mystification. An outcome can be that instead of simply now being people who, compared to the majority, are extra-sensitive listeners, are particularly good at making relationships, and are more effective at helping others to solve problems, they have become 'counsellors' and licensed to help. A licence becomes a danger if:

* those who have it see themselves as qualitatively different from the rest of the population;
* it symbolizes to the non-licensed that they are incapable, or inferior, or calls into question valuable work they may be doing, but are 'unqualified' to do.

It is important to recognize that labelling people can have unfortunate side effects. Let us remember that whatever the nomenclature - counsellor, client or whatever - at a particular time or place, they are just people. All, at some time or other, will be able to give help, at other times will need to seek or receive help. Some are naturally better fitted to help others; some by training can improve their helping skills. All, through increased awareness and skill development, can become more effective helpers than they are now.

Counselling is not only practised by counsellors. It is a widespread activity in the community and appears in several guises. Its constituent skills are described variously as 'talking it over', 'having a friendly chat', 'being a good friend' or simply 'sharing' with somebody. These processes almost certainly include some or all of the skills summarized in figure 4. Often, of course, there are notable exceptions: for instance, we do not listen well; we cannot resist giving our advice, or trying to solve problems for our friends; we find it difficult to drop our facades and roles. Counselling skills training can help reduce our unhelpful behaviours and begin to develop these skills in ourselves, making us more effective counsellors, as well as simply being a good friend. In almost any work involving contact with other people, we would estimate there is a potential counselling component. There is a need for the particular interpersonal skills categorized here as coun-selling skills to be understood and used by people at large, but particularly by all people who have the welfare of others as part of their occupational roles. Specialist 'counsellors' have an important part to play, but it is not to replace the valuable work that is done by many who would not claim the title. Having said that, people sometimes think they are counselling, but in fact are doing things very far removed: disciplining, persuading people to conform to a system, and so on.

Types of counselling

Developmental versus crisis counselling
Counselling can operate either as a response to a situation

or as a stimulus to help a client develop and grow. In the past, counselling has often been concerned with helping someone with a problem during or after the onset of a crisis point: a widow unable to cope with her grief, the boy leaving school desperate because he has no idea what job to choose, the pregnant woman with no wish to be pregnant. This is a legitimate function of counselling, but if this is all that counselling is, it can only ever be concerned with making the best of the situation in which one finds oneself. How much more ambitious to help people anticipate future problems, to educate them to recognize the cues of oncoming crisis, and to provide them with skills to take charge of it at the outset instead of running behind in an attempt to catch up! This is counselling as a stimulus to growth: developmental as opposed to crisis counselling. All successful counselling entails growth, but the distinction between the two approaches is that the crisis approach generates growth under pressure, and since this is often limited only to the presenting problem, the client's behavioural and conceptual repertoire may remain little affected by the experience. There will always be a need for crisis counselling in a wide variety of settings, but the exciting prospect of developmental counselling for growth and change has only recently begun to be tackled.

Individual counselling
As counselling was rooted in psychotherapy it is hardly surprising that the primary focus has been on the one-to-one relationship. There are a number of essential elements in the process. Clients are to be helped to reach decisions by themselves. This is achieved by establishing a relationship of trust whereby individual clients feel that the counsellor cares about them, is able to empathize with their problems, and is authentic and genuine in relating to them. Counsellors will enter the relationship as persons in their own right, disclosing relevant information about themselves as appropriate, reacting honestly to clients' statements and questions, but at no time imposing their own opinions on the clients. Their task is to facilitate the clients' own abilities and strengths in such a way that clients experience the satisfaction of having defined and solved their problems for themselves. If a client lacks information on special issues, is incapable of generating alternative strategies, or cannot make decisions in a programmatic way, then the counsellor has a function as an educator whose skills are offered to the client. In this way the client is never manipulated. The counsellor is negotiating a contract to use some skills which are possessed by the counsellor, and which can be passed on to the client if the client wishes to make use of them.

Individual counselling has the advantages over group counselling of providing a safer setting for some people to lower their defences, of developing a strong and trusting relationship with the counsellor, and of allowing the client maximum personal contact with the counsellor.

Group counselling

Group counselling involves one or more counsellors operating
with a number of clients in a group session. The group size
varies from four to sixteen, with eight to ten being the
most usual number. The basic objectives of group and individual counselling are similar. Both seek to help the
clients achieve self-direction, integration, self-
responsibility, self-acceptance, and an understanding of
their motivations and patterns of behaviour. In both cases
the counsellor needs the skills and attitudes outlined
earlier, and both require a confidential relationship. There
are, however, some important differences (Hopson, 1977).

* The group counsellor needs an understanding of group
  dynamics: communication, decision making, role-playing,
  sources of power, and perceptual processes in groups.
* The group situation can provide immediate opportunities
  to try out ways of relating to individuals, and is an
  excellent way of providing the experience of intimacy
  with others. The physical proximity of the clients to
  one another can be emotionally satisfying and supportive. Clients give a first-hand opportunity to test
  others' perception of themselves.
* Clients not only receive help themselves; they also help
  other clients. In this way helping skills are generated
  by a larger group of people than is possible in
  individual counselling.
* Clients often discover that other people have similar
  problems, which can at the least be comforting.
* Clients learn to make effective use of other people, not
  just professionals, as helping agents. They can set up a
  mutual support group which is less demanding on the
  counsellor and likely to be a boost to their self-esteem
  when they discover they can manage to an increasing
  extent on their own.

There are many different kinds of group counselling. Some
careers services in higher education offer counsellor-led
groups as groundwork preparation for career choices; these
small groups give older adolescents an opportunity to
discuss the inter-relations between their conscious values
and preferred life styles and their crystallizing sense of
identity. Other groups are provided in schools where young
people can discuss with each other and an adult counsellor
those relationships with parents and friends which are so
important in adolescence. Training groups are held for
teaching decision-making skills and assertive skills. There
are also groups in which experiences are pooled and mutual
help given for the married, for parents, for those bringing
up families alone and for those who share a special problem
such as having a handicapped child. All these types of
groups are usually led by someone who has had training and
experience in facilitating them. The word 'facilitating' is
used advisedly, for the leader's job is not to conduct a
seminar or tutorial, but to establish an atmosphere in which

members of the group can explore the feelings around a particular stage of development or condition or critical choice.

Another type of group is not so specifically focussed on an area of common concern but is set up as a sort of laboratory to learn about the underlying dynamics of how people in groups function, whatever the group's focus and purpose may be. These are often referred to as sensitivity training groups (e.g. Cooper and Mangham, 1971; Smith, 1975). Yet a third category of group has more therapeutic goals, being intended to be successive or complementary to, or sometimes in place of, individual psychotherapy. This type of group will not usually have a place in work settings, whereas the other two do have useful applications there. Obvious uses for this type of group occur in induction procedures, in preparation for retirement, in relation to job change arising from promotion, or in relation to redundancy. The second type of group is employed in training for supervisory or management posts, though one hears less about their use in trade unions.

Schools of counselling

Differences in theories of personality, learning and perception are reflected in counselling theory. It is useful to distinguish between five major schools.

1. Psychoanalytic approaches were historically the first. Psychoanalysis is a personality theory, a philosophical system, and a method of psychotherapy. Concentrating on the past history of a patient, understanding the internal dynamics of the psyche, and the relationship between the client and the therapist are all key concerns for psychoanalysis. Key figures include Freud, Jung, Adler, Sullivan, Horney, Fromm and Erikson.

2. Client-centred approaches are based upon the work of Rogers, originally as a non-directive therapy developed as a reaction against psychoanalysis. Founded on a subjective view of human experiencing, it places more faith in and gives more responsibility to the client in problem-solving. The techniques of client-centred counselling have become the basis for most counselling skills training, following the empirical evaluations by Truax and Carkhuff (1967).

3. Behavioural approaches arise from attempts to apply the principles of learning to the resolution of specific behavioural disorders. Results are subject to continual experimentation and refinement. Key figures include Wolpe, Eysenck, Lazarus and Krumboltz.

4. Cognitive approaches include 'rational-emotive therapy' (Ellis), 'transactional analysis' (Berne) and 'reality therapy' (Glasser), along with Meichenbaum's work on cognitive rehearsal and inoculation. All have in common the belief that people's problems are created by how they

conceptualize their worlds: change the concepts and feelings will change too.

5. Affective approaches include 'Gestalt therapy' (Perls), 'primal therapy' (Janov), 're-evaluation counselling' (Jackins), and 'bioenergetics' (Lowen). These have in common the belief that pain and distress accumulate and have to be discharged in some way before the person can become whole or think clearly again.

There are many other approaches and orientations. The existential-humanistic school is exemplified by May, Maslow, Frankl and Jourard. Encounter approaches have been developed by Schutz, Bindrim and Ichazo, 'psychosynthesis' by Assagioli, 'morita therapy' by Morita, and 'eclectic psychotherapy' by Thorne. In the United Kingdom the biggest influence on counsellor training has been from the client-centred school. Behavioural approaches are becoming more common and, to a lesser extent, so are transactional analysis, Gestalt therapy and re-evaluation counselling.

Where does counselling take place?

Until recently counselling was assumed to take place in the confines of a counsellor's office. This is changing rapidly. It is now increasingly accepted that effective counselling, as defined in this chapter, can take place on the shop floor, in the school corridor, even on a bus. The process is not made any easier by difficult surroundings, but when people need help, the helpers are not always in a position to choose from where they would like to administer it. Initial contacts are often made in these kinds of environment, and more intensive counselling can always be scheduled for a later date in a more amenable setting.

What are the goals of counselling?

Counselling is a process through which a person attains a higher stage of personal competence. It is always about change. Katz (1969) has said that counselling is concerned not with helping people to make wise decisions but with helping them to make decisions wisely. It has as its goal self-empowerment: that is, the individual's ability to move through the following stages.

* 'I am not happy with things at the moment'
* 'What I would prefer is ...'
* 'What I need to do to achieve that is ...'
* 'I have changed what I can, and have come to terms, for the moment, with what I cannot achieve'.

Counselling has as an ultimate goal the eventual redundancy of the helper, and the activity should discourage dependency and subjection. It promotes situations in which the person's views and feelings are heard, respected and not judged. It builds personal strength, confidence and invites initiative and growth. It develops the individual and encourages control of self and situations. Counselling obviously works for the formation of more capable and effective individuals, through working with people singly or in groups.

In its goals it stands alongside other approaches concerned with personal and human development. All can see how desirable would be the stage when more competent, 'healthier' individuals would live more positively and more humanly. Counselling may share its goals in terms of what it wants for individuals; where it does differ from other approaches is in its method of achieving that. It concentrates on the individual - alone or in a group - and on one form of helping. Some other approaches would work for the same goals but would advocate different methods of achieving them. It is important to explore the inter-relatedness of counselling and other forms of helping as a way of asking, 'If we are clear about what we want for people, are we being as effective as we could be in achieving it?'

Counselling outcomes

This chapter has defined the ultimate outcome of counselling as 'helping people to help themselves'. A natural question to follow might be, 'to help themselves to do what?' There follows a list of counselling outcomes most frequently asked for by clients:

* increased understanding of oneself or a situation;
* achieving a change in the way one is feeling;
* being able to make a decision;
* confirming a decision;
* getting support for a decision;
* being able to change a situation;
* adjusting to a situation that is not going to change;
* the discharge of feelings;
* examining options and choosing one (Scally and Hopson, 1979).

Clients sometimes want other outcomes which are not those of counselling but stem from one or more of the other forms of helping: information, new skills, or practical help.

All of these outcomes have in common the concept of change. All counselling is about change. Given any issue or problem a person always has four possible strategies to deal with it:

* change the situation;
* change oneself to adapt to the situation;
* exit from it;
* develop ways of living with it.

Is counselling the best way of helping people?

In the quest for more autonomous, more self-competent, self-sufficient individuals the helper is faced with the question 'If that is my goal, am I working in the most effective way

towards achieving it?' As much as one believes in the potential of counselling, there are times when one must ask
whether spending time with individuals is the best
investment of one's helping time and effort.

Many counsellors say that time spent in this way is
incredibly valuable; it emphasizes the importance of each
individual, and hence they justify time given to one-to-one
counselling. At the other end of the spectrum there are
those who charge 'counsellors' with:

* being concerned solely with 'casualties', people in
  crisis and in difficulty, and not getting involved with
  organizational questions;
* allowing systems, organizations and structures to
  continue to operate 'unhealthily', by 'treating' these
  'casualties' so effectively.

To reject these charges out-of-hand would be to fail to
recognize the elements of truth they contain. One respects
tremendously the importance that counselling places on the
individual, and this is not an attempt to challenge that.
What it may be relevant to establish is that counselling
should not be seen as a substitute for 'healthy' systems,
which operate in ways which respect individuality, where
relationships are genuine and positive, where communication
is open and problem-solving and participation are worked at
(see figure 2). 'Healthy' systems can be as important to the
welfare of the individual as can one-to-one counselling. It
is unfortunate therefore that 'administrators' can see personal welfare as being the province of 'counselling types',
and the latter are sometimes reluctant to 'contaminate'
their work by getting involved in administrational or
organizational matters. These attitudes can be very detri-
mental to all involved systems. The viewpoint presented here
is that part of a helper's repertoire of skills in the 'tool-
bag' alongside counselling skills should be willingness, and
the ability, to work for systems change. Some counsellors
obviously do this already in more spontaneous ways; for
example, if one finds oneself counselling truants, it may
become apparent that some absconding is invited by timetable anomalies (French for remedial groups on Friday
afternoons?). The dilemma here is whether one spends
time with a series of individual truants or persuades the
designers of timetables to establish a more aware approach.

One realizes sometimes also that one may, in counselling, be using one's skills in such a way that individuals
accept outcomes which possibly should not be accepted. For
example, unemployment specialists in careers services sometimes see themselves as being used by 'the system' to help
black youths come to terms with being disadvantaged. Such
specialists ask whether this is their role or whether they
should in fact be involved politically and actively in
working for social and economic change.

Resistance to the idea of becoming more involved in
'systems' and 'power structures' may not simply be based

upon a reluctance to take on extra, unattractive work. Some will genuinely feel that this approach is 'political' and therefore somehow tainted and dubious. It is interesting that in the USA during the last five years there has been a significant shift in opinion towards counsellors becoming more ready to accept the need to be involved in influencing systems:

> Their work brings them face to face with the victim of poverty; or racism, sexism, and stigmatization; of political, economic and social systems that allow individuals to feel powerless and helpless; of governing structures that cut off communication and deny the need for responsiveness; of social norms that stifle individuality; of communities that let their members live in isolation from one another. In the face of these realities human service workers have no choice but to blame those victims or to see ways to change the environment (Lewis and Lewis, 1977).

In this country, perhaps a deeper analysis is needed of the 'contexts' in which we work as helpers.

Can counselling be apolitical?

It is very interesting that in his recent book, Carl Rogers (Rogers, 1978) reviewing his own present position vis-a-vis counselling, indicates the revolutionary impact of much of his work as perceived by him in retrospect. Perhaps identifiable as the 'arch-individualist', Rogers signals now that he had not seen the full social impact of the values and the methodology he pioneered. He writes eloquently of his realization that much of his life and work has in fact been political, though previously he had not seen it in those terms. Counselling invites self-empowerment; it invites the individual to become aware and to take more control; it asks 'How would you like things to be?' and 'How will you make them like that?' That process is a very powerful one and has consequences that are likely to involve changing 'status quos'. Clearly processes that are about change, power, and control are 'political' (although not necessarily party political).

From this viewpoint counsellors are involved in politics already. As much as one may like there to be, there can really be no neutral ground. Opting out or not working for change is by definition maintaining the status quo. If the 'status quo' means an organization, systems or relationships which are insensitive, uncaring, manipulative, unjust, divisive, autocratic, or function in any way which damages the potential of the people who are part of them, then one cannot really turn one's back on the task of working for change. 'One is either part of the solution or part of the problem!' We have argued (Scally and Hopson, 1979) that counsellors have much to offer by balancing their one-to-one work with more direct and more skilled involvement in making systems more positive, growthful places in which to live and work.

To counsel or to teach?

Counselling is a process through which a person attains a higher level of personal competence. Recently, attacks have been made on the counselling approach by such widely differing adversaries as Illich (1973) and Carkhuff (Carkhuff and Berenson, 1976). They, and others, question what effect the existence of counsellors and therapists has had on human development as a whole. They maintain that, however benevolent the counselling relationship is felt to be by those involved, there are forces at work overall which are suspect. They suggest:

* that helpers largely answer their own needs, and consciously or unconsciously perpetuate dependency or inadequacy in clients;
* helping can be 'disabling' rather than 'enabling' because it often encourages dependency.

For counsellors to begin to answer such charges requires a self-analysis of their own objectives, methods and motives. They could begin by asking:

* how much of their counselling is done at the 'crisis' or 'problem' stage in their clients' lives?
* how much investment are they putting into 'prevention' rather than 'cure'?

To help somebody in crisis is an obvious task. It is, however, only one counselling option. If 'prevention' is better than 'cure' then maybe that is where the emphasis ought to be. Perhaps never before has there been more reason for individuals to feel 'in crisis'. Toffler (1970) has identified some likely personal and social consequences of living at a time of incredibly rapid change. Many, like Stonier (1979), are forecasting unparallelled technological developments over the next 30 years which will change our lives, especially our work patterns, dramatically. There are so many complex forces at work that it is not surprising that many people are feeling more anxious, unsure, pessimistic, unable to cope, depersonalized, and helpless. Helpers are at risk as much as any, but are likely to be faced with ever-increasing demands on their time and skills. Again, this requires a reassessment of approaches and priorities, which could suggest a greater concentration on the development of personal competence in our systems. We need to develop more 'skilled' (which is not the same as 'informed') individuals and thereby avert more personal difficulties and crisis. One view is that this, the developmental, educational, teaching approach, needs to involve more of those who now spend much time in one-to-one counselling; not to replace that work but to give balance to it.

Personal competence and self-empowerment, which are the 'goals' of counselling, can be understood in many ways. A recent movement has been to see competence as being achievable through skill development. 'Life skills' are becoming as large a band-wagon as counselling has become.

We are producing a series of Lifeskills Teaching Programmes (Hopson and Scally, 1980b) which cover a range of more generic personal skills: for example, 'How to be assertive rather than aggressive', 'How to make, maintain and end relationships', 'How to manage time effectively', 'How to be positive about oneself', 'How to make effective transitions', etc. (figure 3). The programmes attempt to break down the generalization of 'competence' into 'learnable' units, with the overall invitation that, by acquiring these skills, one can 'take charge of oneself and one's life'. We have the advantage, working in a training unit, of being able to work directly with teachers and youth workers on the skills this way. Aspy and Roebuck (1977) have identified that the most effective teachers are those who have, and demonstrate, a high respect for others, who are genuine, and display a high degree of empathy with their students. Many professional counsellors therefore should have the basic qualities required in teaching, and could make appreciable contributions by being involved in programmes in the community which encourage 'coping' and 'growth' skills. More personally skilled individuals could reduce the dependence, inadequacy and crises which are individually and collectively wasteful, and take up so much counselling time.

Towards a 'complete helper'

The argument here is for the development of more complete helpers, more 'all-rounders', with a range of skills and 'tool-bags' full of more varied helping equipment. It is possible to work to increase the level of skill in each particular helping technique and go for 'broader' rather than 'higher' skill development. This diagram (figure 5) could map out for individual helpers how they may want to plan their own development.

On a graph such as this an effective teacher may be placed typically along the line marked 'x'. A full-time counsellor working in a school or workplace may typically be indicated by the line marked 'o'. An organization-change consultant may typically be somewhere along the dotted line.

How much one wants to be involved in helping, at whatever level and in whatever form, obviously depends upon many factors. How much one sees helping as part of the roles one fills; how much helping is part of the job one does; how much one wants to be involved as a part-time activity; how much helping is consistent with one's values, politics and personality; all will have a bearing on where an individual may wish to be placed on the graph. One person may decide to specialize in a particular approach and develop sophisticated skills in that field. Another may go for a broader approach by developing skills from across the range. Yet another may at particular times develop new specialisms as a response to particular situations or as part of a personal career development.

Figure 5

Helpers' skills levels and possible approaches to increasing them
(What skills do I have and in which directions can I develop?)

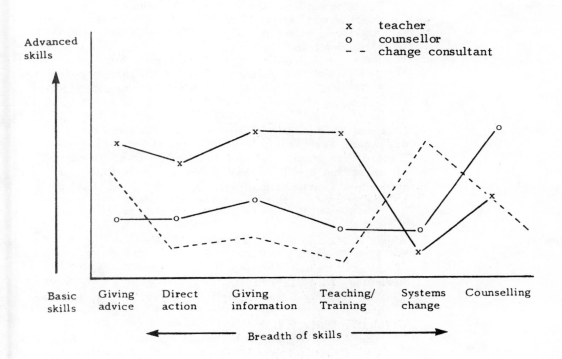

What is advocated here is that basic helping skills can be regarded as essential life skills. These skills can be made available to, and developed very fully in, professional helpers and in those for whom helping is part of their job specification in the workshop, in hospitals, in the social service agencies or in education. They can also be taught to young people in schools and at work.

Counselling in the UK

It is interesting that 'counselling' was a term rarely used in Britain until the mid-1960s. According to Vaughan's analysis (1976):

three factors gradually tended to focus more attention on this area. One was the emergence throughout this century of a wider band of 'helping' professions, such as the Youth Employment Service, the social work services, and psychotherapy, as well as other 'caring' organizations, such as marriage guidance, and more recently such bodies as the Samaritans and Help the Aged. A second was the development of empirical psychology and sociology, which began to offer specific techniques for the analysis of personal difficulties; and a third was the rapid spread from about the mid-1960s onwards of the concept of counselling as a specific profession derived almost wholly from North America, where it had undergone a long evolution throughout the century from about 1910. Thus today we have a situation comparable in some ways to that of the development of primary education in Britain before the 1870 Act. A new area of specialization seems to be emerging.

It is just because a new area of specialization is developing that people already engaged in, or about to involve themselves in, counselling need to think carefully of where and how they wish to invest their time and resources. Counselling clearly is an important way of helping people, but it is not the only way.

References

Aspy, D.N. and Roebuck, F.N. (1977)
Kids Don't Learn from People They Don't Like. Amherst, Mass.: Human Resource Development Press.

Brammer, L.M. (1973)
The Helping Relationship. Englewood Cliffs, NJ: Prentice-Hall.

Carkhuff, R.R. (1974)
The Art of Helping. Amherst, Mass.: Human Resource Development Press.

Carkhuff, R.R. and Berenson, B.G. (1976)
Teaching As Treatment. Amherst, Mass.: Human Resource Development Press.

Cooper, C.L. and Mangham, I.L. (eds) (1971)
T-Groups: A survey of research. Chichester: Wiley.

Egan, G. (1975)
The Skilled Helper. Monterey, Ca: Brooks/Cole.

Hackney, H.L. and Nye, S. (1973)
Counseling Strategies and Objectives. Englewood Cliffs, NJ: Prentice-Hall.

Hopson, B. (1977)
Techniques and methods of counselling. In A.G. Watts (ed.), Counselling at Work. London: Bedford Square Press.

Hopson, B. and Scally, M. (1980a)
Lifeskills Teaching: Education for self-empowerment. Maidenhead: McGraw-Hill.

Hopson, B. and Scally, M. (1980b)
Lifeskills Teaching Programmes No. 1. Leeds: Lifeskills Associates.

Illich, I. (1973)
Tools of Conviviality. London: Calder & Boyars.

Illich, I., Zola, I.K., McKnight, J., Kaplan, J. and Sharken, H. (1977)
The Disabling Professions. London: Marion Boyars.

Ivey, A.E. (1971)
Microcounseling: Innovations in interviewing training. Springfield, Ill.: Thomas.

Kagan, N., Krathwohl, D.R. et al (1967)
Studies in Human Interaction: Interpersonal process recall stimulated by videotape. East Lansing, Mich.: Educational Publication Services, College of Education, Michigan State University.

Katz, M.R. (1969)
Can computers make guidance decisions for students? College Board Review, New York, No. 72.

Lewis, J. and Lewis, M. (1977)
Community Counseling: A human services approach. New York: Wiley.

Loughary, J.W. and Ripley, T.M. (1979)
Helping Others Help Themselves. New York: McGraw-Hill.

Parloff, M.B., Waskow, I.E. and Wolfe, B. (1978)
Research on therapist variables in relation to process and outcome. In S.L. Garfield and A.E. Bergin (eds), Handbook of Psychotherapy and Behavior Change: An empirical analysis (2nd edn). New York: Wiley.

Raths, L., Harmin, M. and Simon, S. (1964)
Values and Teaching. Columbus, Ohio: Merrill.

Rogers, C.R. (1957)
The necessary and sufficient conditions of therapeutic personality change. Journal of Consulting Psychology, 21, 95-103.

Rogers, C.R. (1958)
The characteristics of a helping relationship. Personnel and Guidance Journal, 37, 6-16.

Rogers, C.R. (1978)
Carl Rogers on Personal Power. London: Constable.

Scally, M. and Hopson, B. (1979)
A Model of Helping and Counselling: Indications for training. Leeds: Counselling and Careers Development Unit, Leeds University.

Smith, P.B. (1975)
Controlled studies of the outcome of sensitivity training. Psychological Bulletin, 82, 597-622.

Stonier, T. (1979)
On the Future of Employment. N.U.T. guide to careers work. London: National Union of Teachers.

Toffler, A. (1970)
Future Shock. London: Bodley Head.

Truax, C.B. and Carkhuff, R.R. (1967)
Toward Effective Counselling and Psychotherapy: Training and practice. Chicago, Ill.: Aldine.

Vaughan, T. (ed.) (1976)
  Concepts of Counselling. London: Bedford Square Press.

Questions

1. Distinguish counselling from other forms of helping.
2. How can counselling and helping be 'demystified'?
3. How large a part do you think counselling does and should play in your work?
4. Distinguish between counselling and counselling skills.
5. Who are 'the helpers'?
6. What makes people effective helpers?
7. Compare and contrast two different models of helping.
8. What in your opinion are the legitimate goals of helping and why?
9. How useful a concept is 'self-empowerment' in the context of helping?
10. What are the advantages and disadvantages of individual and group counselling techniques?

Annotated reading

Corey, G. (1977) Theory and Practice of Counseling and Psychotherapy. Monterey, Ca: Brooks/Cole.
  This contains an excellent review of all the schools of counselling described in the chapter. There is an accompanying workbook designed for students and tutor which gives self-inventories to aid students in identifying their own attitudes and beliefs, overviews of each major theory of counselling, questions for discussion and evaluation, case studies, exercises designed to sharpen specific counselling skills, out-of-class projects, group exercises, examples of client problems, an overview comparision of all models, ethical issues and problems to consider, and issues basic to the therapist's personal development.

Corsini, R. (ed.) (1977) Current Psychotherapies (2nd edn). Itasca, Ill.: Peacock Publications.
  An excellent introduction to the main schools of psychotherapy by leading practitioners who have been bullied to stick to the same format. Covers psychoanalysis, Adlerian, client-centred, analytical, rational-emotive therapy, transactional analysis, Gestalt, behavioural, reality, encounter, experiential and eclectic. Contributors include Carl Rogers, Albert Ellis, William Glasser, Alan Goldstein, Will Schutz and Rudolf Dreikurs.

Egan, G. (1975) The Skilled Helper. Monterey, Ca: Brooks/Cole.
  This text is now widely used in counselling skills training throughout the USA. It aims to teach the skills of attending, responding, stimulating and helping the client to act. It emphasizes the importance of teaching the same skills to clients as to counsellors. There is an accompanying training manual packed with group

exercises for the tutor to use to teach the skills in
Egan's model.

Vaughan, T.D. (ed.) (1975) Concepts of Counselling. British
Association for Counselling, London: Bedford Square Press.
A guide to the plethora of definitions of counselling.
Uneven, illuminating, with some useful descriptions of
developments in the UK.

Chapter 16

Office systems
Bruce Christie

It is difficult to imagine an office without a typewriter or
a filing cabinet, yet these items simply reflect a
particular technology, designed to serve fundamental needs
which people in business and organizations have, to
communicate and to handle information. It is old-fashioned
technology and it is rapidly being replaced with systems
designed to serve communication and information handling
better. The office is at the forefront of major changes in
our society. We have moved on from a society dependent upon
an agricultural economy, and lived through our industrial
society. Now we are entering our information society, which
is characterized by an emphasis on information and
communication. In the business world, that information
handling and communication takes place primarily in offices.
The number of office workers in our society has been rising
steadily compared with other kinds of worker and will
continue to do so through the 1980s. These new office
workers will be dealing with information (just as office
workers in Dicken's day) but they will not be using quill
pens to do so; instead, they are increasingly using
sophisticated electronic systems - systems that the science
fiction films of the 1950s show could barely be imagined
just a generation ago.

Before we consider the information-communication needs
that electronic office systems should be designed to serve,
let us look briefly at what sorts of systems are already
beginning to emerge. Office systems can be classified into
two broad categories in terms of the kinds of human
behaviour involved:

* Type A systems are designed to support the need to
interact with other people directly in real time. They can
be regarded as electronic alternatives to meeting face to
face. The most familiar example is the telephone, but the
modern telephone is quite a different animal from the sort
most of us have grown up with. The old electro-magnetic
exchanges are being replaced by computers whose electronic
intelligence allows for new possibilities. For example, you
can press a few buttons and have all incoming calls
automatically re-routed to any extension you choose, so you
need never worry whether someone tried to call you when you

were out of the office. Or your telephone can act as a secretary, repeatedly calling a number that is engaged until it is free, and then calling you to let you know. Or if it gets no answer from one extension, it will try another (if an alternative has been specified by the receiving office), and then another and another, until eventually it finds someone to take your call. In addition to this kind of 'enhanced telephony', as it is called, there are other possibilities: the video telephone, for example, so that people can see each other as well as talk, and teleconferencing, where people in two or more locations hold a 'meeting' using audio systems or audio-video systems. British Telecom's 'Confravision' is an audio-video teleconferencing facility based on broadcast standard (monochrome)/two-way television, to link major cities in the UK.

* Type B systems are designed to support the interaction between people and 'paper'. These are recent electronic developments which make use of microprocessor technology to provide electronic alternatives to written communication and information handling. They are rapidly becoming an essential ingredient in the electronic office. Type B systems are based on modern electronic technology. They are tailored to the office environment and differ from traditional computer systems in many ways. Some of the key differences are listed in figure 1.

Figure 1

Some differences between modern office systems and traditional computer systems

Computer systems	Office systems
operated by specialist computer personnel	operated by secretaries, managers and other office workers
often require special air-conditioned rooms	used in ordinary offices
line printer output is standard	standard output is high quality type on A4 sheets
'unfriendly' dialogue e.g. command language	'friendly' dialogue, e.g. menus

The systems can be regarded in many ways as a logical technological extension to typewriters, filing cabinets, and other traditional office equipment. They deal with all aspects of information handling, including: storage and retrieval of internal information (e.g. personal computers, microform systems); production of documents (e.g. word processing); and communication between offices (e.g. communicating word processors, electronic mail, facsimile).

Some examples of the main types of systems are summarized in figure 2. These are just examples of a whole range of systems that are helping to produce major changes in the business environment. In the next section we look briefly at how psychologists can help in the design of new systems and their integration into organizations.

Figure 2

Examples of key systems

Type A systems

	dyadic	group-to-group	multi-location
audio	enhanced voice telephone	remote meeting table (RMT)	conference call
audio-video	video telephone	arcovision confravision	MRC-TV
face-to-face	meetings	meetings	meetings

Type B systems

	voice	text	graphics
production	dictation speech recognition	word processing	computer graphics systems
storage and retrieval	–	microform videotex STI systems	microform videotex
communication	voice annotation voice mail	communicating word processors electronic mail teletex	facsimile

Analysis of Office Requirements

The design of office systems can be regarded as the design of systems to support human behaviour in an office environment. From this point of view, it can be seen to be essential to understand the behaviour involved in terms of what people are trying to achieve, and fundamental functional aspects of what they do to try and achieve it. In designing office systems, we are particularly concerned to understand office behaviour in terms of the communication and information activities involved. Rather little work has been done on this by psychologists in a way that is of direct relevance to the design of systems, but some information is available.

Time Allocation Studies

A number of studies have examined how office workers allocate their time to different activities. A relatively recent study was done by an IBM team (Engel, Groppuseo, Lowenstein and Traub, 1979) with the express purpose of gathering information of value in the design of office systems. Figure 3 presents their main findings for office principals, organized to bring out the distinction between Type A and Type B activities.

This type of study is quite useful for identifying which activities are the most costly in terms of time. In figure 3, most time is taken up by Type B activities. It is also possible to go further and develop some idea of how much time is relatively unproductive, and which activities are good targets for electronic support. On the basis of figure 3 one might estimate that perhaps 20 per cent of a principal's time is relatively unproductive (i.e. up to one day a week), and that the filing and retrieval of information accounts for a good part of this.

It must be said that estimates of time allocation vary from one study to another and no representative sample survey using adequate methods for data collection and analysis has ever been published. The estimates in figure 3 should be treated with caution.

Time allocation studies do not give any information by themselves about the functional linkages between different aspects of an office worker's activities, and so in principle are limited in their value as far as the design of systems is concerned. They need to be complemented by studies of the sequence of these activities.

At least two very broad approaches to sequential structure in office activities can be distinguished:

* based on system analysis and design methods;

* based on psychological analysis.

At least 30 methods have been developed in the former category. SADT (structured analysis and design technique) is a relatively well-known example. These methods typically conclude with the production of some kind of flowchart or

Figure 3

Allocation of time by office principals (adapted from Engel, Groppuseo, Lowenstein and Traub 1979).

Activities	Average percent of time		
	Level 1	Level 2	Level 3	
Type A Communication	38.2	26.8	19.5	26.5
telephone	13.8	12.3	11.3	12.3
conferring with secretary	2.9	2.1	1.0	1.8
scheduled meetings	13.1	6.7	3.8	7.0
unscheduled meetings	8.5	5.7	3.4	5.4
Type B Communication	38.3	47.4	44.2	44.2
writing	9.8	17.2	17.8	15.6
proofreading	1.8	2.5	2.4	2.3
searching	3.0	6.4	6.4	5.6
reading	8.7	7.4	6.3	7.3
filing	1.1	2.0	2.5	2.0
retrieving field information	1.8	3.7	4.3	3.6
dictating to a secretary	4.9	1.7	0.4	1.9
dictating to a machine	1.0	0.9	0.0	0.6
copying	.1	.6	1.4	.9
mail handling	6.1	5.0	2.7	4.4
Other	23.3	25.9	36.0	29.4
calculating	2.3	5.8	9.6	6.6
planning or scheduling	4.7	5.5	2.9	4.3
travelling outside HQ	13.1	6.6	2.2	6.4
using equipment	.1	1.3	9.9	4.4
other	3.1	6.7	11.4	7.7
	100%	100%	100%	100%
total number of principals	76	123	130	329

Level 1 = upper management
Level 2 = other management
Level 3 = nonmanagement

similar diagram. They are used typically to describe the operation of artificial systems, such as computer systems or telephone switching systems, but they can and have been applied to manual systems in offices. When applied to office activities, the result typically is a normative or prescriptive statement of how management (and/or others) feel that significant aspects of the organization ought to work. In this way they may represent part of the description of the formal organization.

Psychological analysis of sequential structure is concerned much more with what people in offices actually do, and how their behaviour can be examined in terms of roles, rules, goals and other psychological constructs. This approach draws in particular on relatively recent developments in modern social psychology (e.g. Argyle, Furnham and Graham, 1981), treating the office as a set of 'situations' in which behaviour occurs. The methods of analysis used have a history that goes back to the analysis by ethologists of animal behaviour in natural environments.

One important element in the psychological approach typically is the analysis of transitional probabilities, that is the probability that a particular unit of behaviour will be followed by another particular unit. Such analysis can help to identify higher level functional units around which behaviour is organized. For example, in an office environment one would expect to observe a frequent association between reaching for a pen and then making marks on paper: the two form part of the higher level function of writing. The identification of high level functional units through the analysis of transitional probabilities is not entirely straightforward. For example, it is not sufficient to look for frequent associations. Consider an office again. Instead of reaching for a pen and writing, the person concerned may sometimes reach for a keyboard (e.g. on a computer or typewriter) and type. One would expect to observe an especially low frequency of association between reaching for a pen and then typing, precisely because these represent alternative approaches to satisfying a common higher level function (that of generating an item; e.g. letter or other item). Van Hooff discusses the analysis of transitional probabilities in some detail in a valuable handbook of methods of non-verbal behaviour research edited by Scherer and Ekman (1982). The methods required for an adequate psychological analysis of sequential structure in office activities and functions require further refinement but what is even more important is that little or no attempt has been made to apply them to this important class of situations. This area therefore remains a challenge to applied psychologists. In taking up the challenge, it will be necessary to consider to what extent, if any, the psychological approach can usefully be integrated with the approach based on system analysis and design methods.

Some key office functions
Although much empirical research needs to be done to develop a complete analysis of office functions, it is possible to postulate some key elements with a high degree of confidence. These fall into two broad categories of needs, as follows:

The need to INTERACT with other PEOPLE directly in real time, for example:
* meetings;
* telephone calls.

The need to INTERACT with 'PAPERS' or electronic equivalents, for example:
* to create an item;
* to send an item to others;
* to find an item;
* to store an item for future reference (by self or others);
* to use items, e.g. to brief oneself or to make a decision.

Cutting across these distinctions is another distinction, between:

META-ACTIVITY: That system of behaviour that helps a person to keep track of what he or she is supposed to be doing, for example:
* diaries;
* directives from others;
* communications from secretary.

ACTIVITIES: the 'substantive' parts of behaviour.

Knowing which meeting to go to, where, what it is about, and so on, would be an example of what results from a person's meta-activity. Behaviour during the meeting itself would be an example of the substantive part of behaviour, although it may well involve some meta-activity as well (e.g. setting a date for the next meeting).

Much more research needs to be done to develop a more complete statement of what functional elements underlie office activities, and to develop a model of their sequential structure. Such a functional analysis of behaviour in the office would improve the scientific basis for identifying the services that new electronic systems need to provide to support actual office requirements better. In the following sections, we look briefly at what has been learnt so far from research on Type A and Type B office activities and corresponding electronic systems. It must be a personal selection, as space precludes covering the area in any depth. More detailed accounts can be found in Short, Williams and Christie (1976; Type A activities and systems) and Christie (1981; Type B activities and systems).

TYPE A activities and systems

Historical context

The 1960s were in many ways a period of great optimism and idealism. In many areas, things were done just because they could be done. Satellites were launched. The space programme captured public imagination. Large computers were built. 'James Bond' showed off the wonders of the new technological age, and the Americans built the first video telephone (The 'Picturephone'). The first public demonstration of the 'Picturephone' was given in 1962 and wildly optimistic market forecasts later predicted that by the early 1970s the video telephone would largely have replaced the standard voice telephone. Trials of two-way television systems linking major cities both nationally and internationally abounded. The British were among the first with 'Confravision' and the United States as well as many other countries followed. The first paid call in the US on The American Telephone and Telegraph Company's 'Inter-City Visual Conferencing Service' occurred on 25 July 1974.

But the dreams were never realized. Twenty years on, the video telephone is hardly used anywhere in the world and has certainly not replaced the voice telephone. 'Confravision' is still operated but in general teleconferencing is hardly used and has had no discernible impact on business. Economic factors have had a part to play and in this regard the 1980s and 1990s will provide a more favourable environment for teleconferencing as the cost of communications (using satellites, optical fibres, and other systems) is reduced. But psychological factors have played an important role, too, and there is no obvious reason to suppose these will change spontaneously.

Attitudes and performance

One of the factors that needs to be taken into account is what was known colloquially in the 1970s as the 'Gee Whiz Technology' factor. Ask anyone to compare a video teleconferencing system with an audio system (in the abstract) and (s)he will almost certainly say that video is better. (S)he will probably go on to rationalize this evaluation in terms of popular social psychology, especially by saying that visual cues are important in interpersonal communication, and that 'therefore' video must be better than audio-only. Part of this 'Gee Whiz' factor was captured formally in experiments which Champness and his colleagues conducted at University College London's Communications Studies Group (see Short, Williams and Christie, 1976). Champness identified an 'aesthetic appeal' factor measured by semantic differential rating scales such as 'colourless-colourful' and 'ugly-beautiful' which showed consistent differences between different media, with video being rated as more appealing than audio-only. Christie later identified another factor - 'Social presence' - separable from 'aesthetic appeal' but showing similar differences between media. Social Presence is indexed by scales such as 'impersonal-personal' and 'cold-warm'. So people do tend to evaluate video teleconferencing systems more favourably in some respects (e.g. more 'colourful' and 'warmer') than audio-only systems. Despite the differences in attitude, it turned out to be quite difficult to demonstrate any important differences in task performance between video systems and audio-only systems, even under the highly controlled conditions of the psychological laboratory. Even when statistically significant differences were found they were generally small and of doubtful practical significance. This was definitely contrary to what was expected at the time but it was supported by research groups in several different countries and in trials of systems used for real meetings over prolonged periods as well as laboratory studies.

It seems, then, that while visual cues are important in face-to-face interactions in the sense that people do make use of such cues in those circumstances, people can adapt quite readily to situations where visual cues are reduced or absent. They may well judge the situation as 'colder' or less 'colourful', but they can maintain the effectiveness of task performance fairly well. This is especially true where routine, 'task-oriented' interactions are concerned (e.g. getting to know someone) and perhaps less reliably true where more 'person-orientated' interactions are concerned, where visual cues may be more important. These general conclusions are supported further by people's behaviour in regard to the choice of media. Surveys of actual teleconferencing systems show that audio-only systems can be as successful in terms of level of usage as video systems, and in at least one case an organization switched from using a video system to using an audio-only system (better value for money). They are also supported by laboratory studies of such choice behaviour. Both Christie and Holloway (1975) and Christie and Kingan (1977) showed that in a series of choice situations described to subjects, whilst some factors (e.g. travel time, purpose of meeting) affected subjects' choice of whether to travel to a meeting or use a teleconferencing system, the type of teleconferencing system provided did not. (Presumably subjects who chose an audio system in preference to travel would have preferred a video system had there been a valid choice, but as in real life, that was not always the case). These findings suggest that the optimal design decision is to go for a high quality audio system, and to make it as attractive (e.g. colourful, warm) as possible, probably using high quality sound, stereophonic reproduction, and frequency shifting (to avoid howl without clipping speech). This gives a system which is attractive to its users, effective for getting the business done, and relatively inexpensive compared with video systems.

TYPE B activities and systems

Historical context
During the 1970s, the focus of research was on person-to-person communication and teleconferencing. That was where

the money for fields trials and psychological research was being spent. But during the 1960s and 1970s the cost of computers had been falling dramatically and by the close of the 1970s another phenomenon had appeared: word processing. Close on its heels came the personal computer, and other products of the 'microprocessor revolution'. The Information Technology age had arrived.

The new kinds of electronic office systems being developed promise large rewards. In a study for the National Enterprise Board, PACTEL forecast that shipments of word processors alone will have grown from 1.0 billion dollars in 1980 to 4.3 billion dollars in 1985: an average annual growth rate of 34.7 per cent. Competition is high and there is a growing awareness among the major manufacturers that to succeed in the market place their products must not only do what competitive products do (and at a competitive price), they must also do it in a way that will best suit the new types of users, who are not computer specialists and do not wish to become such just in order to use office systems. That is, there is a growing demand for human factors, and leading edge human factors in this area emphasizes applied psychology. Research in this area is embryonic at best, largely because the area is enormous (much larger than the field encompassed by the teleconferencing research of the 1970s – and that consumed over 100 research-years of effort worldwide, just on the human factors side). What follows can only provide a flavour of some of the key issues that are emerging.

Communicating with machines

One of the key issues is how best to arrange for the communication between the human and the electronic system. Some work on this can in fact be traced back to the 1970s when Chapanis and his colleagues did some work on speech recognition and synthesis, stimulated in part by the HAL computer in '2001: A Space Odyssey'. The HAL computer provides a good example of communication between humans and machines. The computer could communicate information to the humans in readily acceptable forms, including spoken natural language; and the humans could communicate information to the computer in very natural ways, including spoken natural language; the computer could even accept drawings and read lip movements. Chapanis and his colleagues (e.g. Ocksman and Chapanis, 1974) conducted a series of experiments in which two people had to co-operate to solve a problem by exchanging relevant information, for example one person might have some components to assemble and the second person might have the instructions. The relevance of the experiments in the present context can be understood if we regard one of the people as playing the role of a perfectly functioning computer like HAL. The 'human' and the 'computer' in these experiments were allowed to communicate using one of several different media; handwritten notes, typed messages, free speech (but a screen to prevent visual contact), face-to-face natural speech, and so on. One of the key findings was that allowing communication by spoken natural language significantly improved the speed with which problems were solved. (Interestingly, in line with what has been said earlier about teleconferencing, allowing visual contact as well as spoken communication did not lead to any significant further improvement.)

User skill levels

More recent research on speech input by others has taken the Chapanis work further and focussed especially on word processing. Some work by Morrison (1981) suggests that the value of speech input for giving instructions to a word processor may depend upon the keyboard skill level of the user. In one experiment, non-typists consistently made fewer errors using speech input than using a keyboard. However, typists did better with speech input only when many commands needed to be used; when only a few commands were available they did better with the keyboard. This example illustrates how the user-system interface needs to be tailored to match the skill level (and other characteristics) of different user groups.

Ease of use

The use of speech input and output is often seen as being one way of helping to make machines easier to use (although this depends partly on the situation), and much current human factors research is concerned with different ways of making electronic systems easier to use. The importance of this has been known for some time. As early as 1967, Rosenberg (1967) was able to demonstrate that ease of use can sometimes be more important than the expected amount of information in determining whether a particular source of information is used. This probably helps to explain why people often seem to rely so heavily on their own files rather than using potentially more effective (but less convenient) sources. In Rosenburg's study, 96 professional personnel in industry and government (52 in research, 44 not) used seven-point rating scales to judge the ease of use and amount of information expected from eight methods of finding information (e.g. 'search your personal library'). They also rank ordered the methods according to their preference for using them in each of three situations (e.g. 'you are working on a design for a procedure or experiment and wish to know if similar work has been done'). A statistically significant association (Spearman rank order correlation of 0.9) was found between order of preference and ease of use but not between preference and amount of information expected (-0.2).

Effect of context

Rosenberg's result might suggest that if the system designer is faced with having to choose between effectiveness (e.g. amount of information retrieved) and ease of use, (s)he should go for ease of use because that is what will affect whether the system is used or not. More recent research (Christie, 1981) suggests the situation is not so simple. Twenty female subjects were asked to consider nine methods of acquiring information (e.g. 'Prestel', 'go and see a neighbour about it') in five situations (e.g. 'the children need new clothes; you want to find out the best place to go to get some'). They rated the methods on several scales, including amongst others:

* how likely it is you would use this method;
* how effective you think it would be;
* how convenient you think it would be.

In contrast with what might be expected on the basis of Rosenberg's results, effectiveness turned out to be at least as important as convenience in most of these 'domestic' situations. Of even more interest, however, is the finding that the relative importance of the two factors depended on the situation being considered. For example, the two were about equally important when seeking information in the form of a new recipe (correlation of 0.8 for both factors) but effectiveness was much more important than convenience in seeking information about clothes for the children. It would seem that in thinking about clothes for their children the subjects were 'good mothers', willing to sacrifice convenience to achieve an effective result. Perhaps the 'recipe' situation was not considered sufficiently important to warrant such a sacrifice. The results of this study suggest one should be cautious about generalizing very far on the basis of an overly simple principle such as ease of use or convenience. Just as one needs to tailor the system to the skill level and other characteristics of the user, so one needs to take account of the context in which the system will be used.

Personalization

As well as tailoring the user-system interface to the skill level of the user and the context in which the system will be used, it can be important to tailor it to the particular idiosyncrasies of the individual user as far as possible to personalize it. No two people are identical, and this is apparent in relation to electronic systems. In teleconferencing, some people prefer desk microphones and others prefer microphones that hang around the neck. When it comes to information systems, some people prefer large screens and others prefer small screens. The differences between people are not just a matter of attitude. They can also affect task performance directly. An experiment conducted by Geiselman and Samet (1982) illustrates the point. They gave some of their subjects an option to construct their own preferred formats for receiving information. Others had to make do with a reasonable but pre-experimentally fixed format. It was hypothesized that personalization would enhance the acquisition and comprehension of the information. The results indicated that the subjects who personalized the format took fewer notes and learnt more. The experiment was concerned with military intelligence but it does suggest that allowing users to personalize the way in which an information system presents information to them may help to take some of the information processing load off them and so help them to use the information more easily and more effectively.

Supporting meta-activity

The examples above are drawn largely from work on the substantive aspects of office activities, but electronic systems can also support meta-activity: the concept of the 'electronic diary' or 'electronic calendar' is an example of this. A recent study by Kelley and Chapanis (1982) points up some of the issues in this particular area and shows how wide a range of individual differences there are in this aspect of behaviour. They interviewed 23 professional persons and found, among other things, that: their respondents often used more than one diary - up to six, in fact; the respondents varied widely in their concern about privacy; some people planned only a day or two ahead, others up to a year or more; the likelihood of an appointment being changed varied widely - from as little as 2 per cent to about 80 per cent. Query patterns, archiving, and the use of notes in diaries also varied greatly. Whatever else they may or may not do, it would seem sensible to design electronic diaries as flexibly as possible to support the needs of users who are likely to vary widely in their patterns of usage.

Other issues

Space precludes a consideration of all the many other research issues that are raised by the emergence of the new information technology. These relate to the use of such systems for creating items of information for storage and retrieval, for communicating information to others, for using information in decision-making, and for using electronic systems in other ways to support behaviour in the office environment. The examples above therefore give only a flavour of what needs to be done and is being done by psychologists working in this area.

Conclusions

The office is at the forefront of a major change in our society towards an 'information society' in which the use of electronic systems is becoming widespread. Psychologists working in this area are helping to ensure that the systems being developed are tailored to the needs of the people using them.

References

Argyle, M., Furnham, A. and Graham, J.A. (1981)
Social Situations. Cambridge: Cambridge University Press.

Christie, B. (1981)
Face to File Communication: A psychological approach to information systems. Chichester: John Wiley.

Christie, B. and Holloway, S. (1975)
Factors affecting the use of telecommunications by management. Journal of Occupational Psychology, 48, 3-9.

Christie, B. and Kingan, S. (1977)
Electronic alternatives to the business meeting: managers' choices. Journal of Occupational Psychology, 50, 265-273.

Engel, G.H., Groppuseo, J., Lowenstein, R.A. and Traub, W.G. (1979)
An office communication system. IBM Systems Journal, 18, 402-431.

Hooff, J.A.R.A.M. Van (1982)
Categories and sequences of behavior: methods of description and analysis. In K.R. Scherer and O. Ekman (eds.), Handbook of Methods in Nonverbal Behavior Research. Cambridge: Cambridge University Press.

Geiselman, R.E. and Samet, M.G. (1982)
Notetaking and comprehension for computer-displayed messages: personalized versus fixed formats. Proceedings of the Human Factors in Computer Systems, ACM Conference, Gaithersburg, Maryland.

Kelley, J.F. and Chapanis, A. (1982)
How professional persons keep their calendars: implications for computerization. Journal of Occupational Psychology, 55, 241-256.

Ocksman, R.B. and Chapanis, A. (1974)
The effects of 10 communication modes on the behaviour of teams during cooperative problem-solving. International Journal of Man-Machine Studies, 6, 579-619.

Morrison, D.L. (1981)
An Evaluation of Speech Input for Text Editing. Unpublished MA Thesis, MRC/SSRC Social and Applied Psychology Unit, Sheffield.

Rosenberg, V. (1967)
Factors affecting the preferences of industrial personnel for information gathering methods. Information Storage and Retrieval, 3, 119-127.

Short, J., Williams, E., and Christie, B. (1976)
The Social Psychology of telecommunications. Chichester: Wiley.

Questions

1. What is the office?
2. How can the analysis of office activities help system designers to identify the services their office systems need to provide?

3. Discuss some of the methodological problems in evaluating communications media in business.
4. Which sorts of variables would you choose to measure, and why, in comparing two office information retrieval systems from the human factors point of view?
5. Are electronic office systems dehumanizing?
6. Video telephones represent a real advance over the standard voice telephone we use today. Discuss.
7. Discuss two important ways in which electronic office systems can be made easier to use.
8. Which is the most important: effectiveness, user's attitudes, or ease of use?
9. What do you consider are the three most important research issues in this area that have been discussed explicitly in this chapter?

Annotated reading

Cakir, A., Hart, D.J. and Stewart, T.F.M. (1980). Visual Display Terminals. Chichester: Wiley.
> A useful reference book designed as a manual covering basic ergonomics of workplace design, health and safety and task organization.

Christie, B. (1981). Face to File Communication: A psychological approach to information systems. Chichester: Wiley.
> Provides a perspective on human factors relating to information technology. Much of it is based on work by the author and his colleagues in an applied context. A useful introduction to the area.

Curtis, B. (1981) (ed.). Human Factors in Software Development. IEEE Computer Society Press. Available from IEEE Computer Society, PO Box 80452, Worldway Postal Center, Los Angeles, CA 90080, USA.
> Not directly relevant to the central topic of office systems but of some indirect relevance as a useful book of readings on human factors of software development.

Jarrett, D. (1982). The Electronic Office: A management guide to the office of the future. Aldershot: Gower with Philips Business Systems.
> An easy to read useful introduction to the technology of the electronic office.

Pritchard, J.A.T. and Cole, I. (1983). Planning Office Automation - Information Management Systems. Manchester: N Publications.
> This provides a useful practical guide to what is going on in the office automation field in terms of the technology available, the main suppliers, national and international activities, and some of the key issues from the point of view of user organizations.

Ramsey, H.R. Atwood, M.E. and Kirshbaum, P.J. (1978). A critically annotated bibliography of the literature of human factors in computer systems. Available from Science Applications, Inc., 7935 E. Prentice Avenue, Englewood, CO 80110, USA (Technical Report SAI-78-070-DEN).

Contains 564 references, with comments, relating to human factors in computer systems covering a period from the late 1960s up to about 1978. A useful bibliography for the serious researcher in this area.

Short, J., Williams, E. and Christie, B. (1976). The Social Psychology of Telecommunications. Chichester: Wiley.

Concerned almost entirely with teleconferencing, this is still just about the best single source of information about the human factors work in this area. Although some work has been conducted since the book was published the area was most active in the period 1970-1975.

Sparck Jones, K. (1981) (ed.) Information Retrieval Experiment. London: Butterworth.

Provides good coverage of the large amount of work done on information retrieval, especially in the area of scientific and technical information retrieval. A very useful book for anyone wishing to go into depth in this particular area.

Part five

Appendices

Appendix I: Introductory readings
Peter Makin

The purpose of this appendix is twofold. First, to give a starting point for those who wish to pursue those areas of psychology which, for reasons of space, it has not been possible to include in the present volume. Second, research does not stand still, and it is desirable that you should be aware of current developments in both theory and research. For this purpose, we list some of the more important journals where you can find the results of the latest research.

Books

General Psychology:
Le Francois, G.R. (1983) Psychology. Belmont, California: Wadsworth.

Ergonomics or Human Factors (the study of the interaction of man and machines):
Oborne, D.J. (1982) Ergonomics at Work. Chichester: Wiley.

Leadership:
Torrington, D.P. and Chapman, J. (1983) Personnel Management. London: Prentice Hall.

Organizational development:
French, W.L. and Bell, C.H. (1978) Organization Development: Behavioural science interventions for organizational improvement. Englewood Cliffs, NJ: Prentice Hall.

Communication:
Porter, L.W. and Roberts, K.H. (eds) (1977) Communication in Organizations: Selected readings. Harmondsworth: Prentice Hall.

Groups in organizations:
Smith, P.B. (1973) Groups within Organizations: Applications of social psychology to organizational behaviour. New York: Harper & Row.

2. Periodicals

In general, those periodicals which publish articles that review whole areas will be of more use and these are listed first. Those that publish research studies should not be overlooked, however, as the introduction sections often give a brief review of the more important books, theories and studies in a particular area.

Academy of Management Journal
Academy of Management Review
Administrative Science Quarterly
International Review of Applied Psychology
Journal of Applied Psychology
Journal of Occupational Behaviour
Journal of Occupational Psychology
Organizational Behavior and Human Performance
Personnel Psychology
Personnel Review

Appendix 2: Psychological testing
Ruth Holdsworth and Peter Makin

Availability

The administration, scoring and interpretation of psychological tests is a skilled operation. In addition, tests could be rendered useless if applicants could purchase them and work out the answers beforehand. For these reasons, the distribution of psychological tests is controlled, and the various companies who publish the tests operate registers of those qualified to order them.

Only professional psychologists who are eligible for Associateship status (ABPsS), or for full membership of one of the Divisions of The British Psychological Society, are able to obtain the whole range of tests. Many of the tests used in industry and commerce are, however, made available to individuals who have successfully completed a recognized training course. Some of the test publishers, whose addresses are given later in this appendix, run such training courses. There are also a small number of independent organizations, for example, the Independent Assessment and Research Centre of Marylebone High Street, London, which is a non-profit making organization which promotes the application of psychological testing. Brief training courses usually last between three and six days, depending upon the particular test(s) involved. (Should you decide to go on such a course, or send one of your staff, you should ensure that it is a recognized course. If in doubt, you should contact The British Psychological Society which, through its Standing Committee on Test Standards, assesses such courses.)

Many of the organizations mentioned also offer their services on a consultancy basis, as do some members of the Division of Occupational Psychology of The British Psychological Society, whose address is given in Appendix 3.

Essential features of tests

Although we are considering mainly published tests in this appendix, it should be borne in mind that what follows can be applied equally well to any form of measurement at work, whether it be a formal test, an annual appraisal, a training school report, etc. For psychological tests, however, the relevant information should be found in the test manual.

Reliability

It is essential that any test performs consistently. A measure that gives wildly different results when it is used to measure the same thing on two separate occasions is obviously not much use. The reliability of tests is usually assessed by comparing the results of two separate administrations to the same group of people on two different occasions. (This is known as test-retest reliability. There are other methods of assessing reliability, but these need not concern us here.) The reliability is expressed as the degree of agreement between the two sets of scores and can range from 0 (no agreement) to 1 (perfect agreement). Because there are always minor variations in any form of measurement, it is highly unlikely that there will ever be perfect agreement but, in order for a measure to be of practical use, a reliability in excess of 0.8 is desirable.

Validity

We have seen that a test, to be useful, has to be reliable. It also has to do the job for which it is intended: in other words, it has to be valid and measure what it purports to measure. A test could be highly reliable yet totally invalid. There are many different types of validity and if you wish to go into this area in more detail you should refer to one of the standard texts on psychological testing, such as Cronbach or Anastasi. Here we will concentrate on those of particular relevance to employer uses.

Face validity

Face validity means 'does the test look as if it is measuring what it is supposed to'. Although it is not perhaps important from a theoretical view that the test items 'look right', from a practical viewpoint this can be important. Whether they are offered a job or not, it is desirable that all the applicants perform as well as they can on the tests and also that they retain a positive opinion of the organization. Both these goals are more likely if they believe that the tests they were given were a fair measure of their potential to do the job. As we mentioned in chapter 4, such high face validity is one of the strengths of 'job sample' tests.

Content validity

For a test to have high content validity it must have a range of items which adequately cover the area it is attempting to measure. To demonstrate, let us consider a test which most people will have experienced more than once: the driving test. Obviously this is very similar to a job sample test in that it involves actual driving but, some would argue, it does not adequately cover the whole range of driving skills. For example, vehicles rarely travel at 29 m.p.h. in 30 m.p.h. areas and there are also informal 'rules of the road' (such as headlight flashing to allow another driver precedence) which conflict with the highway code. In addition, its critics would say, the present driving test does not include any practical test of motorway driving, which accounts for the majority of mileage.

Predictive validity

Obviously the key question that has to be answered by any type of test, be it interview, job sample, references, or psychological test is 'does it predict future performance?' Ideally, the way to determine this would be to subject all applicants to the same test and then to offer all a job, irrespective of their test performance. Then, after an appropriate time, when they had all been trained and given time to 'settle in', performance and test information would be compared. Although the relationship is unlikely to be perfect, we would hope to find that, for example, those who scored low tended to perform below average, while those scoring higher would perform proportionately better. In practice, however, we cannot afford to undertake such an exercise and we have to resort to concurrent validity.

Concurrent validity

The most widely-used method of determining how accurate a test is in indicating future job performance is concurrent validity. The test is administered to all, or a sample of, current employees and then their scores are compared with their recent performance records either in training or on the job. This technique has obvious advantages in that it can give fairly quick results, but it has a major disadvantage which we will now describe.

Suppose that, had we carried out a study of predictive validity, we had found a relationship such as we described above: what results might we have obtained had we used concurrent validity? First, we would have already applied some form of selection test, even if it were only an application form and an interview, and hence would have rejected some probable low performers (and possibly some likely high performers too!). In addition, even once employed, there would have been some continuing selection, with some leaving because they realize it is 'not for them', whilst others are 'let go' (an American euphemism for being sacked). We have hence restricted the people we are going to give the test to those who, in the main, are performing adequately or better; and because those who perform well also score high on the test, the majority of the test scores will also be average to high. The effect of restricting the range of test and performance scores will mean that we will only see part of the picture of the relationship between the two measures. Like viewing a painting or photograph from too close, we will not be able to see the whole pattern properly. Because of this, we may incorrectly conclude that the test is not valid.

Most test manuals should give some information about their validity and you should examine these carefully to see that the test is likely to predict the particular type of behaviour in which you are interested.

Normative data

If you were told that you had obtained a score of 56 on a particular test, what would be your reaction? Most probably you would respond by saying something along the lines of 'is that good or bad?'. In other words, you would want to know how your score compared with other people. Even this might not be enough: for example, if the reply to your question was that your score was in the top 10 per cent of 10-year-old children you might still feel that you needed a more detailed comparison. It may be that the answer you require is how your score compares with others of your sex, age and experience, or with those who already hold a job similar to the one you are seeking. What you should ensure, therefore, is that the test manual gives adequate information in the form of 'norm tables' to enable you to compare a particular score with an appropriate group, whether it be managers, apprentices, skilled craftsmen or whoever.

We have only given here the points to look for as far as the relevant statistical details are concerned. You should also check to see, for example, how easy the test is to administer and score (especially if you intend testing large numbers of people).

It is impossible in this text to list the thousands of tests and inventories currently available. The more established and researched instruments are listed in a book edited by Oscar Buros, 'The Mental Measurement Yearbook' (NJ: Gryphon Press), which should be available in the library of any higher education institution offering psychology as a course.

Test agencies

The major test agencies and developers in the United Kingdom are as follows, and comprehensive catalogues are available from them:

Test Department
NFER - Nelson Publishing Co. Ltd
Darville House
2 Oxford Road East
Windsor
SL4 1DF   Tel: Windsor 69345

Science Research Associates Ltd (SRA)
Newtown Road
Henley-on-Thames
Oxon
RG9 1EW   Tel: Henley 5959

Saville & Holdsworth Ltd (SHL)
Windsor House
Esher
Surrey
KT10 9SA   Tel: Esher 66476

Hodder & Stoughton Educational
P.O. Box 6
Mill Road
Dunton Green
Sevenoaks
Kent
TN13 2XX   Tel: Sevenoaks 50111

EITS
83 High Street
Hemel Hempstead
Herts.
HP1 3AH   Tel: Hemel Hempstead 56773

The following lists include the more commonly used tests. Their inclusion does not carry a recommendation. Would-be purchasers will need to evaluate the relevance of the instrument to their purposes against the criteria of on-going development work and the content of the manual (defining the target population, providing administrative instructions, giving clear instructions for scoring and interpretation, and relevant statistics, such as reliability, validity and norm groups). Only tests for older age groups are included.

Most of the test and inventories listed require specific training and/or experience. Details can be supplied by the test publishers and agencies.

	Total administration time	Target population	Publishers/ Distributors
1. Aptitude batteries			
DEVAT	2-3 hours, depending on group	School leavers of average ability	Department of Employment
General Aptitude Test	2¾ hours	General working population	SHL
Differential Aptitude Tests	Slightly over 3 hours	13-18 years and adults	NFER
Morrisby Differential Test Battery	Approximately 3 hours	13+	EITS

2. Tests of reasoning

These are largely timed group tests.

---

a. VERBAL

Watson Glaser Critical Thinking	Approximately 50 minutes	15+ High Ability Level	NFER
Appraisal Verbal Critical	30 minutes	GCE A Level upwards	SHL
Reasoning Verbal Usage	10 minutes	Minimum qualification of GCE O Level	SHL
Verbal Meaning	10 minutes	GCE O-A Level	SHL
Verbal concepts	15 minutes	GCE A Level upwards	SHL
Moray House Verbal Reasoning Tests	About 45 minutes	Age 8-17	Hodder & Stoughton
APU Vocabulary Tests	15 minutes	11-18	Hodder & Stoughton

b. NUMERICAL (reasoning and arithmetic)

APU Arithmetic Test	25 minutes	11-18	Hodder & Stoughton
Graded Arithmetic Test	30 minutes	7-21	Hodder & Stoughton
Numerical Computation	7 minutes	Minimum qualification to GCE O Level	SHL
Numerical Reasoning	10 minutes	GCE O-A Level	SHL
Number Series	15 minutes	GCE A Level upwards	SHL
Numerical Critical Reasoning	35 minutes	GCE A Level upwards	SHL

c. DIAGRAMMATIC REASONING

Standard Progessive Matrices	No time limit	General population	NFER
Advanced Progressive Matrices	No time limit	Above average ability	NFER

Culture Fair Intelligence Test	12½ minutes	All age range	NFER
Diagramming	15 minutes	GCE O Level upwards	SHL
Diagrammatic Reasoning	15 minutes	GCE O Level upwards	SHL

d. MIXED MATERIAL

AH2/3	28 minutes/ 42 minutes	General population from age 10	NFER
AH4	20 minutes	General population from age 10	NFER
AH5	40 minutes	13+ college and university level	NFER
AH6	43 minutes	High level ability 16+	NFER

3. Tests of special and occupational aptitudes

a. SPATIAL

Revised Minnesota Form Board	20 minutes	15+	NFER
Spatial Reasoning	20 minutes	General population	SHL
Spatial Recognition	15 minutes	General population	SHL
Visual Estimation	10 minutes	General population	SHL

b. MECHANICAL

Mechanical Comprehension	10 minutes	General population	SHL
Bennett's Mechanical Comprehension Test	30 minutes	15+	NFER

c. CLERICAL

General Clerical Test	53 minutes	15+	NFER
Basic Checking	10 minutes	General population	SHL
Checking	7 minutes	General population	SHL

| Classification | 7 minutes | GCE O Level plus | SHL |
| Audio-checking | 10 minutes | General population | SHL |

d. COMPUTER APTITUDE

Computer Programmer Aptitude Battery	80 minutes	For selection of programmers	NFER
Programmers Aptitude Series:			
Level 1	75 minutes	Basic data processing staff	SHL
Level 2	90 minutes	Intermediate staff GCE O-A level	SHL
Level 3	110 minutes	Graduate level	SHL
Computer Operator Aptitude Battery	45 minutes	General population	SRA

4. **Interest inventories**
These predict direction and stability of occupational choice. All except the first are self-report inventories.

Brook Reaction Test	25 minutes	Adults	NFER
Kuder Vocational Preference Record	No time limit 30-40 minutes	School leavers and adults	SRA
JIG-CAL Occupational Interest Guide (+ machine matching)		14+ all educational levels	Hodder & Stoughton
SHL Interest Inventories	No time limit: about 20-40 minutes		SHL
Standard		CSE to GCE O Level	
Advanced		GCE O Level to Graduate/ Professional	
Management		Supervisory to senior	
General Rothwell-Miller Interest Blank	No time limit	General population	NFER
Strong-Campbell Interest Inventory	No time limit	General population	NFER

5. Tests of personality

Eysenck Personality Inventory	No time limit	Wide ability and age range	NFER
Cattell 16 Personality Factor Questionnaire	No time limit 40-60 minutes	16+	NFER
Survey of Personal Values	No time limit 10-15 minutes	16+	SRA
Survey of Interpersonal Values	No time limit 10-15 minutes	Adults	SRA
Occupational Personality Questionnaire	Short and long version	Adults	SHL

(Information about the current status of National Institute of Industrial Psychology Tests can be obtained from the NFER.)

Appendix 3: Useful contacts for help and information
Peter Makin

1. Management education and research	(a) Conference of University Management Schools c/o University of Aston Management Centre Nelson Building Gosta Green Birmingham B4 7DU

(a) Conference of University Management Schools
c/o University of Aston Management Centre
Nelson Building
Gosta Green
Birmingham
B4 7DU

Nearly all the major university business schools are represented on this body. Most offer training courses for managers and also run Master's degree programmes. Over the last few years, there has been a growth in the number of universities offering part-time Master's/ Diploma courses, often by a combination of day and/or evening study. These courses are designed to help the practising manager develop his managerial skills whilst also obtaining a post-graduate qualification.

(b) British Institute of Management
Management House
Parker Street
London
WC2B 5PR

Professional body representing managers. Local organizations are involved in management training.

Management Education Information Unit: has comprehensiv details of management training courses.

Management Research Groups: centrally co-ordinated but locally organized groups providing a forum for discussion of management subjects. Members are usually chief or senior executives of medium-sized companies. Often have links with local universities.

(c) There are also a number of Industry Training Boards which can offer specialized advice within their particular industry.

Personnel and training

(a) Institute of Personnel Management
IPM House
Camp Road
Wimbledon
London
SW19 4UW

Professional body for personnel managers. Local groups organize regular meetings on management topics. Publications include 'Personnel Management' and 'Personnel Review'.

(b) British Association for Commercial and Industrial Education (BACIE)
16 Park Crescent
London

As its name suggests, this organization is concerned with training across a wide field and at many different levels.

Professional psychologists

(a) The British Psychological Society
St Andrews House
48 Princess Road East
Leicester
LE1 7DR

Most British psychologists are members of this society, which has specialist Divisions covering the major areas of psychology. Most relevant for our purposes is the Division of Occupational Psychology, a list of whose members can be obtained from the above address.

(b) International Association of Applied Psychology
c/o Dr G. A. Randell
University of Bradford Management Centre
Emm Lane
Bradford
BD9 4JL

Many occupational psychologists are members of the Occupational Division of this Association.

Index

Index

Index